Joyce's Critics

Irish Studies in Literature and Culture

MICHAEL PATRICK GILLESPIE
SERIES EDITOR

Joyce's Critics

Transitions in Reading and Culture

Joseph Brooker

THE UNIVERSITY OF WISCONSIN PRESS

The University of Wisconsin Press
1930 Monroe Street
Madison, Wisconsin 53711

www.wisc.edu/wisconsinpress/

3 Henrietta Street
London WC2E 8LU, England

Copyright © 2004
The Board of Regents of the University of Wisconsin System
All rights reserved

5   4   3   2   1

Library of Congress Cataloging-in-Publication Data
Brooker, Joseph.
Joyce's critics : transitions in reading and culture / Joseph Brooker.
p. cm. — (Irish studies in literature and culture)
Includes bibliographical references and index.
ISBN 0-299-19604-6 (pbk. : alk. paper)
1. Joyce, James, 1882–1941—Criticism and interpretation—History—20th century.
2. Criticism—Ireland—History—20th century. 3. Criticism—History—20th century.
I. Title. II. Series.
PR6019.O9Z526335   2004
823'.912—dc22   2003022201

Publication of this book has been made possible in part
by the generous support of the Anonymous Fund
of the University of Wisconsin–Madison.

For Liz and Pete

It would be advantageous for the critical comprehension of Joyce generally . . . that a country should be found for him.

—John Eglinton

Words, dimly familiar, but twisted all awry, like faces in a funhouse mirror, fled past, leaving no impression on the glassy surface of my brain.

    I squinted at the page.

    The letters grew barbs and rams' horns. I watched them separate, each from the other, and jiggle up and down in a silly way. Then they associated themselves in fantastic, untranslatable shapes, like Arabic or Chinese.

    I decided to junk my thesis.

—Sylvia Plath

Contents

Acknowledgments   xi
Introduction   3

1. Raising the Wind: Joyce and the Emergence of Modernism   9
2. The Dream of the West: Writing in Transit   52
3. The Men of 1946: Tales Told of Dick and Hugh   97
4. *Tout va bien:* The Arrival of Theory   137
5. When He's at Home: Joyce's Reception in Ireland   183

Works Cited   235
Index   257

Acknowledgments

This book was written at Birkbeck College, University of London, where I would like to thank all my colleagues in the School of English and Humanities for the friendly and stimulating atmosphere they've conjured. But I must mention two names above all: Steven Connor, for his intellectual inspiration and his inability to be uninteresting; and Roger Luckhurst, without whose generous support and encouragement this book might have perished en route.

Other friends and colleagues at Birkbeck kept the intellectual kettle boiling. Cheers to David Deeming, Jason Hall, Kaye Mitchell, Laura Salisbury, Amrita Sidhu, Ana Vadillo, Andrew Wyllie, and a good many more. Paul Sheehan's work on modernism coincided with mine, set an awesome standard, and started a conversation I've tried to keep up with.

In more and less sober surroundings over the years, I have drawn enlightenment from discussions with numerous scholars dedicated to Joyce's work—among them Finn Fordham, Robert Hampson, John Wyse Jackson, Bernard McGinley, and Steven Morrison. Thanks in particular to Andrew Gibson and Declan Kiberd for their advice on the present book and their example as readers of Joyce.

Friends from the University of East Anglia also read drafts of the text and helped in other ways. Nola Merckel has supported this project from the start and has supplied many sources. *Merci beaucoup* to her and to the Eliotian Nigel Parke, the Joycean Richard Robinson, and the Quatermassian Tony Sweeney.

Thanks, finally, are due to my family—especially to my parents, who gave me my first copy of *Ulysses* (I wish I could remember why I asked for it) and to whom I dedicate this book.

Joyce's Critics

Introduction

When Harry Levin published a second edition of *James Joyce: A Critical Introduction* (1960), he professed himself daunted by the textual difficulties that two decades had disclosed. What Levin wrote about understanding Joyce—"I am slightly discouraged—not so much by the complexities of the work as by the shortness of human life" (1960: 195)—could also be said of the task of reading *about* Joyce. As early as 1961, A. Walton Litz thought that the "critical literature [had] reached appalling proportions" (1961: vii). Twelve years later Morris Beja found that "the flood of books and essays [had risen] higher and higher (1973: 26); and by 1985 Richard Brown perceived Joyce criticism as ballooning into its own "partly autonomous language and field of reference" (1985: 2). In a later study Brown amplified this view: "Joyce may well be the most studied, the most taught, the most read-about and the most debated of all the writers of this century. . . . No single introductory (or any other) book could hope to reflect, still less contain, the whole of this still-burgeoning activity" (1992: xvi–xvii). Steven Connor similarly emphasizes that "'James Joyce'. . . now names a peripatetic global institution, a whole hermeneutic culture, a vast and ever-expanding enterprise of exposition and interpretation" (1996: 2). For decades, then, the already "excessive" quantity of writing on Joyce has been exceeding itself, gradually becoming not merely a distracting hindrance but one of the definitive facts about the writer.

That is one reason why this book is not intended as a survey of Joyce criticism, although it does recount a story of the reading of Joyce. It thus joins the kind of (meta-) meta-criticism that has emerged for several other authors—most notably Shakespeare (Holderness 1988; Taylor 1990; Marsden 1991; Bristol 1996), but also such writers as Hardy (Widdowson 1989), Faulkner (Schwartz 1988), and Stevens (Schaum 1988). All these books implicitly claim that the study of the author in question is by now incomplete without the further reflexive move of studying such study itself. The sheer mass and accompanying intellectual or ideological pressure of preexisting commentary make it necessary for criticism to perform a backflip and survey its own history. A recognition of the constructed or preformed character of a reading of literature can teach us the contingency of our own views. Thus, Melita Schaum asserts that "Reexamining Stevens' critical heritage . . . not only affords a glimpse of the critical enterprise in action but brings to light a palimpsest of opinion on which our current versions of the poet may be merely the latest and by no means the last inscription" (1988: 185). Criticizing the critics is a lesson in humility, a salutary warning that the seemingly solid knowledge amassed by the present is as treacherous and changeable a ground as the now quaintly superseded doxa of the past. The reader learns that she is "always the last term of a preceding series even if the first term of a succeeding one," rather than imagining herself to be "first, last, only and alone" (Joyce 1986: 601). As John Serio avers, "[We] recognize that literary theory is as changeable, fluid, and dynamic as the literature it addresses. . . . We realize that if major critics of our time can change their minds about Stevens, so can we" (1988: x–xi).

On this liberal view, a recognition of the fluidity of opinion not only teaches us an ironic humility about our own views but also encourages us to embrace such fluidity and become undogmatically open to change ourselves. But the case for what Peter Widdowson dubs "critiography" (1989: 6–7, 11–16) has also been put more forcefully. Confronted by the mass of commentary that has created the Shakespeare we know today, a cultural materialist like Graham Holderness sees the dissection and critique of that critical heritage as a necessary part of the study of "Shakespeare," an act needed to guard radical critics from blindly reproducing the judgments of their predecessors. Literary works, argue Holderness and Bryan Loughrey, "have no life outside the contexts in which they are read. And the meanings which they generate in and for any given culture are determined cumulatively by a wide range of factors" (1991: 184). A history of scholarly criticism may be only part of such a project, for—at least in Shakespeare's case—the meaning of the author also seems dependent on a host of other factors, such as his role in education and his presence in popular culture.

The kind of critique that follows from this position has often focused on the relation between literature (and its reading or reproduction) and nation. Critics like Chris Baldick (1987), Terry Eagleton (1983: 22–30), and Brian Doyle (1989) have offered insights into the social roots of the rise of "English" as a discipline able to confer on British society an imaginary unity fast being lost by a declining church. Unsurprisingly, Shakespeare turns out to be particularly heavily involved in this process, via what Malcolm Evans terms "a cult of Shakespeare as national hero and, built around this, an English Literature which can be . . . a great source of unity and pride" (1989: 7). For Widdowson something similar is true of Hardy, whose reproduction as "the supreme poet of the English landscape" is intimately related to the anxious construction of a national culture "centred on notions of England and an essential Englishness" in the early twentieth century, "a period deeply riven by domestic and international tensions" (1989: 58, 61). For these critics the analysis of existing readings may contribute to their undoing, and hence clear the ground for more surprising and subversive accounts.

Such work has its value as a model for other critical histories, including that of Joyce. Undoubtedly the variety of interpretations that Joyce's work has provoked will prompt some trepidation in anyone embarking on yet another, as it did for Levin in a less cluttered critical climate. The story of Joyce's readers, in its peculiar diversity, does to some degree have the effect of giddying relativity that Serio describes. But it also has a certain shape, a historical and geographical trajectory, that this book reflects. It is valuable for Joyce's readers to be able to situate themselves in relation to the tradition—a fact demonstrated by the attempts that have already been made to offer such a narrative. Thus, Geert Lernout (1990) and Jeffrey Segall (1993) have discussed Joyce's French and American critics, respectively; Paul Vanderham (1998) has greatly enhanced our understanding of the trials of *Ulysses;* and Joseph Kelly (1998) has investigated key episodes with exemplary thoroughness. But even critics whose main business is interpreting Joyce himself are often drawn to reflect on the critical history. Hugh Kenner, for instance, has frequently oriented his own reading in relation to those of the past (1987a: ix–xv, 1987b: 169–73), while critics attempting to make a polemical break with the tradition have equally felt the need to outline the orthodoxies from which they are departing (Attridge and Ferrer 1984: 3–9; Nolan 1995: 1–22). Clearly this serves a practical function, helping to define new critical initiatives by delineating the limitations of earlier readers. But it also reflects the intrinsic fascination of Joyce's reception. Joyce's fate has been more dynamically changeable than any other modern writer's: during what Levin calls his "quick transit from the *avant-garde* to the academy" (1960: 198) he provoked scandal, nausea, concupiscence, adoration, envy, nationalism, internationalism, and boredom, among much else. To creative writers he has been an example and a burden; in the hands of academics he has been more extensively and diversely interpreted than anyone since Shakespeare. At the end of the 1950s Levin was amused to see Dubliners pointing out "the Martello Tower where Stephen Dedalus lodged" (184); he did not know that it would soon be a Joyce museum, and can hardly have imagined the trade in postcards and teatowels that Joyce would give O'Connell Street's gift shops by the end of the century. To discuss the reading of Joyce is thus to examine several episodes in cultural history. Joyce has provoked much discussion in his own right, but he has also frequently served as the pretext to talk about other things. Over the last century his work has repeatedly become available as a means of plugging in to such major issues as sexuality and censorship, Englishness and the preeminence of the United States, cities and technology, language and meaning, feminism and patriarchy.

And, insistently, Ireland and the legacy of empire. Among my central contentions is that the reading of Joyce has invoked and involved place and nation. His voyage through clashing interpretations is a matter of geography as well as history. Hugh Kenner quotes an article in the London *Times* dated February 1987 whose author "adduced three authors self-evidently as much the property of Europe as of England. His examples? Dickens, Joyce, and Shakespeare"—a reminder of how writers who at one point are left to their colonies can later be audaciously coopted into the English canon. But Kenner's point is the incongruity, the fact that "Joyce wouldn't have deemed himself an English possession" (1987a: ix). Where, then, did he belong? The Anglo-Irish critic John Eglinton wrote in 1929 that "it would be advantageous for the critical comprehension of Joyce generally . . . that a country should be found for him" (1970: 459). Part of the story I am about to consider is this search, a tour of national affiliations. If, as Michael Patrick Gillespie avers, all readings of Joyce "remain transitional" (1989: 2), this has a spatial as well as temporal sense. The peripatetic "reading in public and on the move" that Steven Connor finds in *Ulysses* (1996: 66) has also been a condition for the reading *of Ulysses*.

In chapter 1 one sees Ezra Pound attempting to "de-nationalize" the Irish Joyce into the movement that would later be dubbed "International Modernism," while chapter 2 details the further cosmopolitanism of the journal *transition* and the symbolically important expulsion of Joyce from the English canon by F. R. Leavis. The postwar study of Joyce migrated to an international zone, which happened to be located in the United States. Chapter 3 treats in detail the differing versions of this "international" Joyce constructed by the two preeminent postwar critics, Richard Ellmann and Hugh Kenner. In chapter 4 an alternative national affiliation for Joyce's writing emerges with the adoption of Joyce by French critics in the days of poststructuralism's Parisian ascendancy. Here I discuss the appropriation of Joyce by British critics keen to introduce French theory to England, most notably Stephen Heath and Colin MacCabe. For the radical proponents of "68 thought," bent on attacking as many shibboleths as possible of the English intellectual scene, Joyce was an invaluable weapon. Paradoxically, his association with foreignness enhanced his status once literary theory had become ascendant in Britain.

The circuits of the contemporary Joyce industry are emphatically international. Yet at this moment of globalization, national questions are apt to reappear in unexpected ways. "The answer to whether our world is becoming more local or more global," observes Terry Eagleton, "is surely a resounding yes" (1998: 314). Academics within and outside Ireland have accused the critical tradition of an insidious de-Irishing of Joyce, at the same moment that Joyce's posthumous image has become not only safe but lucrative in Dublin. In the final chapter I explore the complex response to Joyce in Ireland, focusing on the South. It is in the context of independent Ireland's historical development that one needs to place Dublin's recent symbolic reacceptance of Joyce. The flourishing trade in Joyce iconography and heritage is a visible example of this.

Equally telling is the acquisition, in May 2002, of a notebook archive that suddenly made the National Library of Ireland the world's foremost repository of Joyce manuscripts. The change in Joyce's official status could hardly have been more emphatically demonstrated than by this outlay of 12.6 million euros from public funds. At the same time, the most important recent development in Joyce criticism has been what Derek Attridge and Marjorie Howes have dubbed the "Irish turn" (2000: 13). It is here that my book concludes. A homecoming of sorts has been effected for Joyce. But this, like Ireland itself, is not a unitary phenomenon. If Joyce studies have begun to discover a new degree of historical particularity, this may signal the beginning of a long new phase in which old stories are rewritten. In what follows I offer a story of how the reading of Joyce arrived at its current location.

1

Raising the Wind
Joyce and the Emergence of Modernism

> Yes Mr. Joyce, Mr. Pound, Mr. Eliot . . . will be the exotic flowers of a culture that has passed. As people look back at them, out of a very humdrum, cautious, disillusioned society . . . the critics of that future day will rub their eyes. They will look at them, so hopelessly *avant-garde*! so almost madly up-and-coming!
>
> Wyndham Lewis, *Blasting and Bombardiering*

> More than half of modern culture depends on what one shouldn't read.
>
> Oscar Wilde, *The Importance of Being Earnest*

"I think there is a new phase in the works of Mr. Joyce," wrote Ezra Pound, reviewing *Dubliners* in 1914 (1967: 29). Pound's sense of "phases" here is applied specifically to Irish literature, in the development of which Joyce's first published prose marks a break. Yet Joyce has also come to be known as a central figure in that cultural phase whose very identity is rooted in newness: modernism, the moment when, in Tony Pinkney's words, "unavoidable novelty . . . is at last abstracted out as a content in its own right" (1989a: 3). It is in this period that Joyce is first "reproduced": interpreted, acclaimed, denigrated, appropriated, learned, or borrowed from. And Joyce's contemporaries, from various places in the "cultural field" (Bourdieu 1993), did not just read him first: their construction of the work also continues to affect the parameters within which we read it today.

The critical writings of Pound, Wyndham Lewis, and others frequently refer to qualities of newness in contemporary art and to a sense of generational struggle against the literary old guard of post-Victorian England. But it is difficult to find a consistent discourse of the "modern" in the writings of this period, for it is widely agreed that this broad period term was more a retrospective imposition than part of the self-understanding of the figures we now call modernists. "We are accustomed," writes John Harwood, "to thinking of 'modernism' as something that flourished nearly a century ago, but the term itself was not widely employed by literary critics until the 1960s" (1995: 31). For some commentators this kind of back-projection casts doubt on the validity of the label. David Trotter argues that while the term has a useful "descriptive" function, its "explanatory" and "evaluative" functions have got out of hand, encouraging the unwelcome simplifications of "a world-historical march from realism to Modernism and then on into post-modernism" (1993: 4). Yet it is becoming steadily clearer—in work exemplified by Michael North's cultural reconstruction in *Reading 1922* (1999)—that Joyce's writing took its place in a world not only rapidly changing but increasingly self-conscious about its novelty. Whatever we dub this moment in retrospect, the novelty—enthralling or threatening—that Joyce represented and in which his writing seemed to partake was central to his early reception, beginning with the first responses from Ezra Pound.

Like the Side of an Engine: Imagist Joyce

The terms in which Pound describes Joyce's early work are very consistent. His instant response to the first chapter of *A Portrait of the Artist as a Young Man*, which he received in January 1914, was: "I think your novel is damn fine stuff . . . clear and direct like Merimee [*sic*]" (1967: 24). His *Dubliners* review expands on this: "Mr. Joyce writes a clear hard prose. He deals with subjective things, but he presents them with such clarity of outline that he might be dealing with locomotives or with builders' specifications" (27). Pound's 1915 cultural overview for *The New Age* similarly praises Joyce's "hardness and gauntness" and "clear, hard surfaces" as "'like the side of an engine'; efficient" (32–33). In his bid to obtain a grant for Joyce from the Royal Literary Fund the same year, Pound claimed that "His style has the hard clarity of a Stendhal or a Flaubert" (39), and a month later he told Joyce that the *Portrait* was "hard, perfect stuff" (44). After the novel's serialization and New York publication between 1914 and 1916, Pound's review of the English edition (February 1917) was able to treat its qualities—and his own reading of the book—almost as givens. "It is unlikely that I shall say anything new about Mr. Joyce's novel," he begins (88), and is as good as his word in echoing his earlier comments on *Dubliners:* "James Joyce produces the nearest thing to Flaubertian prose that we now have in English . . . hard, clearcut, with no waste of words, no bundling up of useless phrases, no filling in with pages of slosh" (89–90).

Joyce's fiction as construed by Pound shows a persistent resemblance to the art described and prescribed by Pound's own Imagist aesthetics. After the conclusion of T. E. Hulme's poetic career in 1912, Pound was the prime mover of Imagism in poetry. Instrumental in the initial formation of a tiny school of *"Imagistes"* with H.D. and Richard Aldington in 1912, Pound broke with the rest of the movement shortly after the 1914 publication of the first Imagist anthology, for which he had personally secured Joyce's "I Hear an Army Marching on the Land." The movement's first rule—"Direct treatment of the 'thing' whether subjective or objective" (Pound 1954: 3)—suggests the Imagist roots of Pound's praise for the Joyce he also called a "realist" (1967: 28). Pound's order to "Use no superfluous word, no adjective which does not reveal something" (1954: 4) echoes his praise for H.D.'s work in a letter of 1912: "[N]o excessive use of images, no metaphors that won't permit examination. It's straight talk" (Jones 1972: 17). Such pared-down writing is the means to a new objectivity, an encounter with the real unencumbered by excess verbiage; art makes audacious claims to the status of science. Imagism was to avoid excessive "description," leaving objects to speak for themselves ("the natural object is always the *adequate* symbol" [Pound 1954: 5]) rather than shrouding them in adjectives. This archetypal modernist movement—with its manifestos, anthologies, polemical propagandists, and capricious factions—takes its stand against a cloudy and sentimental status quo, or what Pound in characteristically viscous terms of abuse described as "a horrible agglomerate compost, not minted, most of it not even baked . . . a doughy mess . . . blunted, half-melted, lumpy" (Jones 1972: 14).

Pound's subsequent association with Wyndham Lewis's Vorticist movement has been seen as marking an intensification of, rather than a departure from, what he had previously described as Imagist theory (Kenner 1975: 191; Jones 1972: 21; Materer 1979: 112). Michael Levenson offers a useful clarification of this prevalent view. The emphasis of Pound's Imagism, he argues, can actually be divided into two phases: an "Impressionist" stage under the influence of Ford Madox Ford, and—"roughly from the beginning of 1914" (Levenson 1984: 126)—a period in which the work in the plastic arts of Lewis and the sculptor Henri Gaudier-Brzeska provided a more significant model. An important feature of this shift is a change in attitude toward realism. Initially, writes Levenson, the Imagists "made their attack on symbolism from the point of view of realism, and through the Imagist and Impressionist propaganda of 1912 and 1913 runs an aggressively mimetic assumption. Words name things" (132). Pound's second, more "Vorticist," phase, by contrast, becomes aggressively *anti*-mimetic. As early as February 1914, five months before his first review of Joyce, he had declared in the *Egoist* that "Realism in literature has had its run. . . . We have heard all that the 'realists' have to say" (Pound 1914: 68).

This is a rhetoric in tune with the account of modernism that developed later in the twentieth century: as an antimimetic art of alienation and abstraction. Yet Pound also regularly called Joyce a "realist." It is important here to recognize that the realism of the Joyce reviews is of a new, stylized sort. One aspect of Pound's praise seems straightforward enough: Joyce "looks without bewilderment on life" (1967: 33); "He gives us Dublin as it presumably is . . . he deals with normal things and with normal people" (29). But the Imagist aesthetic is not reducible to the mere recording of data, for it simultaneously involves an emphasis on craft. The process of paring down is not simply a brutal reduction to the real but an act of artifice and workmanship—a duality embodied in the persona of the writer so frequently invoked in Pound's polemics: "Papa Flaubert" (248). As much as any other prose writer, Flaubert's literary identity has flickered contradictorily between the reporter's dogged gathering of facts and the aesthete's dedication to the minutiae of the sentence. This oscillation is embodied in numerous statements by the writer himself, from the uncritically mimetic declaration "Let's be magnifying mirrors of exterior reality" (Roe 1989: 28) to the extreme formalism of his famous desire to write "a book about nothing, a book with no external attachment, which would hold together by the internal strength of its style" (Flaubert 1997: 170). Acclaimed as a predecessor by Zola's generation of naturalists, he would also prove open to a contrary appropriation by Roland Barthes, who from *Writing Degree Zero* (1953) onward treats him as the hermetic master of the "problematics of language," an art that "walks forward pointing to its mask" (Barthes 1967: 65). His constant presence in Pound's essays on Joyce is thus highly significant, for it indicates a duality in the apparently singular concept of realism: *at once* an unflinching descent into the sordid business of life and—less obviously—a heightened focus on literary technique. The importance of the latter emerges in Pound's first review when he explains that "The followers of Flaubert deal in exact presentation" (27), with the immediate qualification that "They are often so intent on exact presentation that they neglect intensity, selection, and concentration" (28)—the other, "aesthetic" half of the Flaubertian equation, which Joyce's writing does not neglect. Damian Grant offers one way of framing Pound's demands by distinguishing between versions of realism based on epistemologies of "correspondence" and "coherence," respectively: "In the first case the truth is true *to* something, in the second it is true as a line or edge is said to be true when it is straight, flawless" (1970: 9). Pound's aesthetic plainly has a foot in both camps, its insistence on "the thing as it is" (1967: 28) matched by a formalistic love of "straightness." Joyce's fiction is "true to life"—or so Pound, distant from Dublin, surmises—but it is also "in the true" aesthetically, possessed of a texture and formal perfection quite distinct from that of the traditional realism that has "had its run." In his review of the *Portrait* Pound identifies "the style, the actual writing: hard, clear-cut, with no waste of words" as being "apart from, or of a piece with" Joyce's realism (90). The uncertainty is telling: the aesthetic of "hardness," rather than being mimetically useful, is a style for its own sake, in excess of the duties of narrative. Indeed, it is precisely narrative that Pound evacuates from *Dubliners:* "He is not bound by the tiresome convention that any part of life, to be interesting, must be shaped into the conventional form of a 'story.'. . . '*Araby*,' for instance, is much better than a 'story,' it is a vivid waiting" (28). Pound makes Joyce's tales over into prose equivalents of the haiku-like "intellectual and emotional complex in an instant of time" which is his early definition of the poetic

Image (1954: 4). Pound's reading initially appears to sponsor the most straightforwardly mimetic art possible, but it actually tends in the opposite direction: away from narrative, detail, the "novelistic," toward minimalism ("his exclusion of all unnecessary detail" [1967: 29]), abstraction ("getting at the universal element beneath" [29]), and the "poetic."

This aesthetic maneuver is crucially connected to the most important aspect of Pound's reading, which is directly political. Pound's abstraction of Joyce's stories serves his desire to detach Joyce from an Irish context and place him in a "European" one: "It is surprising that Mr Joyce is Irish. One is so tired of the Irish or 'Celtic' imagination (or 'phantasy' as I think they now call it) flopping about. Mr Joyce does not flop about. He defines. He is not an institution for the promotion of Irish peasant industries. He accepts an international standard of prose writing and lives up to it" (1967: 28–29). Ireland is a backward, rural world of "peasant industries"; Joyce is most emphatically modern in his transcendence of this world and his attainment of the full merit award of the "international standard." The association of the modern with the international, as Michael North has shown, was pervasive in the early twentieth century: not merely in the literal fact of travel but, more importantly, in the imaginary global perspective opened up by increasingly rapid media and communications (1999: 11–19). This international space, North proposes, was precisely what allowed and encouraged the perception of local situations as "backward": "[T]he parochialism of the particular point of view could never have appeared until it had been qualified by exposure to a more cosmopolitan experience" (15). It is not simply the antinomy of the local and the global but also this interaction or dialectic between them that will turn out to be a recurring feature in the reading of Joyce.

Pound's presentation of the national question suggests analogies with other politically loaded interpretive frameworks of gender and of immaturity. The messy fashion in which the Irish "flop about" might be called feminine next to the coded masculinity of Joyce's "hardness"; and they remain locked in childlike "phantasy" while Joyce manfully struggles to live up to the standard of the rest of the world. Cultural historians have made it clear that both these analogies have a long and telling history in Anglo-Irish relations. "All through the nineteenth century," comments Declan Kiberd, "the Irish had been treated in the British media as childlike—'broths of boys' veering between tears and smiles, quick to anger and quick to forget—unlike the stable Anglo-Saxon" (1995: 104). "If the English were adult and manly," Kiberd also states, "the Irish must be childish and feminine. In this fashion, the Irish were to read their fate in that of two other out-groups, women and children" (30). In this context it is plausible to see such analogies at work even in Pound's brief review; but there is one obvious difference between himself and the English subjects analyzed by Kiberd. As an expatriate American, Pound judges Ireland not against the imperial homeland but against a more elusive and ungrounded *international* conceptual space. It is this universal standard, integral to literary modernity, to which an underdeveloped Ireland is unable to rise. If T. S. Eliot, according to a much-cited letter from Pound to Harriet Monroe, had "modernized himself *on his own*" (Smith 1994: 3), the miracle of Joyce's self-propulsion from this parochial situation is that he has also performed the *denationalization* essential to such modernization. Joyce is annexed to the international in one of the foundational moves of his reception, the first—and among the most strident—of the attempts to stake out an "international modernism." Where this left Ireland did not overly trouble Pound. In a *New Age* piece entitled "The Non-Existence of Ireland," published a year after his *Dubliners* review, he declared that Joyce—in his flight from "the local stupidity" of his homeland "into the modern world"—was the only Irishman to be part of the present decade. "He writes as a European, not as a provincial"; and the quality of his work "attests the existence of Mr. Joyce, but by no means the continued existence of Ireland" (1967: 32–33). Ireland, however, has not disappeared from the horizon of the modern world—or from the reading of Joyce—quite as conveniently as that.

Aspect Apoplectic: Early Provocations

Joyce's country of origin was an urgent concern for H. G. Wells, who reviewed *A Portrait of the Artist as a Young Man* for the *Nation* in February 1917. The "peculiar lie of the interest for the intelligent reader," writes Wells, "is the convincing revelation it makes of the limitations of a great mass of Irishmen." The conditions depicted in the novel have "passed almost altogether out of English life"; Stephen Dedalus's life "is like nothing in any boy's experience who has been trained under modern conditions" (1970: 86–88). Where Pound sees Joyce as definitively transcending Irish backwardness, Wells has an anthropologist's fascination with the national "limitations" that continue to mark Joyce's fiction. Unlike Pound, he sees Joyce as deeply implicated in the nation that is his subject matter, a point that emerges in a remarkable passage of political indignation: "[E]veryone in this Dublin story, every human being, accepts as a matter of course, as a thing in nature like the sky and the sea, that the English are to be hated. There is no discrimination in that hatred, there is no gleam of recognition that a considerable number of Englishmen have displayed a very earnest disposition to put matters right with Ireland, there is an absolute absence of any idea of a discussed settlement, any notion in helping the slow-witted Englishman in his three-cornered puzzle between North and South. It is just hate, a cant cultivated to the pitch of monomania, an ungenerous violent direction of the mind. That is the political atmosphere in which Stephen Dedalus grows up, and in which his essentially responsive mind orients itself" (88). For Wells, unlike many later readers of the *Portrait*, Joyce's novel is inescapably political, a warning of the threat still emanating from Ireland less than a year after the heroic failure of the Easter Rising. In a sense this was also the case for Pound: in his review of the novel whose publication he had helped to secure, he remarks that "When you tell the Irish that they are slow in recognizing their own men of genius they reply with street riots and politics" (1967: 89). Pound may well have in mind here the battles over John Synge's *Playboy of the Western World*, in which his sometime mentor W. B. Yeats had been embroiled ten years earlier. Just as Yeats and Synge had been positioned against Arthur Griffith's Sinn Féin in that controversy, Pound sees Joyce as the type of artist taking a stand against nationalism: "Flaubert pointed out that if France had studied his work they might have been saved a good deal in 1870. If more people had read *The Portrait* and certain stories in Mr. Joyce's *Dubliners* there might have been less recent trouble in Ireland. A clear diagnosis is never without its value" (90). Where Pound sees Joyce as a postnational artist, whose writing indeed has an *antinationalist* function, Wells gives every appearance of believing that Joyce himself remains enmeshed in the national politics from which he has emerged. Chris Baldick has noted that Wells was one of "three leading novelists who had large readerships in the United States" (the others were John Galsworthy and

Arnold Bennett) whose journalistic skills were deployed by the British state to sway Irish America against support for republicanism during World War I (1987: 87). In this sense Wells's review is a significant piece of political rhetoric, for it explicitly becomes a warning to an American audience to beware the entreaties of Irish nationalism. The latter, writes Wells, is only superficially a progressive force and "will play into the hands of the Tories by threatening an outbreak and providing the excuse for a militarist reaction in England." Wells concludes that "It is time the American observer faced the truth of that. No reason in that why England should not do justice to Ireland, but excellent reason for bearing in mind that these bright-green young people across the Channel are something quite different from the liberal English in training and tradition, and absolutely set against helping them. No single book has ever shown how different they are, as completely as this most memorable novel" (1970: 88).

For Wells the Irish behave like a separate race, a view that was not unusual in British discussions of the "Irish question" (Cheng 1995: 19–41). A difference so absolutely conceived is not easily transcended, and there is no implication that Joyce has succeeded in attaining the perspective of the "liberal English." The fictional representation of his own youth via Stephen Dedalus seems to Wells precisely to demonstrate Joyce's rootedness in the Irish "training and tradition." Indeed, an earlier paragraph of the review describes Joyce as physiologically different from his potential English audience, whose modernity has cleansed their minds and language: "Like Swift and another living Irish writer, Mr. Joyce has a cloacal obsession. He would bring back into the general picture of life aspects which modern drainage and modern decorum have taken out of ordinary intercourse and conversation. . . . We shall do Mr. Joyce an injustice if we attribute a normal sensory basis to him and then accuse him of deliberate offence" (1970: 86–87). For Wells Joyce's "cloacal obsession" appears to be a distinctively Irish feature, and in this sense it aligns him with his "bright-green" countrymen. Obscenity and "ungenerous violent" nationalism are both, in the eyes of the reviewer, Irish characteristics. So, indeed, is Joyce's formal radicalism: "Like so many Irish writers from Sterne to Shaw Mr. Joyce is a bold experimenter with paragraph and punctuation" (87). In Wells's hands the complex offensiveness of which Joyce's writing would frequently be accused thus acquires a specifically national character. Where Pound's Joyce rises above his origins into modern Europe, Wells's reading locates Joyce's value—and his challenge—in his inescapable Irishness. This is confirmed by a 1928 letter from Wells to Joyce wherein the former explains that "you and I are set on absolutely different courses. Your training has been Catholic, Irish, insurrectionary; mine, such as it was, was scientific, constructive and, I suppose, English. . . . And while you were brought up under the delusion of political suppression I was brought up under the delusion of political responsibility" (Ellmann 1982: 607–8). Wells's comments on the *Portrait*, for all their immoderation, oddly and distantly prefigure the "re-Irishing" of Joyce that would take place in the late twentieth century.

Wells's review provides a focal point in drawing together a number of threats that Joyce's writing is felt to pose: the dangers of obscenity, of formal disruption, and of political rebellion. Perhaps the most remarkable thing about the piece is that despite all this, it is a highly favorable review. Joyce himself, according to Frank Budgen, responded with the correspondingly national retort that "it's Wells's countrymen who build water-closets wherever they go," but added that Wells was "a very appreciative critic of my writings" (1989: 108). When *Ulysses* appeared five years later, Arnold Bennett presented Wells as a "hypnotic influence," the key figure in securing Joyce's growing fame in England: his praise for the *Portrait* had "had very considerable influence upon the young" (1970: 219). But as *Ulysses* began to be reviewed in the early 1920s, the dangers that Wells scented in Joyce's first novel would resurface, in different proportions and combinations, often producing more hostile conclusions. I will consider some signs of this panic in the initial reviews of Joyce's fiction, which are too easily written off as hysterical early responses or the bluff conservatism of Georgian London. In fact, their "hysteria" may have something interesting to tell us about Joyce's writing.

First, however, one ought to recall the circumstances of these early responses. In March 1918 *Ulysses* commenced serialization in the *Little Review*, the bohemian American literary quarterly edited by Margaret Anderson and Jane Heap; and in 1919 the *Egoist* published four episodes. The difficulties encountered by the *Little Review* have been well documented. In January 1919 the issue containing the first episode of "Lestrygonians" was banned from the mails by the U.S. Postal Service; the

May number met the same fate. The January 1920 issue, featuring the third installment of "Cyclops," was also banned, with the U.S. Post Office aiming to put the magazine out of business. The crunch came in August 1920, when Margaret Anderson mailed an unsolicited copy of the *Little Review* to the daughter of a prominent New York lawyer. The magazine contained the final installment of "Nausicaa," whose reader was sufficiently offended to pass it on to her father, "demanding that the magazine be prosecuted" (Vanderham 1998: 37). So it was that the issue came to the attention of New York's district attorney and the New York Society for the Suppression of Vice, resulting in state prosecution of the magazine's publishers. The unsuccessful attempts of the attorney and art collector John Quinn to defend Anderson and Heap in the trials of 1920–21, which Paul Vanderham has skillfully recounted, subtly lay down some of the major themes of the early response to Joyce within an unusually intense and loaded context.

In the protracted struggle to legalize *Ulysses*, Vanderham proposes, one major line of argument drew a strict line between "literature" and (among other things) "obscenity," to the effect that "the literary work, precisely in so far as it is a literary work, cannot be obscene" (1998: 44). Margaret Anderson drew such a circle around the aesthetic in the *Little Review* itself, arguing that "to a work of Art you must bring aesthetic judgment, not moral, personal, nor even technical judgment." Thus, she reasoned, "the words 'literature' and 'obscenity' can not be used in conjunction any more than the words 'science' and 'immorality' can" (53). This style of argument, positing an uncrossable border between literary and other discourses, finally won the day for *Ulysses* in the celebrated Woolsey trial of 1933. Yet in the early 1920s John Quinn was unable to make this case convincingly, and tried several other gambits on the various judges whom he confronted. One was that "there was filth in literature and art, but . . . it was not filth that would corrupt, but rather that would brace and deter" (44). According to this model, the literary could—*pace* Anderson—have "moral" implications, but only through a reinscription of "filth" to reverse the effect that it would have in a nonliterary context. "Nausicaa" could be relied on to produce nausea. "Joyce's treatment of sex," Quinn argued, "would not drive men to whore houses or into the arms of lewd women but would drive them away from them." He also carefully specified the type of reader who would make an appropriate guinea pig: the appropriate test of "Nausicaa" would be "its effect upon the average man or woman, not its effect upon a degenerate on one side, or a convent bred saphead on the other" (45). It is interesting that the robust Quinn envisaged an "average" audience for the novel at all. In his account of the trial the courthouse is overrun by decadence: "There was Heep [sic] plus Anderson, and plus heaps of other Heeps and Andersons. Some goodlooking and some indifferent. The two rows of them looking as though a fashionable whorehouse had been pinched and all its inmates haled into court, with Heep in the part of the brazen madame." Quinn, reports Vanderham, "disliked Joyce's work being associated with Greenwich Village bohemia" (43); his invocation of the "average reader," as against the "degenerate," seems precisely to exclude those supporters of the *Little Review* who were most likely actually to have read Joyce. Philip Moeller, a witness for the defense called by Quinn himself, was reprimanded by the judges for referring to Freud ("a name as new to the judges," opines Richard Ellmann, "and therefore as suspect, as that of Joyce" [1982: 503]), and was told to "Speak plain English if you want us to understand what you're saying" (Vanderham 1998: 49). Quinn's standpoint has a faint resemblance to that of the judge: he yearns for a "plain reader" of *Ulysses,* as a way of legitimating the novel by the normative legal and aesthetic canons of the United States.

The most striking feature of Quinn's defense, however, is its insistent recourse to the notion of "effects." The legal context—the inquiry into the worldliness or social significance of the text—directs discussion of the novel not toward its meaning but rather toward its power to produce reactions in the reader. What is in dispute is the exact nature of those reactions. This is most evident in Quinn's final, comic protest, when he offers up the spectacle of Assistant District Attorney Joseph Forrester as an exhibit for the defense: "Just look at him, still gasping for breath at the conclusion of his denunciation, his face distorted with rage, his whole aspect apoplectic. Is he filled with lewd desires? Does a reading of the chapter want to send him to the arms of a whore? . . . Not at all. . . . He is full of hatred, venom, anger and uncharitableness. But lust? There is not a drop of lust or an ounce of sex passion in his whole body. He is filled with anger and hate. He is my chief exhibit as to the effect of *Ulysses*" (Vanderham 1998: 52). Quinn hits here on the idea of a "bodily" way of reading, in which words generate sensory reactions in their receivers. The attorney's heightened state is not presented as exceptional or reprehensible, but simply as "the effect" of the book that Quinn is out to defend. What Richard Brown, discussing *Ulysses*, has called a "new materialistic [form] of reading that has discernible somatic effects—of reading with the body" (1996: 176), is exemplified by Quinn's description of Forrester. Derek Attridge, discussing the *Portrait*, makes a similar point (2000: 64). Joyce's own work may furnish us with an alternative term for such a mode of reading. During his disquisition on aesthetics in the *Portrait*, Stephen Dedalus distinguishes between proper and improper forms of art: "The feelings excited by improper art are kinetic, desire or loathing. Desire urges us to possess, to go to something; loathing urges us to abandon, to go from something. These are kinetic emotions. The arts which excite them, pornographical or didactic, are therefore improper arts. The esthetic emotion (I use the general term) is therefore static. The mind is arrested and raised above desire and loathing" (Joyce 1992a: 222). In a different context, one can adopt and broaden the term "kinetic" to refer to Richard Brown's notion of a "reading with the body," to denote that kind of text (or mode of reading) that produces effects on the subject such as those described by Quinn. The early history of the reading of *Ulysses* might in one sense be defined as an oscillation between the "kinetic" and "static" descriptions of the text that Quinn and Anderson had respectively advanced.

"Meaning" and "effect" have a vexed relation. John Cowper Powys, a witness called in by Quinn, attempted to exonerate *Ulysses* on the grounds that it could not provoke such responses since it was "too obscure and philosophical a work to be in any sense corrupting," calling it "a beautiful piece of work in no way capable of corrupting the minds of young girls" (Vanderham 1998: 48). Powys's emphasis on "obscurity" echoes Quinn's other line of defense, namely, that the novel would not corrupt anyone because no one would be able to understand it. When passages of "Nausicaa" were read in court, a judge protested that the "ladies" of the *Little Review* should be spared such indecency, and that Anderson, despite being the publisher, had not yet been corrupted because "she didn't know the significance of what she was publishing" (Ellmann 1982: 503). This follows Quinn's logic, which holds that comprehension is essential to corruption. Quinn pushed this line as far as it would go in declaring that he himself did not understand "Nausicaa," because "Joyce has carried his method too far in this experiment" (Vanderham 1998: 49). "Experiment" here is the enemy of obscenity: if a text is too experimental, any obscene content will be irretrievable. Joyce's obscurity and his sexual boldness—both central to the public perception of his modernity—thus seem to push in different directions; or, more cunningly, the former is used (by Quinn, and perhaps even by Joyce himself) as a cover for the latter. Only in Philip Moeller's testimony do the two strands of "experiment" seem to run together: asked about the effect of "Nausicaa" on an average reader, he replied: "I think it would mystify him"—to which a judge impatiently countered: "Yes, but what would be the effect?" (49). It is uncertain whether "mystification" or bafflement is to be considered an "effect" in its own right or simply the cause or condition of one.

The trials raised a number of issues in the reading of Joyce, which will recur in the course of this study. The purely "aesthetic" defense would play its part in Joyce's cultivation of exegetes and critical studies, thereby helping to shape his reading in the academy. The question of Joyce's appropriate or actual readership would recur in early commentaries on *Ulysses*. And the "somatic" model of textual effect, particularly its uncertain relationship with the comprehensibility or otherwise of the Joycean text, would not only trouble Joyce's early readers but would reappear at the much later moment of "theory." What the "Nausicaa" trials help us to see is the uncertainty, and the anxiety, about what it meant to read *Ulysses* during the period of its initial publication.

Invasion of Nuances: The Matter with *Ulysses*

Serialization of *Ulysses* was abruptly halted with roughly half the physical volume of the finished book unpublished, and the first editions were strictly limited: one thousand in February and two thousand (of which up to five hundred were reportedly burned by the U.S. Post Office) in October 1922, five hundred numbered copies in January 1923 (of which 499 were seized by British Customs at Folkestone). "After that," Harriet Shaw Weaver concluded, "the book was banned in England" (Ellmann 1982: 506). In Bruce Arnold's words, sales for the first two years—between February 1922 and the publication of an unlimited edition in Paris in January 1924—thus remained "pitiful [for] a masterpiece so widely and relentlessly proclaimed" (1991: 46). But there is an intimate relation between low sales and proclamations of genius. Pierre Bourdieu describes a "negative relationship ... between symbolic profit and economic profit, whereby *discredit* increases as the audience grows and its specific competence declines" (1993: 48). He posits a "universe sustained by denial of the economy" (50), or by an "anti-economic economy based on the refusal of commerce and 'the commercial' and, more precisely, on the renunciation of short-term economic profits ... and on recognition solely of *symbolic, long-term profits* (but which are ultimately reconvertible into economic profits)" (54).

Bourdieu's model challenges the self-image of high culture and its advocates, but in a sense it also conforms to a traditional view of the avant-garde as the other of commerce. Lawrence Rainey's research has valuably complicated this picture. Modernism, Rainey argues, is not strictly opposed to the marketplace, but occupies a specialized commercial space of its own: "[I]t becomes a commodity of a special sort, one that is temporarily exempted from the exigencies of immediate consumption prevalent within the larger cultural economy, and instead is integrated into a different economic circuit of patronage, collecting, speculation and investment" (1998: 3). In a detailed analysis of the sale of the first edition of *Ulysses*, Rainey demonstrates that Sylvia Beach's tripartite issue—selling at 150, 250, and 350 francs, respectively—transformed the social function of the book. Rather than a novel pitched at the "common reader," it became a luxury good, the purchase of which might cost a week's wages (64). Indeed, it is uncertain whether the bulk of the first edition was bought to be read at all: the majority of those thousand copies went to professional dealers who aimed to sell them at inflated rates as the edition sold out. The book's initial status finds a faint echo even in the paperback *Ulysses* of later years: bought with notorious frequency as a virtuous act or token of sophistication, then left unread on the shelf. A residue lingers even now—for instance, in the lists of previous editions that tend to preface the novel—of the elite status granted *Ulysses* in February 1922.

It is thus a forgotten truth, Rainey argues, that modernist texts were not necessarily *read: pace* New Criticism, their status as specialized commodities or cultural talismans might be far more important than the words on the page (1998: 56, 106). The initial scarcity of *Ulysses* made for such an absence of reading in a still simpler sense, even for those who would have liked to attempt it. Fredric Jameson describes *Ulysses* as "one of those books which is 'always-already-read,' always seen and interpreted by other people before you begin" (1982: 126); and in the first years after its publication this was literally true. The "average man or woman" appealed to by John Quinn could only gain a highly mediated impression of the book. "The extreme difficulty of the work itself, combined with the difficulty of obtaining a personal copy," writes A. Walton Litz, "meant that from the very beginning readers were unusually dependent on the available accounts of *Ulysses*, especially the early essays of Pound and Eliot and Larbaud" (1986: 222). Hugh Kenner concurs: "All the early discussions have this curious property, that readers who had never seen a copy were required to assume Joyce's book was what the protagonist of the moment said it was" (1978: 1). The critic was placed in an unusually authoritative position in relation to text and audience.

Another unusual feature of early discussion was its prolonged, staggered character. "Since it was never properly published," as Bruce Arnold puts it, "it was never properly reviewed. The normal 20th-century process, by which a book is published as a single item, sent out in advance to daily and weekly newspapers, literary journals and other magazines, and reviewed, as strictly as publishers can maintain, on or after the date of publication, was a meaningless concept with *Ulysses*" (1991: 42). Instead, reviews appeared throughout 1922, and commentaries continued to appear in subsequent years: Joyce's "friends and supporters," adds Arnold, "did everything they could to compensate for the irregular emergence of the book by repeatedly getting it reviewed and written about. . . . The book was constantly reviewed throughout the 1920s" (42–43). One should not underestimate the role of these early responses in making the idea of *Ulysses* public. Some of the publicity, of course, was bad—save that, proverbially, there is no such thing. Both positive and negative kinds of media attention served to enhance the book's profile, and Joyce's associates appear to have seen the value of both. As Rainey observes, Beach sought the approval of respected authors like Yeats and Shaw to secure the literary kudos that might justify the book's price (1998: 72). Yet the collations of press that Beach's Shakespeare & Company distributed to the public also included savage attacks from the

Daily Express and *Sporting Times*—and, as photographic evidence reminds us, a placard advertising the latter and proclaiming "The Scandal of *Ulysses*" was hung on the bookshop's wall. The cheeky inclusion of these hostile positions worked, within the publisher's own publicity, to neutralize them—or, more precisely, to appropriate and feed off their energy in a manner reminiscent of *Ulysses* itself. Hostile views might thus be available for appropriation; they might also—in unexpected and even unwitting ways—offer us insights into the meaning of *Ulysses*. In their diversity the early reviews form a powerful and protracted discourse in their own right, which for many readers supplanted rather than supplemented the novel.

If one does not unthinkingly assume that *Ulysses* has always been the canonical classic it is now, it is all too easy to make the opposite error and suppose that Joyce's first reviewers were simply philistines with no appreciation of his greatness. In fact, almost every commentator was prepared to concede Joyce's talent, even those who grudgingly neglected to use the word "genius." The outraged Catholic Shane Leslie granted "the power and litheness of the style" (1970a: 201) and added that Joyce's "genius and literary ability" (1970b: 207) had been apparent since the *Portrait*. Even the dyspeptic reviewer of the *Sporting Times* called him "a writer of talent" ("Aramis" 1970: 192). Yet there is also no mistaking the shock waves *Ulysses* sent through most of its readers, who describe a series of threats like those described in H. G. Wells's review. Holbrook Jackson, reviewing the book in June 1922, was not the only one to find it "an affront" as well as an achievement (1970: 198). The most pressing of these threats—the one, after all, that made the book so hard to obtain in the English-speaking world—was obscenity. "Compared to Joyce," wrote Jackson, "Zola is respectable and George Moore merely mincing." Jackson was, in fact, one of those reviewers who insisted on the artist's prerogative to write as he pleased, declaring that "It is not indecent. There is not a salacious line in it. It is simply naked . . . neither moral nor immoral" (198). Sisley Huddleston, whose notice in the *Observer* was the first to appear, took a similar line: "Obscenity? Yes. This is undoubtedly an obscene book; but that, says Mr. Joyce, is not his fault. If the thoughts of men and women are such as may be properly described as obscene then how can you show what life is unless you put in the obscenity? This may not be your view or mine, but if it is Mr. Joyce's he has no option but to fulfil his mission as a writer" (1970: 214).

In these responses one can discern the stirrings of the strictly aesthetic defense of the novel that would secure its legal status in the 1930s. Margaret Anderson, as has already been noted, insisted on a strict demarcation of discourses in which the literary and the obscene were simply incompatible: if a text could be shown to be literary, there could be no question of its obscenity. Huddleston qualified this view by stating that Joyce's book *did* contain obscene material, but that it was justified by its artistic context: "Surely it is not necessary to say that his purpose is not pornographic? The pornographic writer can always get his books published. If it is desirable he will employ the blue pencil. But Mr. Joyce, unable to obtain publication, would certainly have grown indignant at the idea of the blue pencil" (214–15). Joyce can therefore be distinguished from the professional writer of "dirt" by the artistic seriousness of purpose that paradoxically makes him *more* liable to write obscenely than the cynical, compromising pornographer. Arnold Bennett echoed this logic: "The book is not pornographic, and can produce on nobody the effects of a pornographic book. But it is more indecent, obscene, scatological than the majority of professedly pornographical books" (1970: 221).

The kind of generic distinctions drawn by Huddleston have arguably helped to make *Ulysses* available to us today. For other commentators, however, they did not apply. "Aramis" in the *Sporting Times* refused to recognize an artistic purpose, dubbing Joyce "a perverted lunatic who has made a speciality of the literature of the latrine" and *Ulysses* "rancid," "unprintable," a "stupid glorification of mere filth" (1970: 1920). Shane Leslie called the novel "unquotable" and demanded its destruction (1970a: 201). In such responses one watches *Ulysses* pose problems for classification and reading. Although reviewers unsurprisingly neglected to report any erotic outcome that the book might have had on them, the somatic effects described in the debates on obscenity seemed to spill over into other bodily responses. Prominent among these was disgust, which (as the "Nausicaa" trial had demonstrated) serves as the "healthy" response to obscene material, diametrically opposed to sexual arousal. For the psychologist Joseph Collins, an acquaintance of Joyce's who reviewed *Ulysses* for the *New York Times* in May 1922, "the average intelligent reader will glean little or nothing from it . . . save bewilderment and a sense of disgust" (1970: 222). Leopold Bloom, after all, was "a moral monster, a pervert and an invert," and Joyce clearly knew "how unacceptable the vile contents of that unconscious mind would be to ninety-nine men out of a hundred, and how incensed they would be at having the disgusting product thrown in their faces" (225). S. P. B. Mais in the *Daily Express* also reported that "Our first impression is sheer disgust" (191), and "Aramis" matched Collins's pungency: "I have no stomach for *Ulysses*. . . . The lowest demi-mondaines in Dublin—or, for that matter, in London, Glasgow or Cardiff—would be revolted by many things Joyce writes of. . . . The main contents of the book are enough to make a Hottentot sick" (192–93). What is most striking about these remarks is their visceral quality, the persistent sense that *Ulysses*, even while not having the erotic effects of "depraving or corrupting," was liable to produce violent gut reactions. Disdainfully recording Philip Moeller's courtroom testimony that the book would "mystify" the average reader, "Aramis" retorts that "I fancy that it would also have the very simple effect of an ordinary emetic" (194).

George Rehm's fears seem to hover between the erotic and the emetic, with an unspecified range of dangers floating in the background: "Too many are the possibilities of this human flesh when finally in contact with the crude, disgusting and unpalatable facts of our short existence. One thing to be thankful for is that the volume is in a limited edition, therefore suppressed to the stenographer or high school boy" (1970: 212). The sympathetic Holbrook Jackson added to the variety of physiological reactions that *Ulysses* could produce, calling it "an ungainly, loose-limbed book which falls to pieces as you read it—as, indeed, you do. The very format of the book is an affront. . . . There are the deadliest of Dead Seas in this ocean of prose. You get becalmed in them—bored, drowsed, bewildered" (199). Arnold Bennett also describes a logic of disintegration: "The code is smashed to bits. Many persons could not continue reading *Ulysses*; they would be obliged, by mere shock, to drop it" (221). A certain unexpected transaction becomes possible between what John Quinn had presented as opposites: obscenity and incomprehensibility. While Shane Leslie comforted himself with the thought that "the public is in no particular danger of understanding or being corrupted thereby" (1970a: 203), Bennett suggests that it is a "code" of acceptable communication that is "smashed" by Joyce's boldness. Joseph Collins's description of the average reader who would glean both "bewilderment and a sense of disgust" (1970: 222) likewise allows obscurity and obscenity to coexist.

One reason for this, I wish to suggest, is the motif that runs through the reviews and is shared by Joyce's difficulty and his coarseness, namely the sheer indigestible materiality of his text. This is distinct from—even antithetical to—what Lawrence Rainey identifies as the concretization of the literary undertaken by the modernist market. For Rainey, the legitimation crisis of aesthetic value witnessed in the period prompts a turn to the solidity of the art object. The deluxe book, visibly "a unique and fungible object" (1998: 74), performs a reassuring materialization of quality: the concrete presence of the text underwrites a fetishization of value. *Ulysses* is the main occasion for Rainey's observation. Yet in many of the first edition's readers one can observe an inverse response to the book: its distinctive bulk is not aesthetically reassuring but multiply disturbing. George Rehm, reviewing the novel as early as 13 February 1922, took this objection to an extreme, finding his senses deterred by the very appearance of the words on the page: "[I]t is the unaccustomed eye and not the calloused brain that takes exception to the crude black imprint of hitherto unknown type" (1970: 213). Others were less immediately oppressed by the matter of the novel, but sought metaphors to convey its unassimilable bulk. Terry Eagleton has written of the way that "an 'anti-novel' like *Ulysses* differs from a non-novel like the telephone directory" (1997: 5), but Joyce's early readers sometimes neglected to draw a similar distinction. "As the volume is about the size of the *London Directory*," "Aramis" concludes his review, "I do not envy anyone who reads it for pleasure" (1970: 194). A week later the London *Evening News* played a variation on this image: "The book itself in its blue paper cover looks at first glance like nothing so much as a telephone directory" ("Man About Town" 1970: 194). The first to note the likeness appears to have been George Slocombe, whose remark of March 1922 grows more mystifying the longer it is pondered. *Ulysses*, he writes, is "as large as a telephone directory or a family Bible, and with many of the literary and social characteristics of each" (217).

The comparison of *Ulysses* to the telephone book is in one sense a leveling joke, as modernism's sacred text—family Bible, indeed—is mistaken for a functional, everyday object that barely aspires to the status of "book." Yet it is also a way of responding to precisely the leveling undertaken in *Ulysses* itself, whose bulk, like the directory's, is due to its obsessive all-inclusiveness. "It is not unlikely," writes Joseph Collins, "that every thought that Mr. Joyce has had, every experience he has ever encountered, every person he has ever met, one might almost say everything he has ever read in sacred or profane literature, is to be encountered in the obscurities and in the franknesses of *Ulysses*" (224). "He says everything—everything," exclaims Bennett (221), a remark echoed by Holbrook Jackson: "He has recorded everything" (198). John Middleton Murry, writing two months after the first edition, makes the same observation: "Mr. Joyce has made a superhuman effort to empty the whole of his consciousness into it.... Every thought that a super-subtle modern can think seems to be hidden somewhere in its inspissated obscurities" (197). This is at best a backhanded compliment, for as "everything" comes in, any principle of selection goes out. "In some of his moods," complains Bennett, "the author is resolved at any price not to select.... He has taken oath with himself to put it all down and be hanged to it" (221). S. P. B. Mais likewise complains that for Joyce, "art (if this is art) consists no longer in selection" (191). The book's all-inclusiveness is part of its scandal, for it seems blithely to dispense with the notion of an artistic gatekeeper choosing and forming his materials: "material" is allowed to run riot, bursting the bounds of coherence and raising the specter of an uncontrolled, unstratified world. "*Ulysses*," reports Jackson, "is a chaos" (199). "[W]ithout form," insists Shane Leslie, "there cannot be art. Art must be logical, almost mathematical. Its material, its conditions, its effects must be calculable. Windiness, inconsequence and confusion argue the riot of Nature" (1970b: 211).

Leslie's remarks are telling, for what he calls Joyce's "abandonment of form" (1970b: 211) tends to be described by means of one of two analogies. One is with nonliterary texts, which are not customarily subject to the same constraints of form and selection. "This may, or may not, be literature," Leslie sniffs when faced with "Cyclops": "it is certainly good cataloguing" (1970a: 202). For Arnold Bennett "much of the book is more like an official shorthand writer's 'note' than a novel" (1970: 220–21), while George Moore's reported comments echo the comparisons listed earlier: "[I]t is absurd to imagine that any good end can be served by trying to record every single thought and sensation of any human being. That's not art, it's like trying to copy the London Directory" (Ellmann 1982: 529). The other line of comparison is with the natural world: "Dead Seas in this ocean of prose . . . gulfs and bays which are muddy and noisome with the sewage of civilization . . . a country without roads" (Jackson 1970: 199–200); "a Sahara that is as dry as it is stinking . . . the ocean of inferior writing" (Leslie 1970a: 202–3); "the wide waters and the illimitable stars of this universe" (Slocombe 1970: 218); "the dark flood of . . . consciousness" (Seldes 1970: 236). The liquid character of several of these metaphors is partially echoed in the related invocation of sewage and waste: "the latrine" ("Aramis" 1970: 192), "a French sink . . . a Cuchulain of the sewer . . . the dreary muck-ridden tide . . . the flood of his own vomit . . . an Odyssey of the sewer . . . the *cloaca* . . . who can wade through the spate?" (Leslie 1970a: 201–3; 1970b: 207, 210).

All these descriptions might be summarized in Sisley Huddleston's remark that Joyce had exaggerated "the mysterious materiality of the universe" (1970: 216). Affronted by the novel's insatiable appetite for "everything," its early reviewers present it as spilling over its edges, a viscous unformed tide that might include "artistic" moments—well-formed phrases or passages—but as a whole rejects the principles of construction and restraint necessary for true art. The frequent charge of formlessness is thus closely tied to an emphasis on matter: the stuff that the authentic artist has hitherto shaped and controlled. Jean-François Lyotard offers a suggestive perspective here. "For two millennia," he avers, "there has existed, at least in Western thought, the presupposition, even the prejudice, the ready-made attitude, that the process of art had to be understood in accordance with the principle that there is an opposition between matter and form (or mind)" (1990: 300). This structure is evident in Immanuel Kant's "Analytic of the Beautiful" in the *Critique of Judgment* (1790), in which the experience of beauty aids the "proportioned attunement" of the cognitive powers. In a valid aesthetic judgment the powers of imagination and understanding are quickened by the contemplation of an object with the appearance of "purposiveness," that is, an object that appears significantly formed: "A *pure judgment of taste* is one that is not influenced by charm or emotion . . . and whose determining basis is therefore merely the purposiveness of the form" (1987: 69). Kant's aesthetic judgment is strenuously formalistic, abstracted from the messy complications of content and context and focused on the harmony achieved between the subject's cognitive powers and the object's form: "[I]t brings to our notice no characteristic of the object, but only the purposive form in the [way] the presentational powers are determined in their engagement with the object" (75). As Lyotard comments, what "guarantees the purity of taste [is] the mere consideration for form, the contempt for the properly material quality or power of tangible or even imaginative data" (1990: 300). This contentless harmony nonetheless points beyond itself, as a kind of testimony to the subject's compatibility with the world, a sign of the congruence of mind and nature.

For Lyotard, however, "Since the turn of the century, the arts no longer deal with the beautiful but with something called the sublime" (1990: 297). It is worth recalling Kant's delineation of the sublime. Unlike the beautiful, it "can also be found in a formless object, insofar as we present *unboundedness*"; moreover, "in the case of the beautiful our liking is connected with the presentation of *quality*, but in the case of the sublime with the presentation of *quantity*." Where the beautiful is "compatible with charms and with an imagination at play," the feeling of the sublime is more ominous: "[S]ince the mind is not just attracted by the object but is alternately always repelled as well, the liking for the sublime contains not so much a positive pleasure as rather admiration and respect, and so should be called a negative pleasure." In addition, where natural beauty "carries with it a purposiveness in its form," an object which arouses the feeling of the sublime may appear "contrapurposive for our power of judgment, incommensurate with our power of exhibition, and as it were violent to our imagination" (1987: 98–99). An aesthetic of the sublime would thus involve a forcible outstripping of the cognitive powers, a refusal of the consolations of "form," and an ambiguous effect, alternately fascinating and repellent, on its perceivers. That could also be a description of *Ulysses* as it appeared to its early readers.

Kant, to be sure, is describing responses to the natural world far removed from Joyce's writing; I do not seek to establish that *Ulysses* is "really" a work of the sublime. What Kant and Lyotard help us to grasp is how the novel offended those early reviewers in whose eyes it spurned the need for form, replacing "quality"—artistic construction—with "quantity"—an indiscriminate piling up of every available material. "We call *sublime*," Kant comments, "what is *absolutely large*" (1987: 103). This sheer heaving magnitude of *Ulysses*, what John Middleton Murry calls its "too-muchness" (1970: 197), turns reviewers' stomachs as much as the book's obscenity; indeed the two aspects are related, for much of the language used to describe the book's excess of matter—"dark flood," "muck-ridden tide," "*cloaca*"—also denote its "dirtiness." To reemphasize a point made earlier, there is a surprising compact between the offenses of obscenity and difficulty: in both cases an ill-formed excess of matter obtrudes on "the innocent and defenceless reader" (Bennett 1970: 220), producing visceral or "kinetic" effects rather than the stasis of authentic aesthetic contemplation. Indeed, Joyce's technical innovations and his sexual boldness both appear to provoke an alternation of fascination and repulsion analogous to that described by Kant. Bennett's schizophrenic review is a textbook instance: "My blame may have seemed extravagant, and my praise may seem extravagant; but that is how I feel about James Joyce" (221).

"Words," muses Lyotard, "are matter, nuances, and timbres at the very core of thinking. . . . They are the 'non-will,' the 'non-meaning' of thought, its mass" (1990: 303). As we have seen, it is such a mass of words, what Lyotard dubs "the invasion of nuances," that gets in the way for many of the first readers of *Ulysses*. If matter figures here differently from its role in Lawrence Rainey's account, by the same token it qualifies his emphasis on the smooth workings of the specialist market. The sale of *Ulysses* was indeed abetted by its diverse publicity, but the actual responses often demonstrate a discomfort with the text that Rainey largely leaves unmentioned, and of which one should not lose sight. The motif of materiality washes through this early wave of reaction, whether the book is conceived as tide or desert, as "the boundless ocean heaved up" (Kant 1987: 120) or telephone directory. As we have seen, a related emphasis emerges in the peculiarly somatic reading that the novel seems to impel, with its unpredictably oscillating effects of arousal and emetic, shock and injury. The somatic mode of reading identified by Richard Brown responds to that powerful sense of threat that Joyce's writing posed for H. G. Wells as early as 1917.

As in Wells's account of the *Portrait*, this threat could be multiple. Several of the early reviews present Joyce as a dark, pessimistic writer who "see[s] all things crooked" (Martindale 1970: 205) and has "exaggerated the vulgarity and magnified the madness of mankind" (Huddleston 1970: 216), and whose "vision of the world and its inhabitants is mean, hostile, and uncharitable" (Bennett 1970: 221). More than this, however, Joyce's writing is often associated with political insurrection. For John Middleton Murry—*pace* Pound—Joyce was the antithesis of the "European" tradition, his formal experiments the literary counterpart of political revolt: "He acknowledges no social morality, and he completely rejects the claim of social morality to determine what he shall, or shall not, write. He is the egocentric rebel *in excelsis,* the arch-esoteric. European! He is the man with the bomb who would blow what remains of Europe into the sky.... His intention ... is completely anarchic ... just as Mr. Joyce is in rebellion against the social morality of civilization, he is in rebellion against the lucidity and comprehensibility of civilized art" (196). For Murry Joyce's anarchism is fortunately a shade too idiosyncratic to take full political effect: in what has since become a much-pondered paradox, "modernism" is radical and ineffectual for the same reasons. Other reviewers were less sanguine about Joyce's harmlessness. "Reading Mr. Joyce," S. P. B. Mais memorably declared in the *Daily Express,* "is like making an excursion into Bolshevist Russia: all standards go by the board" (191). Shane Leslie, with a vivid line on all of Joyce's offenses, took up this theme a few months later (October 1922): "Here we shall not be far wrong if we describe Mr Joyce's work as literary Bolshevism. It is experimental, anti-conventional, anti-Christian, chaotic, totally unmoral" (1970b: 207). That same month the poet Alfred Noyes assailed "the 'literary Bolshevism of the hour'" in the *Sunday Chronicle.* Alongside the now familiar attacks on the book's "foulness" and "disorder," Noyes's piece is notable for its association of Joyce with a broader movement of "Metropolitan criticism" that takes Joyce seriously while, like "Bolshevik Russia," denigrating Dickens (1970: 275). The nationality of Joyce's work once again becomes an issue here: *Ulysses* is emblematic of a growing assault on the English literary tradition.

"I myself can remember a time," T. S. Eliot mused in the early 1930s, "when [Pound] and I and our colleagues were mentioned by a writer in *The Morning Post* as 'literary bolsheviks'" (Smith 1994: 29). Wyndham Lewis may once have called Ezra Pound "a Trotsky of the written word" (1982: 288), but the political trajectory of much Anglophone modernism retrospectively gives Noyes's description an ironic look. In the years before *Ulysses,* Joyce had indeed been promoted as part of an avant-garde full of verbal abuse for the existing order; but by the same token he was assimilated to a classicist aesthetic whose self-justifications became the hegemonic form of Anglophone modernism. Before considering the diverse reflections on *Ulysses* offered by Ezra Pound, T. S. Eliot, and Wyndham Lewis, it is necessary to take a brief detour back into the development of this aesthetic.

Craft and Violence: The Meanings of "1914"

Early in 1917, around the time of the English publication of the *Portrait,* Pound wrote to Margaret Anderson: "I want an 'official organ' (vile phrase). I mean I want a place where I and T. S. Eliot can appear once a month (or once an 'issue') and where Joyce can appear when he likes, and where Wyndham Lewis can appear if he comes back from the war. . . . DEFINITELY a place for our regular appearance and where our friends and readers (what few of 'em there are), can look with assurance of finding us" (1967: 91).

By this point the quartet that Lewis would retrospectively dub the "Men of 1914" (1982: 249) is reliably gathered, a common feature of Pound's communications in the period. But in what sense this group actually existed is debatable. In the terms that Raymond Williams proposes in *Culture,* the group seems to veer between "School" and "Independents," "Alternative" and "Oppositional," "organized around some *collective public manifestation*" or merely "not easy to distinguish from . . . a group of friends who share common interests" (1981: 62–73). Indeed, considering that the four never occupied the same room at the same time, to call them a group of friends seems excessive; yet Dennis Brown, for instance, treats them as no less than a "work-group" whose output in fact forms a single, multiauthored text fueled by ceaseless rivalry and "emotional bonding" (1990: 1–7). What is clear is that the unity of the group was a potent piece of rhetoric, insistently implied in the documents turned out by Pound's typewriter through the 1910s. Joyce was one of those "blessed" in the first issue of *Blast* (July 1914, the same month Pound's review of *Dubliners* appeared), which leads Brown to characterize the magazine as "the visible expression of the grouping together of the four most revolutionary writers in English Modernism" (46). In April 1916 Pound wrote to Harriet Shaw Weaver that "Next to Lewis and Joyce [Eliot] seems to me the best of the younger men. NOT weedy" (Lidderdale and Nicholson 1970: 121); in December 1918 he told Marianne Moore that he had "got Joyce and Lewis, and Eliot and a few other comforting people into print" (1982: 143). His review of the *Portrait* made the notional grouping public by linking Joyce, Lewis, and Eliot to their nineteenth-century forebears Flaubert, Dostoyevsky, and Laforgue, respectively (1967: 89)—a typical gesture that simultaneously gives the modernists the authority of tradition and asserts their shared membership of a "younger generation." Thanks to Pound, Joyce's first prominence in English and American circles was in association with this kind of generational aggression. As early as the *Dubliners* review, Pound had implicitly signaled his own membership of the group with the claim that Joyce's "rigorous selection . . . marks him, I think, as belonging to my own generation, that is, to the 'nineteen-tens,' not to the decade between 'the 'nineties' and today" (30). In 1920 Pound was harping on the same theme: "In both Joyce and Lewis we have the insistent utterance of men who are once and for all through with the particular inanities of Shavian-Bennett, and with the particular oleosities of the Wellsian genre" (1954: 425). Wells and Bennett, as we have seen, had their own views to offer on Joyce's writing. But at this point I wish to consider the cultural—and ultimately political—affiliations implied by Joyce's pressganging into the Men of 1914.

"You will be astonished," Lewis warns at the start of his autobiography, "to find how like art is to war, I mean 'modernist' art" (1982: 4). Pound's attempt to breach the strongholds of literary London through the 1910s produced a stream of pronouncements bristling with martial overtones. In the 1918 summary article "Joyce" he asserted that "the lovers of good writing have 'struck'; have sufficiently banded themselves together to get a few good books into print, and even into circulation. The actual output is small in bulk, a few brochures of translations, Eliot's 'Prufrock,' Joyce's 'A Portrait,' and Wyndham Lewis's 'Tarr' (announced), but I have it on good authority that at least one other periodical will start publishing its authors after the War, so there are new rods in pickle for the old fat-stomached contingent and for the cardboard generation" (1967: 133–34). The violence of Pound's polemics in this period inevitably suggest Lewis's analogy between the battles of literary London and the carnage of Europe in 1914–18. In an essay written in February 1914 Pound had asserted that "the artist has at last been aroused to the fact that the war between him and the world is a war without truce. That his only remedy is slaughter"; henceforth he "must live by craft and violence" (1914: 68). Paul Fussell claims that the entire "adversary habit" that dominates the thought of Pound and Lewis (emerging in Lewis's later review *The Enemy*) is inspired by the conflict (1975: 106). For Dennis Brown the parallel is irresistible: "Part of Pound's tactics was to conduct a war of his own—unlike the Great War, one of aggressive advance and consolidation rather than slogging attrition and defence. . . . [He] led the group (especially when Lewis went to the Front in 1916) in terms of Fight/Flight assumptions. . . . Pound's literary *élan vital* was as geared to advance as the French cavalry in 1914" (1990: 51–52).

Yet a contradictory view is also possible here, namely that the experience of war actually calmed the modernists down. Pound's "war without truce" was announced six months before Britain declared war on the Central Powers. Within a year Pound would write that "The political world is confronted with a great war, a species of insanity. The art world is confronted with a species of quiet and sober sanity called Vorticism" (1915: 277). *Pace* Lewis, Pound's emphasis now is modernist art's *unlikeness* to war. Despite his own previously cited claims, Dennis Brown calls Pound's grouping "a kind of internationalist counter-culture, to whom the War would increasingly appear as an abomination" (1990: 51). Lewis himself remembers that events in Europe dwarfed London rhetoric: "The War had washed out the bright puce of the cover of the organ of the 'Great London Vortex.' Too much blood had been shed for real . . . to startle anybody" (1982: 90). "Before the war," argues Michael Levenson, "the modernists had assumed the role of violence-inciting artistic *provocateurs* whose aim was to startle the culture out of lethargy. But after August 1914, lethargy was no longer the dreaded ill. The problem for the moderns became what posture to adopt in the face of general social disarray" (1984: 140).

One is thus presented with an avant-garde whose rhetoric could be both analogous to and divergent from the war. What is the significance of this paradox? First, the antagonistic mind-set of the Men of 1914 is opposed to official society and the "mass" mentality that reaches its apotheosis in the war, as evidenced by Lewis's scornful depiction of London's "war-crowds" in July 1914 (1982: 78–83). The aggressive individual is appalled at the "foolishness" of institutionalized aggression, the "carnivals of mass-murder" (85). War is declared upon war. This leads to a second observation. Of the "war-crowds" Lewis writes: "The police with distant icy contempt herd London. They shift it in lumps, passim, touching and shaping it with heavy delicate professional fingers. Their attitude suggests that these universal crowds are out for some new vague Suffrage. . . . Is this opposition correct? In ponderous masses they prowl, with excited hearts. Are the crowds then female?" (78). Lewis goes out of his way to give the crowd a gender, depicting it as the "lumps" of raw material upon which the unlikely artists of the police go to work. This typifies one of the predominant rhetorics of his and Pound's writings, namely "icy contempt" both for the crowd and for the feminine. Among the more recent commentators who have explored the link between the politics and the aesthetics of "1914," Andreas Huyssen's judgment that modernism "constituted itself through a conscious strategy of exclusion, an anxiety of contamination by its other: an increasingly consuming and engulfing mass culture" (1986: vii) is echoed by Peter Nicholls, who finds this animus toward "mass" society encoded in a practice of style: "Mass production is swiftly elided with the democratic masses, and a merely representational art equated with the equally hollow forms of contemporary politics" (1995: 190). The antimimetic emphasis stirring within Pound's construal of the early Joyce thus has an ideological meaning: mimesis, Nicholls argues, is associated with the "imitative" life of the undifferentiated crowd, against which the "strong and authoritative . . . self" (193) of the artist must take a stand. Michael Levenson describes the antimimetic correlative of this when he concludes that the art of Lewis and Henri Gaudier-Brzeska "had severed realistic correspondence and realistic responsibility. . . . It substituted a pursuit of abstraction for the pursuit of representation; it deserted 'life.'" The lesson for literature was that "it was no longer obliged to justify its technical experiments on the grounds of greater realism, that it might now insist on the autonomy of form" (1984: 125). Gaudier-Brzeska, writing in *Blast* 1, defined "sculptural feeling" as "the appreciation of masses in relation. . . . the defining of these masses by planes" (1914: 155). Vorticism, Pound subsequently declared, was interested in the "creative faculty as opposed to the mimetic" (1915: 277). The thrust of the aesthetic of "1914" was thus away from mimesis, copying, "life" and toward abstraction, form, "planes."

Huyssen proposes that the mass culture of modernist paranoia was associated and even identified with the women who were seen as its principal consumers: "[T]he political, psychological, and aesthetic discourse around the turn of the century consistently and obsessively genders mass culture and the masses as feminine, while high culture, whether traditional or modern, clearly remains the privileged realm of male activities" (1986: 47). This is indeed the other feature of Nicholls's account of the Men of 1914's aesthetic politics, in which "style" was pitted against the feminine. The hardness and clarity celebrated in Pound's reviews of Joyce was opposed to formless matter. This is a venerable polarity whose prevalence in ancient Greek philosophy Marianne DeKoven finds unmasked by Luce Irigaray's *Speculum of the Other Woman:* "[M]asculine (self-)representation defines (refines) itself in opposition to maternal materiality as pure intellect, ideality, and reason. . . . Matter is, for Plotinus, at once liquid and feminine-maternal. It is incapable of form, but is the necessary medium upon which form imprints itself" (DeKoven 1991: 30, 32). DeKoven, however, is concerned to point out the specific inflations and inflections of such a model at the historical moment of modernism, as are Huyssen and Nicholls. In Nicholls's account "that triumph of form over 'bodily' content on which one major strand of modernism will depend" (1995: 4) reaches its apotheosis in the associated aesthetics of Pound, Lewis, and Eliot, for whom "what really counted was the 'organisation of forms,' the power of design as the 'composition and symmetry and balance' of structures . . . which might function to order the flux and chaos of modern phenomenal life. . . . To articulate 'form' is consequently to effect that displacement by which we are able to 'contemplate' (in Eliot's word) the flux of sensation in which we are normally immersed" (196).

If one aspect of "1914"—of Poundian Imagism or Lewisian Vorticism—was couched in the heated language of the *guerrier*, the other gravitated toward the cold calculation of the craftsman. The one leaps over the top, firing off manifestos at literary London; the other retreats disdainfully into the studio to work in solitude. It could be argued that the latter historically succeeds the former, but there are also continuities between the two. Both are antagonistic to the "herd," or "mob"; both are implicitly masculinist. If the former rhetoric is a polemical avant-gardism analogous to Futurism (not least in its violent antagonism to F. T. Marinetti's movement, whose meetings Pound and Lewis disrupted), the latter may be defined as modernist classicism. As early as 1912 this had been adumbrated by T. E. Hulme, who came to counterpose the classical to romantic art, calling for a period of "dry hardness" in verse (1960: 126). Hulme's assertion that "after a hundred years of romanticism, we are in for a classical revival" (113) was echoed by Lewis, who sealed the classicist tag on "1914" in *Blasting and Bombardiering*: "What I think history will say about the 'Men of 1914' is that they represent an attempt to get away from romantic art into classical art" (1982: 250). As we have seen, Pound's early reviews of *Dubliners* and the *Portrait* epitomize this aesthetic: toward abstraction, clarity, hardness and against the mob rule he perceives in Ireland. The "rhetoric of later Rome," Pound declares, was "the seed and the symptom of the Roman Empire's decadence and extinction. A nation that cannot write clearly cannot be trusted to govern, nor yet to think" (1967: 90). But with the arrival of *Ulysses* we face another paradox. The press's response to Joyce's book frequently described it in precisely the terms against which his contemporaries' aesthetic had been set. *Ulysses* was heaving, uncontrolled, a defeat for "form" at the hands of "matter." From the point of view of the classicist modernists Pound, Eliot, and Lewis—all veterans of the same "youth racket" as Joyce—this would seem to be an aesthetic problem, for Joyce produces the very opposite of the classical art they had espoused thus far. How did Joyce's three contemporaries respond? The answers are significant both for his subsequent reception and for the development of the idea of modernism.

Calling Your Time: Classicists of 1922

When, in June 1922, Ezra Pound gave notice of the completed *Ulysses*, he continued to present the text according to his own preferences. "*Ulysses* is, presumably, as unrepeatable as Tristram Shandy; I mean you cannot duplicate it," he proclaimed (1967: 196); but he did not hesitate to duplicate his own comparison of Joyce to Flaubert, which had dominated his view of the writer for almost a decade. This has been partly explained as a kind of blindness on Pound's part, a typically stubborn refusal to recognize the changes undergone by his former protégé. "In effect," comments A. Walton Litz, "his later essays of 1922–23 are simply a working-out of the view of *Ulysses* already established in 1918–19. . . . Pound's first and lasting impression of *Ulysses* was based on the earlier and plainer versions of the first nine episodes, before Joyce had revised them to harmonize with the more complex second half of the novel" (1974: 10). But the reassertion of the Flaubert-Joyce link also has a deeper significance, in Pound's need for this immense, new, and immensely novel book—"first of the new era" (Pound 1967: 199)—to conform to the cultural and political project that he continued to pursue. If the Joyce of *Dubliners* had seemed to Pound to be an invaluable acquisition, a prize writer of prose, the Joyce of *Ulysses* was an essential cultural ally, too important to let slip. What Pound's latest invocation of "Papa Flaubert" does is to make *Ulysses* a critique of modernity: an "inferno," not an encomium, a satire of degradation, not a capitulation to it.

The strategy this time, therefore, is to compare the novel to another text of Flaubert's, as Pound maintained what Eliot might have called his continuous parallel between Joyce and the nineteenth century. If *Dubliners* could be mapped onto *Madame Bovary* and the *Three Tales*, and the *Portrait* onto *A Sentimental Education*, this latest book could be shown to resemble Flaubert's unfinished *Bouvard and Pécuchet*. This not only provides a suitably comic counterpart to *Ulysses* but encourages a reading of the novel as pure satire, a lingering mockery of bourgeois stupidity: "Messrs Bouvard and Pécuchet are the basis of democracy; Bloom also is the basis of democracy; he is the man in the street, the next man, the public, not our public, but Mr Wells' public; for Mr Wells he is Hocking's public, he is *l'homme moyenne sensuel;* . . . the Daily Mail reader, the man who believes what he sees in the papers" (1967: 194). Bloom faces a chain of rejections here. The despised advertising man is "not our public"—the readership of the *Dial,* for instance—but that of Wells: a figure who, like Wells's work, sums up the leveling banality of the democratic age. But the ignominy continues, for even Wells would disavow Bloom and see him as someone else's constituent. Joyce, on this reading, is brutally assaulting "the public" and "democracy." In "Cyclops," Pound avers with some relish, "satire on the various dead manners of language culminates in the execution scene, blood and sugar stewed into clichés and rhetoric; just what the public deserves, and just what the public gets every morning with its porridge, in the Daily Mail and in sentimento-rhetorical journalism; it is perhaps the most savage bit of satire we have had since Swift suggested a cure for famine in Ireland" (198). *Ulysses* as read by Pound, then, is a profoundly political text in its bludgeoning of what Nicholls calls "the hollow forms of contemporary politics" (1995: 190). Toward the end of his article Pound calls the novel "an epoch-making report on the state of the human mind in the twentieth century" (1967: 199). In Pound's eyes the book works to confirm the divide between cultural haves and have-nots, the "party of intelligence" (89) and the "imbeciles" who inhabit most of the world (115).

Pound is evidently untroubled by what many reviewers had considered the overwhelming sprawl of the book. After all, as early as March 1917 he had informed Joyce that he had begun "an endless poem, of no known category . . . all about everything" (1967: 102), so the bulk of *Ulysses*—"the size of four ordinary novels" (198)—does not dismay him. Evidently this is simply the scale needed to batter contemporary society comprehensively, to show nothing less than "the whole occident under the domination of capital" (198). This polemical function is the key to the relation of Pound's reviews to the style of modernism he had promoted. As we have seen, there were two faces to this avant-garde: the antagonistic as well as the aloof. Pound's reading of *Ulysses* secures its place in the "1914" canon not as a serene masterpiece but as the culmination of the antisocial agonistics that had dominated *Blast* almost a decade earlier.

What kind of text might be suited to this role? Pound's reading has often been described as a "realist" or "novelistic" one, but realism for Pound is not a straightforward category. One of the most interesting features of his reading is his struggle to think his way beyond the novel form. Indeed, as Paul Sheehan (2002) has demonstrated, the novel qua form, with its innate predisposition toward narrative, always posed a problem for modernism. One reason for this is that the novel's narrative character seemed to encourage responses—empathy, suspense, and the like—associated with precisely the mass culture identified earlier as one of modernism's targets. David Trotter has noted the difficulty that "the novel's addiction to romance" presented for writers attempting to be "serious," and has pointed to the surprising homologies between the narratives of D. H. Lawrence and popular fiction (1993: 43, 184–93). Another allegory of the novel's risky relation to the popular is *Madame Bovary*, which for Andreas Huyssen (1986: 44–47) is the founding instance of a male modernism's denigration of the mass and the female. "Flaubert's 'hardness,'" writes Peter Nicholls, "is recognizably modernist in its way of pitting style against debased forms of cultural imitation. . . . [F]or while Emma Bovary's career is the very embodiment of a secondhand desire derived from romantic fiction, [Flaubert] . . . tacitly proposes a 'genuine' aesthetic as a ground of critical distance" (1995: 20). If the novelistic genre itself is implicated in this feminine world, then a "genuine" aesthetic must reinvent the novel—or indeed produce something that is not a novel at all. When Suman Gupta writes that "both Eliot and Pound were cognizant of the difficulties of confining *Ulysses* within a definition of the novel" (1993: 233), one should perhaps conclude that the novel's difficulty was modernism's opportunity.

"In this super-novel," Pound writes, "our author has also poached on the epic" (1967: 197). But he also asserts that Joyce "has done an inferno" (198), and the French version of his article claims that "Joyce a complété le grand sottisier" (206), confronting the world with "une encyclopédie imbécile—sous la forme de fiction" (208). Pound trawls the possible genres to describe *Ulysses*, and finds the book overspilling each one—but the best description of this might be the "encyclopedia" itself, conceived as an inclusive catalogue of styles and details. (The book, writes Pound, "does add definitely to the international store of literary technique" [196].) This is the final significance of Pound's invocation of Flaubert's unfinished last work, whose monotonous narrative was intended to degenerate into a series of textual scraps—"a collection of transient propositions," according to Jonathan Culler, "which are piled up, exposed as rubbish and thus made available for durability" (1988: 179). In Pound's *Ulysses* reviews, the "modernist encyclopedia" is the fulfillment of the lists and columns of "transient propositions" that did the polemical work in *Blast*.

If the problem of genre is latent in Pound's response to *Ulysses*, it is conscious and explicit in T. S. Eliot's. "I am not begging the question in calling *Ulysses* a 'novel,'" he insists in "*Ulysses*, Order and Myth," "and if you call it an epic it will not matter." But it does matter, to judge by the theory of literary history that Eliot deftly produces: "If it is not a novel, that is simply because the novel is a form which will no longer serve; it is because the novel, instead of being a form, was simply the expression of an age which had not sufficiently lost all form to feel the need of something stricter. Mr. Joyce has written one novel—the *Portrait;* Mr. Wyndham Lewis has written one novel—*Tarr.* I do not suppose that either of them will ever write another 'novel.' The novel ended with Flaubert and with James" (1975: 177). Eliot posits a catastrophic fall from "order," a modern counterpart to the dissociation of sensibility. An earlier age—presumably from the rise of the novel to the end of the nineteenth century—"had not sufficiently lost all form" and could thus find unforced expression in the novel, with the order of the age spontaneously manifested as order in the text. But the twentieth century has itself "lost all form" and if directly transmuted into art will produce mere formlessness. In itself this last claim is not so far from Joyce's hostile critics. Eliot's contribution to the argument is to insist that *Ulysses,* rather than capitulating to formlessness as Richard Aldington had complained, imports the necessary structure from the *Odyssey.*

Eliot was not the first to have noticed the Homeric parallels. Most notably Valéry Larbaud, in a lecture on Joyce delivered in December 1921, had explained (with Joyce's authorization) that the "key" was "in the door, or rather on the cover": the title would explain the book, in which "everything which appeared arbitrary and sometimes extravagant is really deliberate and premeditated" (1970: 260). Eliot had published a section of Larbaud's talk in the *Criterion* of October 1922 and refers to it early in his own essay; Arnold Bennett shows himself aware of Larbaud in his review, a year and a half before Eliot. So although Joyce reported himself disappointed with the lack of "Homeric" responses a year after publication (Ellmann 1982: 527), Eliot's focus on "myth" is not a decisively new element. What is striking about the focus is less its novelty than its narrowness, its refusal to take in any other aspects of the text in an article published twenty-one months after Joyce's book appeared. As Michael Edward Kaufmann has pointed out, Eliot promised to write a review of *Ulysses* for most of 1922. In May he claimed to be "toiling over it fitfully," and five months later he was still "struggling with a notice of *Ulysses.* . . . I find it extremely difficult to put my opinion of the book intelligently" (Eliot 1988: 526, 594). Kaufmann proposes that this tardiness is related to the development of *The Waste Land,* which was not published in book form until early 1923—when it was accompanied by Eliot's footnotes. The latter, Kaufmann suggests, played a role in Eliot's understanding of his own poem analogous to that of the *Odyssey* in his understanding of *Ulysses:* both "created an image of the Modernist work . . . as unified, elaborately patterned, autonomous, an image that many continue to accept as Modernism" (1992: 80). One can add that until he hit on the Homeric emphasis, Eliot was unable fully to deal with *Ulysses*. In 1918 he had written of its "attractive terror . . . repel[ling] the majority of men" (Kelly 1998: 71). In September 1922, while still "toiling" and "struggling" with his review, he discussed the book with Virginia Woolf in terms different from those of the article he eventually produced: Joyce, Woolf recorded him as saying, had "showed up the futility of all the English styles" and had "destroyed the whole of the 19th century" (1978: 75, 74). Even "*Ulysses,* Order and Myth" itself begins by acknowledging that "it has given me all the surprise, delight, and terror that I can require" (Eliot 1975: 175), a comment that Jonathan Levin has glossed as "distinctly romantic": "The constant pursuit of surprise, delight, and terror . . . the abandonment to experiences that are invariably accompanied by them, bespeaks a fundamentally different sensibility than that which seeks compulsively, and with a sense of impending sociocultural disaster, to create order out of chaos. . . . Such a sensibility values experience itself, whatever unfamiliar shape it may take, over the desire to impose a more satisfying, more familiar shape on it" (1992: 140).

There are two sides, in short, to Eliot's response to *Ulysses*. One is well known and, as Kaufmann says, has become definitive of modernist aesthetics. The other is more subterranean: Eliot appears startled, disturbed, even terrified by Joyce's destructive text. This second reaction is closer, in fact, to the shocked, somatic recoil of the reviewers I discussed earlier. What this helps us to see is the relation between that "kinetic" response and the "static" one enshrined by Eliot's article: the latter is a defensive formation produced *against* the former, a prevention of the troubling effects that so many other readers had described. In Kantian terms, it could be said that Eliot converts an experience of the sublime (nature can count as dynamically sublime, writes Kant, "only insofar as we consider it an object of fear" [1987: 119]) into a judgment of the beautiful.

The defensive character of Eliot's response may explain the vehemence with which he asserts the wider significance of Joyce's "mythical method," as a solution to the problem of the "modernist novel" that I noted in connection with Pound. Where Pound sees a teeming, polemical *Ulysses* reinventing the encyclopedia, Eliot rejects the novel still more emphatically and identifies the "epic" as the privileged new genre of the postnovelistic age. Indeed, he lets the antinovelistic cat out of the bag with his revealing comments that the novel is not even a "form" at all—a fundamental handicap given the paramount importance of form to this classicist aesthetic—and that the mythical method will replace the "narrative method" (1975: 178). One could not find a clearer statement of modernism's generic problem—or its solution.

Eliot's essay not only expounds the aesthetic issue in stark, stripped-down terms but performs a similar operation on *Ulysses* itself, guarding against the "kinetic," fastidiously avoiding any reference to the diverse contents and idioms of the book, and substituting structure for texture. If Pound's review of the complete *Ulysses* remains rooted in his reading of Joyce in the 1910s, Eliot's manages the feat—in some ways even more retrogressively—of producing a text in line with the "dry hardness" of Hulmean classicism. It is commonplace in discussions of "*Ulysses*, Order and Myth" to point out that Eliot's account seems designed to justify his own *Waste Land*. But more broadly, it achieves the feat of making Joyce safe for the aesthetics of "1914," which, to repeat Michael Levenson's words, "substituted a pursuit of abstraction for the pursuit of representation" and "insist[ed] on the autonomy of form" (1984: 125). Where Pound's *Ulysses* provides satirical "violence," Eliot's demonstrates classical "craft."

Eliot's essay is an exemplary case in the history of Joyce criticism. It is the starkest and most influential instance of the abstraction of Joyce—of a practice of reading and writing that would tend toward generalities rather than specifics, broad allegorical structures rather than the work's texture. The other two important dichotomies observed thus far can be aligned here: the Eliotic tradition will favor stasis over kinesis and global distance over local proximity. Pound and Eliot, writes Joseph Kelly, "changed Joyce from an Irish writer into an avant-garde, cosmopolitan writer, shucking off his provincial husk" (1998: 9). It may well be asserted that these emphases find a warrant in Joyce's work itself. But they downplay what Andrew Gibson (2002) has more recently reasserted as the *particularism* of Joyce's writing, its immersion in specific historical and geographical situations and their attendant mass of detail.

In the final irony of the present investigation, it was the remaining Man of 1914 who best articulated this. It was left to Wyndham Lewis to challenge Pound and Eliot's successful assimilation of the book, in a tirade that presented *Ulysses* as too much in tune with contemporary fashion. Lewis had met Joyce in 1920 and become a sometime drinking companion, but in 1927 his lengthy critique entitled "An Analysis of the Mind of James Joyce" appeared both in his new magazine *The Enemy* and in his vast and recondite philosophical polemic *Time and Western Man*. "I regard *Ulysses*," Lewis writes, "as a *time-book*" (1993: 81). The philosophical "Time-school" or "Time-mind" of which Joyce is a literary representative reaches from Henri Bergson—"the perfect philosophic ruffian" (166)—to Albert Einstein, with thinkers such as A. N. Whitehead and Oswald Spengler also dissected in the course of the book. Bergson inaugurates the time-school with his misguided reaction to "mechanistic," Newtonian accounts of the universe, against which he poses that realm of freedom experienced in the *durée:* an organic flux of intuitive time unconstrained by the "spatializing" reifications of clock time. Yet this plunge from the "mechanical" to the "organic," Lewis asserts, is bogus: "The ['time'] doctrine . . . is labelled 'organic': and its advertisement is that it is *life,* as contrasted with the mechanical 'deadness' of materialist science. . . . What you pay for the pantheistic immanent oneness of 'creative,' 'evolutionary' substance, into which you are invited to merge, is that you become a phalanstery of selves. . . . [But] it is very clear what you *lose.* By this proposed transfer from the beautiful *objective, material* world of common-sense, over to the 'organic' world of chronological mentalism, you lose not only the clearness of outline, the static beauty, of the things you commonly apprehend; you lose also the clearness of outline of your own individuality which apprehends them" (165–67). Lewis sees in the time-school a merging of the human subject into its surroundings, indeed, into an unfolding cosmic process. Rather than offering freedom from determinism, he argues, such a move only makes the human all the more determined, revealed as the helpless accomplice of forces beyond it. The "organism" of the time-school thus turns out to be "perfectly *mechanical*" (174), a covert attack on human agency and the clear distinction between subjects and objects. Lewis's sense of the public mind as irrational and manipulable was a very contemporary view. As Michael North has shown, the 1920s were marked by concern that "public opinion" had degenerated from reasoned debate to a "public unconscious," a thing of phobias and prejudices (1999: 64–86).

Lewis's account of Joyce's own mind ranges carelessly across various features of his art that seem to have little to do with the "time-school." One comes closer to the crux of the matter with Lewis's assertion that Joyce's stylistic daring conceals an uninspired mind: "[H]e has practised sabotage where his intellect was concerned, in order to leave his craftsman's hand freer for its stylistic exercises. . . . Daring or unusual speculation, or an unwonted intensity of outlook, is not good for technical display, that is certain, and they are seldom found together. The intellect is in one sense the rival to the hand, and is apt to hamper rather than assist it" (1993: 92). As "*the craftsman*, pure and simple" (88) Joyce lacks intellectual dynamism of his own. This is how the "time-mind" has been able to possess him, filling the vacuum in his head: "It is such people that the creative intelligence fecundates and uses. . . . He is only a tool, an instrument, in short. . . . [T]he craftsman is susceptible and unprotected" (88). Joyce thus begins to figure as the opposite of Lewis's hard, critical intelligence: his possession by the drifting influence of the time-mind is a parable of the passive, anti-agential time doctrine itself.

Worse still, in Lewis's view, is the actual content of *Ulysses*, which Eliot had strategically avoided. In line with his description of Joyce's passivity, he claims that the book is an inflated, if covert, example of naturalism: an acquiescent notation of literary material, unshaped by artistic will. This, in turn, produces an impression of random, unmediated matter: "[I]t lands the reader inside an Aladdin's cave of incredible bric-à-brac in which a dense mass of dead stuff is collected, from 1901 toothpaste, a bar or two of Sweet Rosie O'Grady, to pre-nordic architecture. . . . The amount of *stuff*—unorganized brute material—that the more active principle of drama has to wade through, under the circumstances, slows it down to the pace at which, inevitably, the sluggish tide of the author's bric-à-brac passes the observer, at the saluting-post, or in this case, the reader. It is a suffocating moeotic expanse of objects, all of them lifeless, the sewage of a Past twenty years old. . . . At the end of a long reading of *Ulysses* you feel that it is the very nightmare of the naturalistic method that you have been experiencing" (89). Lewis, in fact, reproduces with a sardonic rather than outraged air one of the major objections of the early reviewers five years previously: a suffocating despair at the seemingly endless materiality of the book. He brings two new features to this critique. One is simply his status as a "Man of 1914," the last to respond to *Ulysses* (of which Pound had asserted that "all serious men of letters, whether they write out a critique or not, will certainly have to make one for their own use" [1967: 194]). Eliot's article was a repudiation of ill-informed complaints of formlessness: a recuperation of *Ulysses* for classicist modernism, one that we may suspect was hard to secure in the face of the "terror" of the text. The effect of Lewis's attack is to undo Eliot's effort, banishing Joyce from the developed modernist aesthetic rather than taking the trouble to assimilate him. To be sure, Eliot's has become the more canonical account. But just as Fredric Jameson describes Lewis as "blurting out" the ideological presuppositions suppressed in less extreme thinkers (1979: 23), one may see him as blurting out all the material that Eliot had to work to suppress in order to process a classicist Joyce. Whatever its own blindnesses, Lewis's critique, unlike Eliot's praise, sees in Joyce the prominence of the particular, of historical specificity and textual detail.

One such specific dimension again proves tellingly difficult to ignore, as it had for H. G. Wells. One of Lewis's first moves is to discuss Joyce in relation to other Irish writers, who "descended into Piccadilly Circus, thenceforth watched by an Empire on which the sun never sets" (1993: 74–75). Eliot mentions Yeats as "the first contemporary to become conscious" of the need for the mythical method, but he never adverts to his and Joyce's Irish background. For Lewis, by contrast, "Joyce and Yeats are the prose and poetry respectively of the Ireland that culminated in the Rebellion" (75). Joyce is not to be thought of as a Sinn Féiner: "In spite of that he is very 'irish.' He is ready enough, as a literary artist, to stand for Ireland, and has wrapped himself up in a gigantic cocoon of local colour in *Ulysses*" (76). Lewis by no means sees nationality as a primal identity that writers spontaneously express: in an age of globalism, he insists, nationalism becomes "artificially fostered," as in the "artificial, pseudo-historical air" of the Easter Rising (78, 76). He thus shows no sympathy for republicanism. Richard Ellmann, commenting on Lewis's account of his first meeting with Joyce, ventures that "to be Irish was to be too Irish for Lewis's taste" (1982: 495). Lewis's sense of the interdependence of the local and the global nonetheless adumbrates a more complex account of Joyce's relation to Ireland than that of the modernist internationalism initiated by Pound.

The other, related, effect of Lewis's critique is to locate Joyce in a new intellectual context. Bergson, Proust, Gertude Stein—all signify for Lewis the decadent Parisian atmosphere of *faux*-revolution or "high-bohemia," of which *transition* is a notable feature. Lewis's quest for a space "with nothing but air and rock, however inhospitable and featureless, and a little timeless, too" (1993: 89), "the physical world" (110) of ruthless externality, is the zenith of that masculinist modernism outlined earlier, in which not only mass culture but most of the avant-garde can be written off as formless, fluid, and feminine. The stream of consciousness in *Ulysses* is not only a sludge of matter but "the einsteinian flux. Or (equally well) it is the duration-flux of Bergson.... And into that flux it is you, the reader, that are plunged ... down into the middle of the stream.... [T]he method of *Ulysses* imposes a softness, flabbiness and vagueness everywhere in its bergsonian fluidity" (100–101). It is not difficult to see the gendered implications of this account. Lewis feminizes *Ulysses*, makes of it a flowing, passive stream of a book. Marianne DeKoven has pointed out the significance of such imagery for modernism, in which "threatening desire, gendered female, is imaged as a turbulent flood" (1991: 34). Once again, nothing could be further from Eliot's account. But Lewis inadvertently sets up a new chain of associations for Joyce, which will only be fully realized in the moment of "theory." Paul Edwards argues that French feminism, with its "invitation to plunge into a pre-logical non-system of signification [is] in a direct line of succession" from Bergson and the "time-school" (Lewis 1993: 479). Tony Pinkney summarizes the change in critical outlook that occurred later in the twentieth century: "[T]he reactionary politics of the modernist Right seems chiefly a matter of a hypertrophied, centred, 'male' identity—all that is captured in the Eliotic, Hulmean, Yeatsian and Poundian poetic themes of 'hardness', 'dryness', impersonality, objectivity, 'presentation.' Against this frenetic masculinism, the progressive modernist text ... will unleash the creaturely forces of Nature, the body, sexuality, the 'feminine'; the great modernist role-model was no longer Eliot's Tiresias . . . but rather Joyce's Molly Bloom" (1989b: 6). Lewis would not live to see such a day, though he appears to have thought it had already arrived in the 1920s. His "Analysis of the Mind of James Joyce" takes "1914" to its apogee and adumbrates the realignment Pinkney describes: with enemies like the Enemy, Joyce would have no shortage of friends.

To recap, for many reviewers Joyce raised more than one problem. The highbrow author of "erudite nonsense" (Slocombe 1970: 218) was also explosively somatic, a writer liable to produce shocks and vomiting. Modernism, for these commentators, is at once an aloof elite—a *cénacle* distant and detached from the general public—and a fashion associated with "the New York intelligentsia" ("Aramis" 1970: 193), "the new fashionable kinematographic vein" ("Man About Town" 1970: 194), and "the youthful dilettantes in Paris or London" (Leslie 1970a: 202). Michael North has shown how, in the media of 1922, *Ulysses* and *The Waste Land* could figure not as aloof and obscure examples of "high modernism" but as part of the contemporary: as avatars of novelty analogous to jazz music (1999: 140–47). The analogies were loose and imprecise, more a matter of generational association—of an imagined connection with youth—than with textual specifics or authorial intention. Nonetheless they formed part of the horizon for the public perception of Joyce as he became an object of notoriety and fascination. The *Daily Express* headline "An Irish Revel: And Some Flappers" inadvertently sums this up (Mais 1970: 191).

In one sense what makes Joyce most obscure—his style—is directly opposed to what most plainly makes him a public figure: his obscenity. As John Quinn sought to argue in the "Nausicaa" trials, the latter would depend on a lucidity absent from Joyce's writing; but there is also a submerged link between the two qualities. Both, like the sublime modernism described by Lyotard, overwhelm and destabilize the reader to "kinetic" effect, in an excess of matter that throws the "literary" status of *Ulysses* into doubt; both pornography and the avant-garde are decried as a threat to social order. And for H. G. Wells, as we saw, both qualities were oddly linked to Joyce's Irish provenance.

All this was downplayed by Pound and Eliot. Despite the striking differences in their readings, both writers viewed Joyce as a detached critic of the contemporary rather than as threateningly at one with it. "*Ulysses,* Order and Myth" remains the starkest statement of this recuperation: rescuing Joyce from the sphere of the novelistic, it evacuates particularity from the text. This would be an enduring gesture. Analogously, one witnesses the beginnings of modernist internationalism in these critics: Eliot never mentions Ireland, and Pound had been publicly internationalizing Joyce since 1914. But Irishness is one of the many features of Joyce unassimilable to a classicist aesthetic that Lewis "blurts out." Inadvertently Lewis paves the way for later critics who will treat Joyce as other than the classical, "static" artist that a major strain of modernist aesthetics required him to be. In the next chapter, however, such strategies will be observed still at work in consolidating Joyce's reputation.

2

The Dream of the West
Writing in Transit

> [L]iterature is not split up by political frontiers.
> Ezra Pound, "Past History"

> The campus calls them.
> *Finnegans Wake*

"International Modernism": so criticism came to name the work, selected and canonized, of Joyce's generation. Michael North has demonstrated just how important—and how rapidly changing—a sense of international space was in public consciousness and culture during Joyce's own working life. Drawing on Raymond Williams's emphasis on travel and estrangement as the keys to modernism (1989a: 45–46), North finds mobility and transit pervasive—not only as physical facts but as aspects of feeling and perception—in the early twentieth century. The advent of network broadcasting, he suggests, created a new kind of community, "one that linked different localities and even different countries with a simultaneity that made physical travel seem antediluvian by comparison" (1999: 15–16). North's account echoes the geographer David Harvey's theorization of "time-space compression" as a defining force of modernity. Communications, transport, and the flow of capital, Harvey proposes (1989: 260–83), have accelerated experience and shrunk space, and placed ordinary life against a global horizon. For both North and Harvey literary modernism takes place in this new global arena, from which its experimentation with spatial and temporal categories is inseparable. Joyce's writings appear to illustrate these developments with particular clarity. In *Ulysses* and *Finnegans Wake,* in particular, critics have found what Williams calls the "modernist universals" (1989a: 47), the bid for an art that would transcend place and time; and these polyglot texts seem to exemplify the linguistic border crossing described by Williams and lived by Joyce himself, replicating international space at the level of the word.

The beginnings of such an internationalization of Joyce by his contemporaries has already been observed. This emphasis will recur, indeed intensify, in this chapter as one reads Joyce's readers in the era of *Work in Progress.* The reading of Joyce has itself had an international character: nodes of interpretation and appropriation emerge and shift from Dublin to London and from Paris to Boston. But to say this is also to name specific places. The international and the national, the global and the local are themselves inseparable, as in David Harvey's dialectic: "[T]he diminution of spatial barriers has provoked both an increasing sense of exclusionary nationalism and localism, and an exhilarating sense of the heterogeneity and porosity of cultures" (1996: 246). The international is invented and experienced in national contexts; the modernist universals are promoted in particular situations. This chapter will explore the movement of Joyce's work, first through a series of particular critical contexts and then outward across geographical space. I shall first examine the advocacies of Joyce put forward by his associates in the late 1920s and early 1930s, drawing out the different approaches to his writing that they initiate and encourage. I will then turn to Joyce's reception in the academy, which is gradually assuming its role as the main site for the production of literary criticism. The developing perception of Joyce as an international writer informs the contrasting responses to his work in England and the United States. I shall consider a selection of commentaries that, firstly, crystallize a critical position with particular clarity and, secondly, have tended to retain some force or status after the moment of their publication. The five sections of this chapter are thus organized around five representative readers of Joyce: Eugene Jolas, Stuart Gilbert, Frank Budgen, F. R. Leavis, and Harry Levin. Around these central figures I will try to paint a broader picture and point to other writers influenced by them or working in the same milieu.

Joyce had already encouraged certain writers to praise his work. Notably, in response to "*Ulysses*, Order and Myth," he hoped that Eliot would coin a catchphrase such as "two plane," since the public needed a new term on which to focus every six months (Joyce 1975: 297). But the author's orchestration of his commentators becomes more intensive after Wyndham Lewis's intervention, with a series of sustained advocacies openly primed and prompted by Joyce: the volume of essays *Our Exagmination Round his Factification for Incamination of Work in Progress* (1929), Stuart Gilbert's *James Joyce's "Ulysses"* (1930), and Frank Budgen's *James Joyce and the Making of "Ulysses"* (1934). I begin with the Parisian literary review *transition*, which from 1927 to 1938 played a major role in the centrifugal expansion of Joyce's reputation.

The International Style: Revelations of the Word

Eugene Jolas, as Sydney Bolt notes, was "born cosmopolitan" (1992: 204) in the United States and raised in France, subsequently spending much of the 1920s moving between the two countries (his memoirs are entitled *Man from Babel*). As literary editor of the *Chicago Tribune*'s Paris edition, he published a series of articles under the rubric "Rambles Through Literary Paris," interviewing Surrealist authors and sometimes discussing *Ulysses*, which was still only available in France. Jolas's desire for a magazine of experimental literature emerges from this transatlantic experience, in which he had come to interpret and report the European scene for an English-reading public. Back in the United States in early 1926, Jolas discussed the country with Sherwood Anderson, who "argued that the American character and pattern of life came almost exclusively from the American soil" (McMillan 1975: 14). But Jolas, writes Dougald McMillan, "knew well how deep the roots of America were buried in Europe. He could not limit his concern to either continent, but was seeking a way to build a bridge between Europe and America" (14). When Jolas, his wife Maria, and the journalist Elliot Paul conceived of a new literary review, the titles they initially favored were *Bridges* and *Continents*. The magazine *transition*, then, was intended to occupy an unusual geographical site, mediating and ferrying ideas and writing across national boundaries and between continents. It is one of the most concerted attempts to create a textual space of international modernism—a space that functioned above all to channel European writing to the United States. As we saw in chapter 1, the critical internationalization of Joyce began as far back as 1914, but *transition* represents another, more extensive stage in the writer's elevation to this realm.

Joyce was rarely absent from *transition* during its twenty-seven issues. Before 1939 it was the major outlet for what would become *Finnegans Wake*. Articles advocating his new work also became a regular feature (there were over one hundred), and the "Work in Progress" corner of the review expanded to include curiosities like Stella Steyn's illustrations of "Anna Livia Plurabelle" and César Abin's caricature of the author. In the words of McMillan, "*transition* became, as the French critic Marcel Brion said, 'la maison de Joyce'. . . . Indeed, the name Joyce became so synonymous with *transition* that attackers could or would not tell them apart" (1975: 179). A number of the explicatory articles are now best known from their appearance in the *Exagmination*, which was intended as a defensive response to public hostility. The book is exemplary of the kind of interpretation and advocacy that Joyce received in *transition* and retains a unique status as the only authorized account of *Finnegans Wake* to appear. What are the aesthetic and cultural connotations of the *transition* and *Exagmination* position?

First, an affirmation of the review's internationalism. Samuel Beckett's "Dante . . . Bruno. Vico . . . Joyce" avers that "no creature in heaven or earth ever spoke the language of *Work in Progress*," but that "it is reasonable to admit that an international phenomenon might be capable of speaking it" (1983: 30–31). For Frank Budgen the *Work* is similarly an exemplary text of modern cosmopolitanism, of Harvey's "annihilation of space": "Technical progress has brought the sundered tribes of Europe nearer together. Their interests interlock and their thought and speech interpenetrate in spite of wars and customs barriers. . . . All languages and dialects are there for [Joyce] to draw on at will" (1961: 38–39). Victor Llona makes this connection plainer still. Wondering whether Joyce makes too great a multilingual demand on his readers, he concludes that "in this departure he but anticipates the trend of the times, which assuredly leans to a thorough internationalization in speech as in everything else" (1961: 100). Joyce's writing becomes the native style of the twentieth century, at once incorporating the new range of linguistic material available to the artist and promising to serve as a primer for the tongue of the global village. In the 1920s, Michael North notes, the belief was widespread that "this wider and more complicated world needed a less ambiguous means of public communication" (1999: 108); hence the intensity of interest, in the interwar years, in forging a universal language. Joyce's engagement with this prospect is raised by Robert McAlmon, who tries to draw a fine distinction: "[H]e does not want to create a new literary esperanto, but he wishes to originate a flexible language that might be an esperanto of the subconscious" (1961: 110). Stuart Gilbert is similarly ambiguous on this point, warning that "it would be wrong to see in *Work in Progress* . . . any sort of propaganda for an international tongue, a new Volapük or Esperanto" (1961: 57), but conceding that "the Irish writer's vocabulary is world-wide—*Work in Progress* may well be easier reading for a polyglot foreigner than for an Englishman with but his mother tongue" (58). Llona tentatively hints at a national origin for the international polyphony: Joyce's daring is greater than that of Rabelais because the French author "had perhaps a much greater reverence than Mr. Joyce, an Irishman of revolutionary tendencies (in literature, at least), could possibly entertain for the King's English" (98). In the course of his critique of Joyce, Wyndham Lewis had argued that globalism produced a heightened sense of nationality as its dialectical by-product. Llona is one of the first of many to make the opposite claim about Joyce's writing, namely that a specific national situation lies behind the drastic "internationalization" performed on the English language.

The politics of *transition*, however, did not descend to such local matters. Indeed, Eugene Jolas's direct polemical engagement with Sean O'Faolain, the Dublin intellectual and veteran of 1916, is readable as a repudiation of "parochial" Irish concerns from a cosmopolitan standpoint. In January 1929 O'Faolain wrote in the *Irish Statesman* that Joyce's new work was too often "empty of content" and hence "ceases to serve any useful purpose" (1970: 397). Yet even as O'Faolain, writing in the first decade of the Irish Free State, rebukes Joyce's lack of accountability to the real world, he reclaims his "revolt against the despotism of fact" for a national tradition of doomed dreamers: "[H]e is here very much of his race, has his forebears in old Irish legend—is he not of the clan of Brendan who sailed for Ui Bhreasail, Bran who sailed for the Land of Heart's Desire, Ossian searching for the Land of the Ever Young . . . dreamers of the unattainable all[?]" (1970: 398). O'Faolain's chiding reclamation of Joyce for the motherland is one source of the energy with which Jolas replies in both *transition* and the *Irish Statesman*, asserting that language is more fluid and promiscuous than O'Faolain understands. English, Jolas argues, has admitted and naturalized a slew of foreign words: "Mr. O'Faolain will probably object that he is not supposed to know Scandinavian in order to understand a work of English literature. But it is equally apt to say that a knowledge of Latin and Greek, and a light smattering of other languages, is no longer sufficient in an age that is rapidly coming to a complete internationalization of the spirit" (1961: 81–82). For Jolas the Irishman O'Faolain's thesis of the immobility of language is unequal to the transnational hybridity of Joyce's prose, and indeed of twentieth-century culture. In this respect Jolas echoes the founding critical gesture with which Ezra Pound had lifted Joyce from an Irish into an international arena.

"The real metaphysical problem today," writes Jolas, "is the word" (1961: 79). The best-known flaring of this insistent theme came in 1929 with the "Revolution of the Word Proclamation," a twelve-point list that appeared at the head of a double issue of the magazine, whose signatories included four of the *Exagmination* contributors. The artist, the proclamation declares, "has the right to use words of his own fashioning and to disregard existing grammatical and syntactical laws." He or she is absolved of the need to contact a wider audience: "The writer expresses. He does not communicate"; "The plain reader be damned." The opening statement that "the Revolution in the English language is an accomplished fact" is a sign of how much the manifesto was, like the *Exagmination*, an apologia for what Joyce was already doing. If the assertion of artistic autonomy upholds his right to be difficult, the sixth proposition on the list seems most directly inspired by *Work in Progress:* "The literary creator has the right to disintegrate the primal matter of words imposed on him by text-books and dictionaries" (McMillan 1975: 49). Other *Exagmination* contributors echo Jolas's insistence on the unit of the word (McAlmon 1961: 110; Rodker 1961: 144; Budgen 1961: 39). And the word is also a major focus of the best-known essay on *Finnegans Wake*, Beckett's "Dante . . . Bruno. Vico . . . Joyce": "Here is the savage economy of hieroglyphics. Here words are not the polite contortions of 20th century printer's ink. They are alive. They elbow their way on to the page, and glow and blaze and fade and disappear" (1983: 28).

In Patricia Waugh's words, "Jolas established a modernist commitment to the notion of aesthetic autonomy or the idea of the materiality of the word" (1997: 1). Yet this particular avant-garde rhetoric differs notably from that which dominated my discussion in chapter 1. From Imagism to the "mythical method," the "Men of 1914" version of modernism pitted "form" against "matter," ultimately fissuring on the problem of assimilating *Ulysses* to this model. *Work in Progress* proved still harder to take. In 1926 Pound admitted that he could "make nothing of it whatever" (1967: 228); ten years later Eliot asserted that due to Joyce's failing eyesight "what I find in *Work in Progress* is an auditory imagination abnormally sharpened at the expense of the visual" (1975: 262–63). The abstraction favored by the "Men of 1914" line was precisely the aesthetic foe for Jolas. As Dougald McMillan has pointed out, the valorization of the word that he encouraged represents an alternative berth for Joyce in a separate wing of modernism: "The attitudes of the imagist movement pervaded the works of the best poets of the language ... [who] contrasted the concision and 'hardness' of the image with the 'soft' inadequacy of words.... [I]t was primarily *transition* that re-established the importance of 'the word' which had suffered so much in the exaltation of the image in the first quarter of the century" (1975: 2, 5). The *transition* line promotes a notion of words as "matter." Stuart Gilbert refers to "a constructive metabolism of the primal matter of language" (1961: 57). Beckett, too, refers admiringly to Shakespeare's "fat, greasy words" and Dickens's fidelity to "ooze squelching" in the course of describing Joyce's language as "a quintessential extraction of language and painting and gesture, with all the inevitable clarity of the old inarticulation" (1983: 28). Eugene Jolas writes that Joyce "gives his words odors and sounds that the conventional standard does not know.... They have the tempo of the Liffey itself flowing to the sea" (1961: 89). Jolas's reference to "the spontaneous flux of his style" (90) answers Lewis's rejection of Joyce's surrender to Bergsonian "flux." These readers defend Joyce precisely by claiming him for an artistic attitude that Lewis abhors.

This contrast was made explicit, with several essays in the *Exagmination* tilting at Joyce's critics (MacGreevy 1961: 127; William Carlos Williams 1961: 184). In particular, Marcel Brion's essay accepts wholesale

Lewis's claim that Joyce belongs to the "time-school" but inverts the valences of this assertion. Brion's musings (1961: 25–26) could be a caricature manifesto dreamed up by Lewis. "I imagine," Brion remarks, "that Joyce could compose a book of pure time"; indeed, "*Work in Progress* is essentially a time work. . . . [T]ime appears to be its principal subject" (1961: 31). The *transition* line on Joyce thus directly inverts that proposed by the "Men of 1914." Pound had called for a strong controlling consciousness, the "fury of intelligence" (Nicholls 1995: 196). Once again *transition* presents a contrast, for the Jungian Jolas's constant emphasis is on the unconscious wellsprings of art. This statement from *transition* 18 is characteristic: "The absolute importance of the dream for the creative artist must now be assumed. . . . The dream is pure imagination. At the limit of the creator's spirit there is always the pre-logical" (McMillan 1975: 57). Jolas's ultimate goal, as he explained in *The Language of Night* (1930), was a new romanticism. Joyce was thus valuable not least for his unprecedented attempt "to describe that huge world of dreams, that a-logical sequence of events remembered or inhibited, that universe of demoniacal humor and magic which has seemed impenetrable so far" (1961: 91).

Commentators frequently seek to detach and distance Jolas from Joyce, presenting the former as an overexcited ingénu whom the latter could turn to his own uses. Michael Finney's disdain for Jolas's "naive philosophy of linguistic nihilism" and "transparently sophomoric" rebelliousness (1978: 40, 44) is widespread. But as this brief review of *transition*'s promotion of Joyce has made clear, Jolas helped to create a critical space more congenial to *Work in Progress* than Joyce's erstwhile contemporaries. The different responses to the work from Jolas and Pound reflect not merely different temperaments but different strands of modern literary doctrine. The magazine's account of Joyce can, finally, be seen as both continuing and breaking with modernism's previous development: reinforcing the cosmopolitan internationalism that had already marked Joyce's elevation, yet explicitly challenging the aesthetic of classicist modernism with a new romanticism, reinstating the sticky materiality of the word as the key means of the avant-garde. One can discern here an early instance of the kind of counterreading of modernism that has deployed Joyce against rather than alongside some of his most influential contemporaries, and opposed the conservative constructions of the period propagated by Eliot and his followers. A later and more extensive case will be considered in chapter 4, when the reading of Joyce arrives at the age of theory.

Every Grain of Sand: Gilbert's Modern Classic

Stuart Gilbert was an unlikely stalwart of *transition*. His private diary reflects disparagingly on the magazine's contributors: "They can't express themselves so as to be understood, get tied up in knots; sound and fury" (1993: 6). His treatment of Joyce was correspondingly different in emphasis from that encouraged by Eugene Jolas. Gilbert's book *James Joyce's "Ulysses"* (1930) is in a sense an immense elaboration of Eliot's construal of that novel seven years earlier. Gilbert had been in contact with Joyce since 1927 and assisted in the translation of *Ulysses* into French. His study grew out of conversations with Joyce about the precise meaning of passages, for "only when the implications of the original are fully unravelled does one start looking for approximations in the other language. Thus I made a point of consulting Joyce on every doubtful point . . . and never 'passing' the French text unless I was sure we had the meaning of each word and passage quite clear in our minds" (1963: 8). The major implication of this is immediately evident. Far more than any previous commentator, Gilbert stakes all on scholarly thoroughness and hermeneutic accuracy. His study sets a vital precedent for the intensity of attention subsequently accorded Joyce: it is a book of over three hundred pages dedicated to one novel, which, following a sober exposition of background, treats each chapter of *Ulysses* in turn. The epitome of Gilbert's book is the five-page list of rhetorical forms that concludes his chapter on "Aeolus": at the heart of his project is the discovery and presentation of raw information inaccessible to the uninitiated. Gilbert's book is the beginning of a gradual process of intensified textual scrutiny. In 1974 a collection of eighteen essays on *Ulysses*, with a noted critic taking on each chapter, still required justification for the inflated importance allotted to the text (Hart and Hayman 1974: vii), whereas by the mid-1990s a series of discrete collections of essays, each volume dedicated to just *one chapter* of the novel (Gibson 1995, 1996), raised few eyebrows. Gilbert, then, heralds a long-term trend toward completeness and totality in the understanding of Joyce, the belief that his work not only bears but demands exhaustive explication. This drive for total understanding would prove paradoxical, for the more that was explained about Joyce's writing, the more there remained to be said: the explanation of a given correspondence or reference raised as many questions as it answered, fueling more interpretive books and articles and, eventually, a subgenre of metacommentaries on the state of Joycean commentary.

Gilbert himself, following up leading questions from Joyce in the late 1920s, was a long way from such a situation. When his study first appeared, *Ulysses* was still banned in the Anglophone world. In the early 1930s T. S. Eliot at Faber and Faber would suggest to an unbending Joyce the possibility of publishing parts of the novel in England (Ellmann 1982: 653). In a sense, despite Joyce's refusal, Gilbert's study is that book, an edited text of *Ulysses* punctuated with extensive commentary. In the 1930 preface Gilbert explains "the unusual circumstance that, though *Ulysses* is probably the most discussed literary work that has appeared in our time, the book itself is hardly more than a name to many. I have therefore quoted freely from the text, so that those who are unable to . . . acquire the original, may, despite the censorial ban, become acquainted with Joyce's epic work" (1963: 7). This produces another "unusual circumstance," in which the critical study becomes a surrogate *Ulysses*, a kind of "reader's edition" akin to the *Shorter Finnegans Wake* produced by Anthony Burgess some decades later. (In 1932 Charles Duff called Gilbert's book "the best substitute for the original" [McCarthy 1991: 23].) In chapter 1 I noted the high importance assumed by early reviews of *Ulysses*, given the book's unavailability to a general readership. Gilbert takes this situation to its logical conclusion, generating a book that commences by telling the story of the novel in four pages, then recapitulates it at length—half the length of *Ulysses* itself, in fact, and less trouble to read. Once again, when dealing with Joyce, an unusual relationship obtains between text, commentary, and reader.

Gilbert's reading of Joyce differs from that of Jolas and the other "verbal revolutionaries." Michael Finney notes that Gilbert sought to play a mediating role in the storms over the "revolution of the word': in late 1929 he confessed in *transition* that "for some of us, and with reason, the word 'revolution' has an ominous resonance," and that if the verbal revolt involved wanton destruction, "the chorus of communation [*sic*] which greeted our announcement . . . would have been amply justified"

(1978: 48–49). Gilbert's habitual tone is elaborately sober: discussing Joyce's anatomy of rhetoric in "Aeolus," he asserts with an extravagant flourish that "our modern Aeolists ensure with punctual emphasis our daily gasp, relayed on wings of wind from a land of darkness, or loose on us a wallet of *canards* bound with a silver thong" (1963: 171). The grand primness contrasts subtly but tellingly with Jolas's penchant for excited overstatement: Suzette Henke even suggests that Gilbert's contribution to the *Exagmination* "sounds very much like a parody of the arrogant asseverations of the *Wake*'s Professor Jones" (1991: 68). Something more than just stylistic idiosyncrasy is at work here. Gilbert's background included "a longish judicial career in the East" (1963: 8), specifically nineteen years as a judge in Burma, where he first read *Ulysses*. He came to Joyce as a figure of the imperial establishment, and his diary of the period is given to reactionary bile like the following: "Reflections on the Socialist victory in England. The workers will have more to eat but less pleasure in it. They will create the decor but dirty it with their mud and spittle. . . . [T]hey will assert themselves bloodily and take politeness for the mark of weakness. And they may bust the pound" (1993: 11–12). Unsurprisingly, Gilbert was not given to Jolas's brand of revolutionary pronouncement. Asked in May 1929 to sign the proclamation "praising the New Word," Gilbert wondered: "Why don't they learn the old ones first?" (10). The Blakean additions he made to the manifesto accordingly downplay its modernity in order to place it in a longer historical perspective (McMillan 1975: 48). This also describes a major tendency in Gilbert's book on *Ulysses*, which is above all an emphatic reassertion of the "classical" reading of Joyce. References to the symmetry and harmony of the novel are frequent: "a knowledge of each part is necessary for the understanding of the whole" (1963: 37). Reproducing for the first time a table of correspondences and Homeric parallels for the benefit of the reading public, Gilbert emphasizes "the symmetry of the technical structure," down to "Wandering Rocks," an episode "reproducing in miniature the structure of the whole" (39). He draws the lesson that "there could be no greater error than to confuse the work of James Joyce with that of the harum-scarum school or the *surréaliste* group . . . whose particular *trouvaille* was a sort of automatic writing, no revision being allowed" (39).

The antiromanticism—so radically different from Jolas—was deliberate. In a 1952 preface Gilbert elucidated: "[I]n those early days most readers and many eminent critics regarded *Ulysses* as a violently romantic work, an uncontrolled outpouring of the subconscious mind, powerful but formless. Thus it was necessary to emphasize the 'classical' and formal elements, the carefully planned layout of the book, and the minute attention given by its author to detail" (1963: 10). At one point Gilbert distinguishes Joyce's poetry from what he calls "the modernist school" (40). Joyce, of course, would later become closely associated with this term; but for Gilbert "modernism" refers to the worst of modern writing, an undisciplined contemporary literature ("at its worst a spate of mere verbiage" [40]) from which Joyce must be sharply differentiated. Unlike this juvenile modernism, Gilbert argues, Joyce has a full sense of his forebears: "James Joyce is, in fact, in the great tradition which begins with Homer; like his precursors he subjects his work, for all its wild vitality and seeming disorder, to a rule of discipline as severe as that of the Greek dramatists; indeed, the unities of *Ulysses* go far beyond the classic triad, they are as manifold and yet symmetrical as the daedal network of nerves and bloodstreams which pervade the living organism" (40). One could not ask for a starker statement of the classicist reading of Joyce. The bulk of Gilbert's book is a detailed demonstration of this position, via elaborate Homeric reference and explication. For Gilbert, behind Dublin the *Odyssey* always lurks: "[A]s so often in *Ulysses,* what seems meticulous realism is profoundly symbolic" (132), and any detail can be decoded and traced back to its secret source. Gerty MacDowell's ironing recalls the cleanliness of the seafaring Phaeacians (250); "[Bloom's] meeting with Dlugacz, a reminder of racial affinities, symbolizes the Recall of Odysseus from the far island of Calypso eastwards to his own country" (132); and "the brazen walls of the palace of Aeolus have, perhaps, their counterpart in the tramlines ... which encircle the office" (165). In an ingenious interpretation of the "McIntosh" question, Gilbert argues that in both "Hades" and the *Odyssey* an interpolation concerning a "mystery man" is "enclosed at both ends by the same line" (154): the shadowy weight of Homer thus stands behind the most innocuous textual details.

The evident aim of this is to reemphasize the unsuspected degree of what Eliot called "order" in *Ulysses,* expunging the random along with the romantic. As with Eliot, a discrepancy emerges between public judgment and the private reflections that produced it: the composed, conservative tone of Gilbert's book is the respectable front of the dyspeptic reactionary of his Paris diary. It is thus possible to discern an authoritarian politics in his classicist treatment of Joyce. But this treatment had other hidden motives too, according to Gilbert's 1952 preface: "[W]e who admired *Ulysses* for its structural, enduring qualities and not for the occasional presence in it of words and descriptive passages which shocked our elders, were on the defensive, and the pedant's cloak is often a convenient protection against the cold blasts of propriety" (1963: 10). Two points should be emphasized here. One is Gilbert's deployment of the distinction in the *Portrait* between "stasis" and "kinesis," to which I referred in the first chapter. Repeatedly citing Stephen Dedalus's undergraduate theories—and hence setting a precedent for their "authorized" use as a metastatement on Joyce's work—Gilbert explains that "Aesthetic emotion is *static*. . . . Such a conception of the function of the artist presided over the creation of *Ulysses*. . . . The artist's aim, then, is to ban kinetic feelings from his readers' minds, and in *Ulysses* we find the ideal silent stasis of the artist nearly realized, his personality almost impersonalized" (30–31). The book's only vestige of the kinetic, Gilbert assures us, is a Swiftian loathing: "[T]here is not the least pornographical appeal" (31). He repeats this assertion a little later: "It must not be forgotten that Joyce regarded aesthetic beauty as a *stasis;* kinetic art, pornographical or didactic, is, for him, improper art" (45). Gilbert's classical *Ulysses* is specifically devoid of those bodily effects of which, as we have seen, it had frequently been accused. It sheds that special status in which, for John Quinn or the *Sporting Times*, it seemed to provoke a "reading with the body," and becomes a book for the intellect's luminous apprehension.

Gilbert's emphasis on artistic wholeness proved well-judged: it functioned as a vital tool in the overturning of the American ban on *Ulysses* in December 1933. As Paul Vanderham demonstrates, the claim that the text was a unified work of art was instrumental in securing its status as a discursive mode not to be confused with pornography or other kinetic forms. Morris Ernst, the lawyer arguing the case for *Ulysses* against the United States, maintained that a complete understanding of *Ulysses* ran deeper than a superficial response to a given sentence, involving instead an apprehension of the book's complex unity. Ernst drew specifically on

Gilbert's book to make his case that "it is not only the language that is baffling; the construction is almost unbelievably involved" (Vanderham 1998: 100). Vanderham summarizes the unique importance of Gilbert's *Ulysses* as follows: "[If] understanding *Ulysses* requires detailed knowledge of its schematic complexity, as defined by Stuart Gilbert, then very few readers, and certainly no reader approaching the novel for the first time (without, that is, the aid of Gilbert's book), can be said truly to understand *Ulysses*.... [But Ernst] is also claiming that *Ulysses* is indeed a coherent artistic whole.... Gilbert's discussion of the elaborate schematic complexity of *Ulysses* provided Ernst with an economical means of putting Judge Woolsey in mind of the elaborate coherence of the novel as a whole" (101). The use that Ernst and Woolsey made of Gilbert's *Ulysses* dramatically demonstrates the pragmatic function of his book in particular, and of classicist avowals of the formal coherence of *Ulysses* in general, in establishing Joyce's status as readable and, eventually, canonical.

Gilbert's purpose was indeed to show Joyce as "an artificer, maker of labyrinths" (1963: 206), a writer of control, symmetry, "*pointilliste* precision" (10). Yet it is also possible to see his book as having a different effect, at once stabilizing and destabilizing *Ulysses*. The extent of the Homeric correspondences that he offers makes the text appear more tightly controlled, but their obsessiveness can come to seem parodic, promising an infinity of further hidden parallels to the reader with sufficient imagination or an alternative literary framework. Terry Eagleton captures something of the Gilbert-effect: "[I]f a world of intricate symbolic correspondences is to be constructed, some kind of mechanism or switch-gear will be necessary by which any one element of reality can become a signifier of any other; and there is clearly no natural stopping place to this play of allegorical signification, this endless metamorphosis in which anything can be alchemically converted into anything else" (1990: 320). Gilbert might have retorted that he indeed had a natural stopping place: James Joyce, who gave "his full approbation" (1963: 10) to the book. Yet doubt has been cast on major elements of his approach. By the 1950s it was argued that Joyce had pulled Gilbert's leg in directing him to Victor Bérard's study *Les Phéniciens et L'Odyssée* (McCarthy 1991: 30). Far more outlandish than this, however, is Gilbert's insistence that

Ulysses is underpinned by "esoteric"—mystical and Oriental—thought. Joyce's echoes of Homer's story, Gilbert avers, illustrate a belief in reincarnation: "[T]he soul passes through a rhythmic series of what theosophists . . . style *manvantara* and *pralaya*, the days and night of Brahma, alternate periods of activity and repose" (1963: 43). Gilbert continues: "The soul . . . is linked up by a bond, closer than that of birth or atavism, with its pre-incarnations, and an uninterrupted chain of existences on the immaterial plane" (56). In general, Joyce's *Ulysses* expresses a sense of cosmic harmony in which, "like the seed of the lotus or the grain of sand, the smallest particle of creation bears within it the secret of the whole" (53), and clues to this philosophical undercarriage appear in the book's references to the East: "Mr Bloom's spiritual home lies farther east than Attic Olympus; rather, one may surmise, on the flowery slopes of Mount Meru where Devas in dazed contemplation await Nirvana" (142). This legacy of Gilbert's time "east of Suez" (8) has been difficult for later readers to take seriously. It is not made easier to swallow by the fact that *Ulysses* mordantly parodies "pralaya" by likening it to the "modern home comforts" of "*talafana, alavatar, hatakalda, wataklasat*" in the mock séance to which Paddy Dignam returns (Joyce 1986: 247–48); nor by the association of Eastern mysticism with the Anglo-Irish fraction to which Joyce was an outsider. In *Dublin's Joyce* Hugh Kenner would describe "the most elaborate legpull of [Joyce's] career" as his "permitt[ing] a *Transition* fellow-traveller, Stuart Gilbert, to believe that his useful book was the authorized exposition of *Ulysses*," with esoteric sources as the prize jests (1987a: 361). But if even an interpretation apparently sanctioned by Joyce can be suspected of such arbitrariness, then others who have followed Gilbert's lead and produced elaborate readings without the author's imprimatur are still more doubtful.

The example that best demonstrates the ambiguity of Gilbert's legacy—its simultaneous production of control and uncertainty, system and arbitrariness—is Richard Levin and Charles Shattuck's 1944 essay "First Flight to Ithaca." This ambitious rereading endeavors to show "that *Dubliners* has an architectural unity in a secret technique—that, like *Ulysses*, only far more obviously and demonstrably, as is our purpose here to make plain, *Dubliners* is based upon Homer's *Odyssey*" (1948: 49). After all, "in the vast, at-first-sight seeming chaos of *Ulysses* there is nothing of direct reference to Homer, and there is such rich loading of other kinds, literary and philosophical, that if Joyce had not announced his intention through [the title] and other means, it is unlikely that any reader would have discovered it" (47). Most notable among these "other means" was Gilbert, who "published what we may accept as the official interpretation: Gilbert's job was to show the world what it had missed, and among the items in his study the Homeric parallels bulk large" (48). The authors' account of the Gilbert effect is telling: "So, in 1930, Joyce-Gilbert finally told all that had not been guessed about *Ulysses*—and here and there, one may reasonably suspect, tossed in a joker, just to keep the game going" (48). The revelation of "all," therefore, need not end speculation about the book so much as fuel it further; rather than closing the workshop of interpretation, Gilbert provides a whole new set of tools with which Joyce's body of work can be repeatedly disassembled and reassembled. This includes—as in Gilbert's use of the *Portrait* to illuminate *Ulysses*—the transfer of parts from one job to another; thus, Levin and Shattuck have no qualms about using "Homeric parallels" to restart *Dubliners*. On the face of it their grounds appear thin: "Joyce's lifelong interest in the *Odyssey*," after all, already does duty to "explain" *Ulysses*, so does not demand to be transferred back to the earlier work. Yet as pages of exegesis mount up, Levin and Shattuck might well be thought to make a fair case for the parallel. As Patrick Parrinder confesses, a theory like theirs "can neither be proved or refuted" (1984: 51). Their patient enumerations admittedly tend to slide into bathos. "Polly's brother Jack, a horse-race addict, who dislikes Bob, is Aphrodite's uncle Poseidon, patron of horse races, who hates Ares for the slaying of his son Halirrhothius"; "Odysseus is separated from Aeolus for something beyond ten days; Chandler from Gallaher for eight years"; "Both have failed to do something important—Maria to bring the plumcake, Odysseus to bury Elpenor" (Levin and Shattuck 1948: 68, 71–72, 77). But the blend of pedantry and bathos casts Gilbert in a new light, retrospectively illuminating the element of arbitrariness that underlies his—or, one might say, Joyce's—whole project. With Joyce dead and only textual hints to manipulate, there is indeed no natural end to the extravagant multiplication of plausible interpretations.

Joyce reportedly told Samuel Beckett that he "may have oversystematized *Ulysses*" (Ellmann 1982: 702). The same could be—indeed, has been—said of Stuart Gilbert. But if part of Gilbert's legacy was to bestow on Joyce's work a modicum of the respectability it needed—not least in the Woolsey judgment—it also produced a new sense of crazed, unbounded hermeneutic possibility, the start of a safari of symbolism in which there is always more "system" where that came from. Gilbert discloses correspondences and grids to demonstrate Joyce's artistic control, but in doing so he hints at the potential for the uncontrolled generation of such readings. Four decades later C. H. Peake would sigh at the results: "'[S]ymbolic' and far-fetched criticism continues to dominate, and to flourish on Joyce's works as on the works of no other writer.... [M]any unlikely and wild interpretations . . . are now treated as recognized truths" (1977: viii). Even as it began to be an object of mockery for its occultism and poker-faced pedantry, Gilbert's book, with its chapter-by-chapter progression and patiently completist exegesis, was a fair sign of the shape of things to come.

Character Building: The Budgen Version

In a different sense this is also true of Frank Budgen's book on *Ulysses*, a memoir of walks and talks that in several ways complements the Gilbert case for Joyce's defense. A Cornish painter and sculptor, Budgen has constant recourse to a vocabulary of lines and angles, planes and pictures. The book commences *in medias res*, with Budgen at his desk in Zurich. While a colleague tells him about Joyce, "I looked past the dark blue silhouette and profile of King George V at the yellow, white and blue sky, green lime trees, trickling Sihl and dark railway sheds" (1989: 9). Budgen's style of thought and writing persistently tends toward such visual detail. Joyce's arrival in the book is heralded by another densely kaleidoscopic description: "He was a dark mass against the orange light of the restaurant glass door.... His hair is dark enough to look black in this light. His beard is much lighter, orangey-brown and cut to a point.... [H]is eyes are a clear, strong blue . . . in a moment of suspicion or apprehension they become a skyblue glare. The colour of his face is a bricky red, evenly distributed" (11–12). The same principle pervades Budgen's record of conversations with Joyce. Upon hearing of Joyce's deployment of the *Odyssey* as a "ground plan" for the novel, Budgen reflects: "A train of vague thoughts arose in my mind, but failed to take shape definite enough for any comment. I drew with them in silence the shape of the Uetilberg-Albis line of hills. The *Odyssey* for me was just a long poem that might at any moment be illustrated by some Royal Academician. I could see his water-colour Greek heroes, book-opened, in an Oxford Street bookshop window" (15). Budgen's thoughts here become a utensil for sketching, an addition to the palette with which he outlines an imagined landscape. Correspondingly, Joyce's literary innovation (the "mythical method") provokes a specifically painterly reflection. Budgen's questions to Joyce invite and elicit the use of such a visual vocabulary from the writer himself. Seeking elucidation of Joyce's notion of the "completeness" of his protagonist, Budgen supposes that, "For example, if a sculptor makes a figure of a man then that man is all-round, three-dimensional" (17). Joyce responds: "I see him from all sides, and therefore he is all-round in the sense of your sculptor's figure. But he is a complete man as well . . ." (17–18). In Budgen's version Joyce goes out of his way to emphasize the fleshy physicality of his characters: "If they had no body they would have no mind," to which Budgen helpfully adds, "That's the painter's form of leverage" (21). Later in the book Joyce explains his decreasing interest in the character of Stephen Dedalus: "He has a shape that can't be changed" (107). Budgen draws his own distinction: Leopold Bloom "is as plastic as Stephen is pictorial" (60). It is as though Budgen's account, like a chapter of *Ulysses* itself, has painting as its "Art" or the plastic arts as its "Technic," seeping through the prose, coloring the book's vocabulary and subtly tilting its way of seeing Joyce. There is something almost self-parodic about Budgen's expression of relief that Joyce does not have the air of a well-known writer: "He might easily be a painter" (12).

The growing enthusiasm with which Joyce not only encouraged the book but actively primed it makes it partly, in Clive Hart's words, "a collaborative effort" (Budgen 1989: xiii), another exercise in the kind of critical ventriloquism that Joyce had recently practiced through Stuart Gilbert. Joyce's hand in the work, and the sheer insistence of Budgen's penchant for visual metaphors and "externals," suggest a concerted rather than merely contingent attempt to offer a particular reading of the novel and its author. What is at stake here, and what effects does Budgen achieve?

Where Gilbert's was a structural and symbolic exegesis, Budgen's can be described as a novelistic reading. Like Gilbert, he spends much space narrating and quoting from the book, similarly producing a surrogate *Ulysses* in the process. Parts of the book consist almost entirely of summary and quotation (1989: 77–91). But Budgen rarely recounts Homeric situations: his *Ulysses* is a freestanding story not ceaselessly shadowed by its model. Budgen cleaves to the aesthetics of the realist novel, stressing character and environment. He conceives of *Ulysses* as a landscape with figures, with the canvas of Dublin—"We see the city as a whole, in a wide sweep" (72)—bearing characters sketched in differing degrees of detail, from the many-sided Bloom to lesser characters: some "portrait studies," others "drawn on the flat with a few suggestive lines," and still more grotesques and caricatures (68). Above all Leopold Bloom—"By the end of the day we know more about him than we know about any other character in fiction" (66)—comes to the fore as the heart of the text: "Joyce's first question when I had read a completed episode or when he had read out a passage of an uncompleted one was always: 'How does Bloom strike you?'. . . Technical considerations, problems of homeric correspondence, the chemistry of the human body, were secondary matters" (106–7).

The novel form, writes Ian Watt, is "distinguished from other genres . . . by the amount of attention it habitually accords both to the individualisation of its characters and to the detailed presentation of their environment" (1987: 17–18). In Watt's influential account, the realist novel is marked by its reference to particularity, to individual character, and to social environment. Raymond Williams further emphasizes that this form has tended toward the enlargement of attention, toward an ever-widening range of social levels: "[C]ertain kinds of subject were seen as realism. . . . The most ordinary definition was in terms of an ordinary, contemporary, everyday reality, as opposed to traditionally heroic, romantic, or legendary subjects. In the period since the Renaissance, the advocacy and support of this 'ordinary, everyday, contemporary reality' have been normally associated with the rising middle class, the bourgeoisie" (1975: 300–301). Williams elsewhere amplifies this view of realism, noting that "this movement of social extension—'let not your equals move your pity less'—is a key factor in what we can now identify as a realist intention." He further adds that a defining trait of realism in history has been its "emphasis on secular action," in which "a human action is played through in specifically human terms—exclusively human terms" (1989c: 228–29).

To be sure, all these alleged features of realism raise as many questions as they answer. But their relevance here is that, according to Frank Budgen, *Ulysses* also participates in such a project. In his contribution to the *Exagmination,* he finds "a large humanity in Joyce's work. None of his contemporaries is so free from highbrow snobbishness and the superiority complex. The characters in *Ulysses* are of the common run of average humanity. Joyce didn't find them at hunt balls, country house parties and the Chelsea Studios of millionaire dilettanti but in trams, pubs, shops and the common streets and houses where the mass of the people spend their lives" (1961: 40–41). In *James Joyce and the Making of "Ulysses"* Budgen again speaks up for the momentousness of the apparently mundane: "[I]f we enumerate the things that happen in *Ulysses* most human beings will agree that of themselves . . . these happenings are important" (1989: 74). After listing the outstanding events of the novel, Budgen goes further: "Alongside these larger actions there are actions that may be called common only because they are being constantly performed by many people all over the world. They are not and never were unimportant. . . . If the experience is common why does Joyce narrate it? Because he is building with an infinite number of pellets of this clay of common experience the character of Leopold Bloom" (75). Joyce is affiliated to a version of the tradition of the realist novel, with its dedication to lived particularity, rounded character, human (as against divine) scale and agency, and an inclusive social range. Indeed, Ian Watt himself comes to a similar conclusion when his history of the novel touches on Joyce. Bloom, writes Watt, is the epitome of unheroic ordinariness, yet still "infinitely various" and more interesting than his Homeric prototype—which makes him typical of "the novel in general" (1987: 207). *Ulysses* is thus most "novelistic" in its insistent attention to the humble and quotidian—precisely the case implied by Budgen.

Budgen's *Ulysses,* as a novel with fully realized characters, is ultimately readable by a wide public. Rather than symbol hunting and the proliferation of parallels, Budgen encourages a reading that relates the book to readerly experience. Even "Circe," he assures us, "would not move us at all if it were not nature, our own and that of all men. The observed fact is that hallucination is common human experience. . . . Joyce shows it as being a common experience of sane men" (1989: 251). This last line is the keynote of Budgen's approach, which attempts to bridge the gap between Joyce's esoteric reputation and the robust reader for whom Budgen stands in. As Hugh Kenner puts it, "he makes the strange book seem an eminently natural one for a normal man to have conceived" (1987b: 4). Budgen is one of the first and most enduring to outline a "popular Joyce" who might be savored as well as studied: he avows his appreciation of the book's "popular character," like "those old popular songs which tell of tragic happenings to a jolly tune and a ringing chorus of tooralooralay" (1989: 135). In a later essay on *Finnegans Wake* he insists still more emphatically on the writer's essential accessibility: "Joyce worked with the material of the marketplace, and if he is not understood there, it is certainly not on account of any preciosity in himself. . . . [H]is own experience was at one with that of his fellow-men. All the more strange that he should be sometimes regarded as a dweller in an ivory tower" (339).

Along with this sketching of a "popular Joyce" comes a subtle shaping of Joyce's political profile. The conception of the novel sketched above may be described as a democratic one, with its generous attention to the overlooked crannies of urban existence. To enlist Joyce to this generic mode is also to imply an outlook: "The prevailing attitude of *Ulysses* is a very humane scepticism—not of tried human values, necessary at all times for social cohesion, but of all tendencies and systems whatsoever. . . . [T]he prevailing mood is humour" (Budgen 1989: 73). This liberal and humanist account is a long way not only from the *Ulysses* that Shane Leslie thought he was reading—"experimental, anti-conventional, anti-Christian, chaotic, totally unmoral" (1970b: 207)— but from the satirical "inferno" that Pound considered it to be (1967: 198). If Stuart Gilbert's mission was to calm the text into mythic order, Budgen soothes it away from such allegations of ideological extremity and reveals its humane comedy. This is not to convict him of a total neutralization of the question of Joyce's politics, though by the time of Joyce's death he confessed himself "guilty of helping to create the impression that Joyce was nonpolitical" (1989: 339). Budgen had been active in socialist politics (viii), and his emphasis on the demotic and ordinary in Joyce's writing can be viewed as a mild attempt to claim Joyce for the political Left. More precisely, it works to exonerate Joyce from charges of elitism or mandarin contempt in the 1930s, a decade when the literary world was unusually politicized. (This strategy is summed up in Joyce's own remark, first recorded by Eugene Jolas and cited in many subsequent political readings: "I don't know why they attack me. Nobody in any of my books is worth more than a thousand pounds" [Jolas 1948: 14].)

In this respect Budgen joins another noted commentator from this period, the New York–based critic Edmund Wilson, whose *Axel's Castle* (1931) was the first book-length attempt to group and define the "modern movement." Wilson, too, was a man of the Left—according to Daniel Aaron, by 1930 "his socialism [had] changed from pink to red" (1979: 181)—and his book concludes with the suggestion that the modern writers he so admires represent "things that are dying—the whole belle-lettristic tradition of Renaissance culture perhaps . . . more driven in on itself, as industrialism and democratic education have come to press it closer and closer" (1961: 235). *Axel's Castle* is hence an immanent critique of modernism, sympathetic to its artistic achievements while viewing it as socially inadequate. Yet Jeffrey Segall has demonstrated that in the context of the literary debates of the American Left at this time, Wilson's was effectively an apologia for the modernists—most notably Joyce, who was being attacked as a decadent bourgeois writer by Communist critics from Karl Radek in the USSR to the U.S. Marxists of *The New Masses* (Segall 1993: 30–35, 91–95). When the *Marxisant* Wilson calls Joyce "the great poet of a new phase of the human consciousness" (177–78), he is staking Joyce's claim to be objectively "progressive" in a way not reducible to his political beliefs. But like Budgen, he also reads *Ulysses* as a fanfare for the common man, an advisable criterion for the socialist critics of the period. Joyce's achievement is "to have exhibited ordinary humanity without either satirising it or sentimentalising it"; his protagonists "are certainly not either unamiable or unattractive—and for all their misfortunes and shortcomings, they inspire us with considerable respect" (176, 175). In Leopold Bloom, "the typical modern man," one sees "the possibilities of that ordinary humanity which is somehow not so ordinary after all"; and even Molly Bloom's "gross body" is "labouring to throw up some knowledge and beauty by which it may transcend itself" (178, 179, 180). What looks like simply a deft introduction to Joyce, therefore, also has its polemical side as a demonstration of his worth to progressive readers. Wilson's criticism, based on book reviews rather than academic research, is noteworthy for its accessible, synoptic manner, offering helpful summaries of otherwise forbidding works. Wilson, like Budgen, thus adumbrates a readable, "popular" *Ulysses*—though rarely so vividly as in his imaginary Hollywood adaptation of *Axel's Castle*, in which Joyce was to be represented by the Marx Brothers (Meyers 1995: 144).

Budgen's is a novelistic reading in another sense, too. For his own book is also in part a narrative of scenes and conversations, fleshed out with his brand of descriptive passages. *James Joyce and the Making of "Ulysses"* is not only a detached, self-effacing exegesis but a kind of fiction itself, in which the interpreter is a literary protagonist as well as occupying a safely metalinguistic post beyond the text. Budgen's "character and environment" approach to *Ulysses* is echoed by his own tale, in which he and Joyce are figures in a carefully colored and shaped landscape. His book has a dual focus, oscillating from book to man, from a recital of the events of "Cyclops" to a reflection on the bars of Zurich. Budgen's most intriguing effect of all is hence to make Joyce into a "character," through a regular supply of anecdotes and character traits that occasionally threatens to become a disjointed list: "Joyce himself never or rarely swore by one god or nine. . . . He has little feeling of attachment to animals. Flowers appeal to him but little. Only for trees among all organic forms has he a pronounced sympathy. . . . Joyce is a superstitious man . . ." (1989: 197).

In fact, this is logically connected with the overall thrust of his interpretation. The humanism that Budgen finds in *Ulysses* is matched by the figure of Joyce: the author is personified, revealed as a personality existing on the same plane as Budgen or his reader. If *Ulysses* is "humane," the desanctified Joyce is "human": less the invisible god of creation than the man in the street. Rather than viewing this as the revelation of the "real" Joyce, one can see it as a retrospective effort to fashion a character, a persona, to which his writing might be made answerable. The initiation of a humanist reading of Joyce's work requires not only a new emphasis on character in the work itself but also the invention of a human figure to explain and anchor it—what Michel Foucault describes as "a complex operation which constructs a certain rational being that we call 'author'" (1991: 110).

Foucault's reflections on authorship also propose that the author's real function is to foreclose the dangerous open-endedness of writing through "a limitation of the cancerous and dangerous proliferation of significations . . . the principle of thrift in the proliferation of meaning" (118). In one sense this is indeed the purpose of Gilbert and Budgen, namely to provide "authorized" explanations and thus grant a certain fixity to a bewilderingly indeterminate text. Yet just as Gilbert's search for order sets in motion a slew of hitherto unimagined interpretations, so Budgen's anecdotes have an inviting, suggestive quality. A phrase reported to be Joyce's can be used to put the seal of authenticity on an interpretation, but the very range of its deployment places this "fixing" role in question. The following recollection is a notable example: "'I want', said Joyce, as we were walking down the Universitätstrasse, 'to give a picture of Dublin so complete that if the city one day suddenly disappeared from the earth it could be reconstructed out of my book'" (Budgen 1989: 69).

This moment has proved fruitful for subsequent readers. In 1977 C. H. Peake quoted Joyce's statement to explain the importance of the "arts" in the *Ulysses* schemata, as giving an "impression that the condition of all the fields of intellectual endeavour in Dublin has come under scrutiny," for this is "a novel in which the city is presented as a powerful, even a dominant, force in the working out of the action—as the hostile being against which the two protagonists contend" (1977: 152). For Frank Delaney, who reproduces the quotation on the back of his coffee-table guide to Dublin, Joyce's words justify his "plain man's guide to the novel," for *Ulysses* is usable as "a guidebook, a literary Baedeker, by which a trip to Dublin becomes enlivened" (1983: 11). Hugh Kenner draws the opposite significance from Joyce's statement, reading it as a comment on the wreckage of Easter 1916. It is the very real upheavals in Dublin, rather than its continuity since 1904, that make *Ulysses* a valuable record: "Most of *Ulysses* in fact was written in the knowledge that all the cityscapes . . . would never be seen again as they had been" (1987b: 93). James Fairhall's historicist reading follows Kenner, again quoting Budgen and glossing that "[Joyce's] pre-war self probably never imagined that dull, solid, colonial Dublin was in danger of vanishing. But after the Easter Rising, the Russian Revolution, and the continuing slaughter of the Great War, many things once thought permanent were receding into memory or had taken on an air of mortality" (1993: 194). Jeri Johnson, noting that the Budgen anecdote "is, by now, infamous," adds the extra wry twist that "some places which had disappeared in the interim have reappeared of late in the wake of Dubliners' recognition that Joyce's Dublin, like Dickens's London, draws the tourists" (1993: xxv). Finally, in Frances L. Restuccia's psychoanalytic study, Budgen's anecdote has sunk deep enough into the Joycean unconscious to be tacitly referred to without citation, in the claims that "Joyce fanatically wanted to rebuild Dublin exactly" and erects "a literary simulacrum of Dublin" (1989: 107, 139).

More traces of this or other Joycean bons mots could be dug up easily enough. What the example of Budgen shows is that as Joyce becomes a "character," he becomes quotable. His "nonfictional" words illuminate his published works; but the anecdotes turn out to be almost as ambiguous as the work itself, always available for further reinterpretation. With Budgen's fund of stories and one-liners, the author reappears behind his handiwork, a presence to whom the texts can be made answerable—but also a fertile and inviting text in his own right.

Thus far I have analyzed a number of attempts to win Joyce critical legitimation, partly provoked by existing hostile readings. In *transition* one saw a neoromantic avant-garde ranged against the aesthetics of the "Men of 1914," while reasserting the internationalism of Joyce's work. This rhetoric is largely based on *Work in Progress*—demonstrating that different appropriations of Joyce favor different periods of his work and construct desirable versions of modern writing from these specific preferences. Gilbert and Budgen's claims for Joyce rest centrally on *Ulysses* and exemplify the different directions in which claims for that book could go. Gilbert insists on the classical stasis of Joyce's work and proved effective in enhancing Joyce's claim for the modern canon. Budgen treats *Ulysses* as a humane realist novel, of interest to the common reader and distinguished by the everyman figure at its center. Both critics act as spurs to subsequent readers: the one legitimating the ingenious search for patterns and correspondences, the other fashioning a Joycean persona that will prove helpful to those seeking an originating presence behind the text. "At about this time," writes Hugh Kenner, Joyce "left the Book of Bloom to fend for itself" (1987b: 4). *Ulysses* would demonstrate its vaunted transnational character by fetching up in the United States, at the center of the universities' new attention to modern literature. But in Britain Joyce's status was less certain.

Anglo-Saxon Ingratitude: Leavis and His Legacy

"Our time, in literature," writes F. R. Leavis toward the end of *D. H. Lawrence: Novelist*, "may fairly be called the age of D. H. Lawrence and T. S. Eliot" (1964: 317). It was in part due to Leavis's own efforts that the period could not, fairly or otherwise, be called the age of James Joyce. What Francis Mulhern has called the moment of *Scrutiny* lasts, in one sense, from 1932 to 1953, the years in which the pioneering, polemical journal dominated by Leavis commenced and ended; but it can also be said to extend well into the review's afterlife. Raymond Williams, a graduate of and teacher in Leavis's Cambridge, remarked that by the early 1970s "Leavis had completely won" in debates on the novel, such that even his opponents "were in fact reproducing his sense of the shape of its history" (1979: 245). Francis Mulhern places more stress on Leavis's adversarial, "outlaw" relation to the dominant culture, but also notes that "by the late forties" *Scrutiny*'s adherents were "represented at every level of the national educational system, from professorial chairs to the classrooms of unnumbered secondary schools" (1979: 312). Mulhern further states that "by the end of the war, *Scrutiny*'s 'vanguard' campaign against the old regime had succeeded; within a further few years, the rebellious ideas of the thirties had become dominant in the teaching of English. The literary canons established by Leavis became highly influential, his critical methods even more so; and the broad cultural themes of his journal became commonplaces of secondary education. Many accepted them literally and in their entirety; reformed or diluted, debased or syncretized, they became the faith of a whole profession" (319).

This faith was not short-lived. Writing in 1979, Lesley Johnson noted that "[Leavis's] influence in certain universities throughout English-speaking countries has been prodigious.... [T]here are no doubt many examples of teachers in the schools greatly influenced by Leavis, working in an isolated manner for the promulgation of his ideas" (114). Leavis himself always maintained the stance of an embattled outsider, an awkward thorn in the flesh of the metropolitan establishment. But this did not prevent his ideas from securing academic hegemony. As late as 1983 Terry Eagleton could venture that "English students in England today are 'Leavisites' whether they know it or not, irremediably altered by that historic intervention" (31). Having rapidly ascended from a position of militant marginality in the early 1930s, Leavisism achieved dominance for decades in literary studies in England. During that period this country produced little work on James Joyce. This was no coincidence.

References to Joyce in *Scrutiny* and Leavis's writings are scarce. The writer who had been the prime exhibit of the *Egoist*, the *Little Review*, and *transition* barely registers in the index of the Cambridge journal. However, in the September 1933 edition of *Scrutiny* Joyce did earn an eight-page review article entitled "Joyce and 'The Revolution of the Word,'" which was to remain Leavis's most sustained statement on Joyce. Leavis's judgment is largely negative. He nods respectfully at *Ulysses*, whose "Proteus" episode contains prose "of a Shakespearian concreteness," a "rich complexity" and "intensely imagined experience." Toward the end of the essay the book seems to be characterized as one of modern literature's finer achievements; like many of Joyce's harshest detractors, Leavis concedes the writer's "genius" (1933: 194). But even this novel displays signs of a worrying trajectory: "A certain vicious bent manifested itself very disturbingly in *Ulysses*, in the inorganic elaborations and pedantries and the evident admiring belief of the author in Stephen's intellectual distinction" (197). As for what followed it, Leavis begins by suggesting that the *Work in Progress* is "in any bulk, not worth the labour of reading" (193) and proceeds to outline his disagreement with those Joycean devotees who have compared their master to Shakespeare. Shakespeare's technical innovations and lexical leaps, Leavis argues, were strictly in the service of the message or idea they sought to convey: "[T]he words matter because they lead down to what they came from. . . . [I]t is the burden to be delivered, the precise and urgent command from within, that determines expression—tyrannically." Shakespeare was a writer "whose medium was for him strictly a medium"; for Joyce, by damning contrast, "the interest in words and their possibilities comes first" (194). In the ongoing *Wake*, words are savored for their own sake, material signifiers sundered from the meanings with which they ought rightly to be coupled. The Joycean word, allowed to revolt against referentiality, is confronted only with its equally autonomous fellows; language grows sick on its own narcissism. Leavis's key terms to describe this state of affairs are "contrived," "external," and "mechanical," and all three are significant. Joyce's "contrived" method of writing, in which material is worked over and revised at leisurely length, militates against directness and spontaneity of expression, substituting for them a "deliberate, calculating" (Leavis 1933: 195) care which is viewed as the hallmark of modernism after Flaubert. The "internal" sources of Shakespeare, the "uncompromising, complex and delicate need" from which his poetic felicities were born, are accordingly relegated and supplanted by an excess of self-consciousness and "external" craftsmanship. A "mechanical" approach brutally ousts the organic and authentically human wellsprings of art, as the text is transformed from vivid expression to reified artifact.

Such a description of Leavis's reservations may seem to risk exaggerating his distrust of Joyce's later work. But if anything, the danger is of understatement. It is in this review that Leavis chooses to make some of his most full-bloodedly organic pronouncements; subsequent histories of *Scrutiny* (Mulhern 1979; Parrinder 1991) would make surprisingly frequent reference to this brief article in explaining Leavis's social thought. Allowing himself "a brief reflection on the conditions of Shakespeare's greatness" toward the end of the piece, Leavis sketches the outline of his whole conception of language, literature, and history. Shakespeare "incarnated the genius of the language," taking advantage of the "genuinely national culture"; the greatness of Elizabethan literature was due to "a national culture rooted in the soil. . . . [T]he popular basis of culture was agricultural" (1933: 199). "The strength of English," Leavis asserts, "belongs to the very spirit of the language—the spirit that was formed when the English people who formed it were predominantly rural" (200). This "spirit" is also, paradoxically, the sign of the English language's bond with the body. "How closely the countryman's life and language grow together; they are like flesh and bone," the farmer Adrian Bell is cited as observing. "They grow together," Leavis adds, "just as mind and body, mental and physical life, have grown together in those [English] phrasal verbs" (200). Within a few months Bell's essay "Change in the Farm" (March 1934) would be intoning that "[E]ven in splitting logs, in some measure man passes into axe and axe into man. How complex a harmony then is man and scythe; every swing an unconscious reiteration of natural law" (Mulhern 1979: 61). It is against such Adamic ruralism that the "Revolution of the Word" essay pits Joyce, whose "mechanical" writing turns out to be metaphorical for something still more sinister: "When one adds that speech in the old order was a popularly cultivated art, that people talked (so making Shakespeare possible) instead of reading or listening to the wireless, it becomes plain that the promise of regeneration by American slang, popular city-idiom or the inventions of transition-cosmopolitans is a flimsy consolation for our loss. . . . [T]he possibility of . . . a like richness of life, of emotional, mental and bodily life in association, is hardly even imaginable. Instead we have cultural disintegration, mechanical organization and constant rapid change" (Leavis 1933: 200).

James Joyce, then, stirs Leavis to a rhetorical miniature of his entire social and cultural stance. The decadent dissolution of Joyce's later writing becomes metonymically attached to all the ills of modernity that texts like *Mass Civilization and Minority Culture* (1930) and *Culture and Environment* (1933) have already dissected. Joyce's writing is accused of a kind of formalism, a fetishism of word over world and signifier over signified, which takes to an extreme the general alienation and decline of literary language that Leavis sees as occurring since the Elizabethans. In Joyce's free-floating text there is no chance of a cratylistic bond between body and language such as the rural laborers of a lost England enjoyed; and his rootless modernity is also decisively urban, an idiom born of the "constant rapid change" and linguistic promiscuity of the international metropolis. Leavis makes no mention of the specifically Irish dimension of Joyce's life and work: what Joyce represents is not colonial particularity but "transition-cosmopolitan" generality. An implicit rivalry hovers between *Scrutiny* itself, rooted in the English provinces, and the Parisian *transition:* a conflict between English common sense and French self-indulgence that would continue to resound through literary studies.

The dichotomy seems decisive. But we should also note the curious points of contact between Joyce and Leavis. It was Leavis, of all people, who in the summer of 1926 requested the police's permission to import a copy of *Ulysses,* to be discussed in a lecture course in the autumn term. The bookseller Charles Porter, writing to the authorities on Leavis's behalf, also requested that the book be made available to students, even if only by placing one copy in the library. This extra plea was a liberty too far for the Home Office, where officials were especially alarmed at the prospect of female students encountering the book: "A lecturer at Cambridge who proposes to make this book a textbook for a mixed class of undergraduates must be a dangerous crank," opined an official (Travis 1998: 3). The director of public prosecutions, who had effectively issued the ban in 1922, warned Cambridge's vice-chancellor A. C. Seward of the danger to the university's reputation, and instructed the local chief constable to keep an eye on Leavis (MacKillop 1995: 88–91). The episode enhanced Leavis's then racy reputation and contributed to his sense of persecution: he worried that his association with Joyce would make his university post more tenuous (MacKillop 1995: 91, 107, 119).

Furthermore, the reflections on language in his 1933 review might, with only a slight twist, be read to Joyce's advantage. The compact that Leavis seeks between word and thing, language and body, echoes the very critical standpoint he is rejecting, best summarized by Beckett: "Joyce has desophisticated language. And it is worth while remarking that no language is so sophisticated as English. It is abstracted to death" (1983: 28). Beckett's affirmation of a primal, "desophisticated" language, concrete rather than "abstracted," presents Joyce not as a detached technician but as a verbal conjuror, summoning the mysterious essences of words—"the old inarticulation," "hieroglyphics." In this, as we have seen, Beckett is an eloquent spokesman for a neoromantic view of Joyce as tapping the primordial secrets of the tongue. Since Leavis, writing in 1933, is responding specifically to this reading of Joyce—his biographer tells us that he carefully marked this passage of Beckett's essay (MacKillop 1995: 215)—one may surmise that he does not so much react violently against the *transition* theory as anxiously seek to demarcate his own view from it. In the essays by Jolas and Beckett, both of which he quotes, Leavis may detect not something radically unlike his own thought but an eccentric parody of it that must be spurned all the more decisively. Against Beckett's notion of "desophistication" he insists that "[i]t is, on the contrary, plain that the whole phenomenon is one of sophistication, cosmopolitan if not very subtle, and, so far from promising a revival of cultural health, is (it does not need Lawrence's nostril to detect) a characteristic symptom of dissolution" (Leavis 1933: 198). The initial threat of *Ulysses* was bound up with its effect on the body, what I have termed its kinetic quality. Leavis's repulsion of Joyce thus has a touch of perversity about it, for the terms with which he seeks to set his healthy English canon apart from the decadent Irish Parisian sometimes seem to apply to both. If *transition* presents a counterreading of modernism, so does Leavis; yet he fails to see the possible points of connection between the verbal romanticism of the Parisian journal and the organicism of his own. Curiouser still, the literary enemy for both stances turns out to be the same, as one can see from an examination of Leavis's later remarks on Joyce and the place he assigned him in modern writing.

Leavis's relation to modernism in general remains ambiguous. Patrick Parrinder describes *New Bearings in English Poetry* (1932) as "an incisive primer of the modernist poetic" (1991: 248), and John Docker's postmodernist polemic treats the Leavises as its prime exhibit of "literary modernism" (1994: 15–23). Yet as Alan Sinfield has pointed out, "Four defining characteristics of Modernism, as generally understood, did not match Leavis's views: cosmopolitanism and internationalism; self-conscious experimentation with language and forms; the idea of the artwork as autonomous; and the concept of the artist as alienated by the special intensity of his (usually his) vision of the 'modern condition.' Leavis wanted literature to be central in an English tradition, and therefore it should be English, relatively comprehensible, concerned with positive moral values, not avant-gardist" (1989: 182). In effect, *Scrutiny* could handle some versions of modernism and not others: as Terry Eagleton has observed, it was capable of "embracing the 'modernist' (*The Waste Land*) but also repulsing it (*Ulysses*) from a 'traditionalist' standpoint" (1976a: 14). The most fundamental polarization was that between Joyce and the writer whom Leavis called "the great creative genius of our age" (1964: 317), D. H. Lawrence. In Lawrence he famously found a modernism after his own heart: a writer who wrote prolifically, passionately, and unevenly, whose most celebrated achievements turned on the contradictions of a changing rural England, and who presented the novel as the privileged medium of Leavis's most prized category, "Life." One must not overlook the real complexity of these figures: the organicist Leavis worked to modernize Cambridge English; the English Lawrence cursed his country and died in exile. Yet the dichotomy erected by Leavis is unmistakable and uncompromising. Looking back at his 1930 pamphlet on Lawrence twenty-five years later, Leavis wrote that "my essay was . . . a serious tribute to a great writer by someone wholly convinced of his greatness, and convinced that he demanded much further study—that he would repay endless frequentation as Joyce would not. (Those two, it seems to me, were pre-eminently the testing, the crucial authors: if you took Joyce for a major creative writer, then, like Mr. Eliot, you had no use for Lawrence, and if you judged Lawrence a great writer, then you could hardly take a sustained interest in Joyce.)" (1964: 10). In one stroke Leavis establishes two main currents within modern prose that are mutually exclusive. The Lawrentian and Joycean never shall meet, and for a long period the bulk of literary criticism in England took the former path.

For Leavis Lawrence looks back to the line of novelists that *The Great Tradition* (1948) identifies as possessing "a vital capacity for experience, a kind of reverent openness before life, and a marked moral intensity" (1962a: 17). Formally adding Lawrence to the pantheon, Leavis feels compelled to justify this choice against the claims of Lawrence's nearest rival: "It is this ['religious'] spirit . . . that makes him, in my opinion, so much more significant in relation to the past and future, so much more truly creative as a technical inventor, an innovator, a master of language, than James Joyce" (36). Extending his fifteen-year-old strictures against *Work in Progress* back to *Ulysses,* Leavis finds "no organic principle determining, informing, and controlling into a vital whole, the elaborate analogical structure, the extraordinary variety of technical devices, the attempts at an exhaustive rendering of consciousness, for which *Ulysses* is remarkable, and which got it accepted by a cosmopolitan literary world as a new start. It is rather, I think, a dead end, or at least a pointer to disintegration—a view strengthened by Joyce's own development" (36). Joyce is not an entirely isolated literary freak. Leavis's work offers an alternative, less vital wing of modernism as Joyce's context, which helps one locate the place he occupied on the English map after *Scrutiny*. A key figure here is T. S. Eliot, toward whom Leavis's attitude changed unpredictably over the years (Bergonzi 1986: 85–112). By the 1950s Leavis is taking every opportunity to score points at Eliot's expense, and a crucial divergence between the two hinges on Joyce. From "*Ulysses,* Order and Myth" in 1923 to *After Strange Gods* ten years later, from the Faber publication of Stuart Gilbert's guide to *Ulysses* (1930) and sections of *Work in Progress* to his tribute, just after Joyce's death, to "the greatest man of letters of my generation" (Eliot 1948), Eliot remained loyal to Joyce. Leavis, in turn, came to associate the two. For *The Great Tradition* Joyce's influence has been pernicious, joining with a strain in Eliot's writing to produce nihilistic, life-denying imitators (Henry Miller, Djuna Barnes) "in whom Mr. Eliot has expressed an influence in strongly favourable terms" (Leavis 1962a: 36). Nor does the chain of guilt stop there. In a critique of

After Strange Gods (*Scrutiny*, September 1934), a terrier-like Leavis had seized on and savaged Eliot's invocation of Wyndham Lewis against Lawrence (1962b: 240–47); in his 1955 study of Lawrence he connects the remaining dots. From the first chapter onward, Eliot's "attitude to life . . . of distaste and disgust" and his writing's "slow meticulous labour of calculating judgement" (1964: 25–26) lead him to be identified with Flaubert, who is explicitly presented (as he was in *The Great Tradition*) as Lawrence's antithesis. Patrick Parrinder observes that Leavis's polemic against Flaubert as "high priest of modernist fiction" is also directed against "Joyce as Flaubert's successor" (1991: 253). Leavis's insistent invocation of Flaubert as, in Francis Mulhern's words, "the incarnation of formalism and moral anomie in the modern novel" and "the symbolic antithesis of 'the great tradition'" (1979: 259–60) thus indirectly restates his view of Joyce.

Leavis soon resumes open attack on "the contrivances of Joyce, where insistent will and ingenuity so largely confess the failure of creative life." This time the target is coupled with "the technique of the *Cantos*, where, by Eliot's own account, he is not interested in what Pound says, but only in the way he says it" (1964: 28). Attacking Flaubert and Eliot again in the next chapter, Leavis scornfully remarks that "it is hard to respect the conception of proper training or of tradition that finds a superiority of moral sensibility over Lawrence in Wyndham Lewis, Pound, or Joyce" (78); and toward the end of the book he again notes of Lawrence "how radically unlike (his unlikeness being his greatness) . . . Eliot, Wyndham Lewis, Pound and Joyce this writer is" (261). This collocation is familiar from chapter 1 of the present study. Leavis has finally staged an improbable reunion of the "Men of 1914," regrouped as the enemy of Lawrence and Leavis's "English modernism"—almost thirty years after Pound had given up on *Work in Progress* and Lewis had launched his own attack on *Ulysses*. If Eliot's standing can survive Leavis's hostility, Joyce's posthumous critical fate looks less assured, as he is placed at the center of the contrived and mechanical modernism that England can do without. Distrusted for his technical perversity and impenetrable eccentricity, he and the cranky and politically explosive Lewis and Pound are expelled from the main current of English writing.

If Joyce does not qualify for Leavis's formidably exclusive pantheon, neither does he entirely drop out of the literary picture. As higher education expands after the war, literary guides and introductions proliferate, and several postwar surveys of English literary history find a place for him, if little sympathy for *Finnegans Wake*. Walter Allen in *The English Novel* (1954) treats Joyce as a great if still mysterious talent, the diametrical opposite of his peer, Lawrence: "[T]hey are so removed from each other that comparison is impossible" (1958: 357). Ifor Evans's *Short History of English Literature* (1940) again pairs him with Lawrence but recognizes "a fierce and absolute genius that is difficult to follow" (1963: 214). In the Leavisite Boris Ford's *Pelican Guide to English Literature* (1961) the socialist critic Arnold Kettle's essay on Joyce echoes Leavis's terms: "[T]he very consistency of his total effort, the very completeness of the structure he creates has in it something inhuman, leaving one in the end with the feeling that he who accepted so boldly all the implications of his exile . . . had flinched at nothing except life itself" (1973: 331).

A similarly guarded admiration can be detected in Raymond Williams, the post-Leavisian critic who exerted the greatest influence on the postwar academic Left. Williams admitted that at Cambridge University's Socialist Club, "by the second year [1940–41] Joyce was without question the most important author for us. *Ulysses* and *Finnegans Wake* . . . were the texts we most admired, and we counterposed to socialist realism" (1979: 45). "Nearly all socialist writers of the time," he adds, "were excited by Joyce" (278). In the 1950s, three decades after Leavis's run-in with the Home Office, Williams lectured on Joyce for adult education and British Council classes (Inglis 1995: 151, 158), and in *The Long Revolution* (1961) he finds a small place for *Ulysses* in a discussion of the realist novel, characterizing it as "the realist tradition in a new form, altered in technique but continuous in experience." This implicitly endorses the Budgen defense of Joyce as a humanist writer in the novelistic tradition who achieves the totalizing vision crucial to Williams's socialist conception of realism: "[T]here are three ways of seeing . . . yet the three worlds, as in fact, compose one world, the whole world of the novel." Yet Williams still follows Leavis's judgment in expressing his unease at the book's later elaborations: "*Ulysses* does not maintain this balance throughout; it is mainly in the first third of the book that the essential composition is done" (1975: 310). Where Joyce is concerned, Williams thus makes only a partial break with Leavisite orthodoxy, a judgment confirmed by *The English Novel from Dickens to Lawrence*

(1970). A self-conscious rewrite of the Leavisian Great Tradition, the book proudly and extensively reinserts Dickens and Thomas Hardy as dynamic voices of social change in England. Yet while Lawrence duly receives his chapter, Joyce is only briefly grafted on as a chronicler of urban consciousness. Tellingly, Williams again sticks to the early chapters of *Ulysses* rather than taking on the later formal ruptures, and if the book contains "an ordinary language, heard more clearly than anywhere in the realist novel before it," *Finnegans Wake* echoes "the strains already evident in the later sections of *Ulysses*" and slides into an alienated "surrogate, a universal isolated language" (1987: 167–68). Despite Williams's achievement in developing cultural criticism beyond Leavis's models, his treatment of Joyce stands as an example of the tenacity of that earlier Cambridge response. It would be left to the next generation of English critics to complete the break with Leavis, as we shall see in chapter 4. It remains ironic that the man who came to the attention of the state for trying to import Joyce was also the one who, as much as any English critic of these decades, deported him. But Joyce's work would find another home soon enough.

Envoi: Dublin, Texas

"There is . . . a Joyce industry. . . . Joyce foresaw this when he kept adding to his puzzles, saying that he would ensure his fame by keeping the professors happy; and, sure enough, they now know so much about *Ulysses* that they call 'the older studies' merely 'the work of cultivated amateurs'" (Kermode 1959: 675). These words sound contemporary to us, but Frank Kermode wrote them upon the publication of Richard Ellmann's biography. As early as 1959 Kermode found the novel passé: "The power of *Ulysses* to possess a man's mind seems to have flagged: the book has dated. . . . If you were ever flushed and excited by *Ulysses* you are probably now over forty; if you ever tried to live by it, over thirty. Under thirty, people seem to be a little bored by Joyce's endless experimentation. . . . [T]he young are not much interested in the vast ambition of Joyce, his desire to make of a book an entire self-supporting world. . . . One reads *Ulysses* on a cosmic scale or not at all; and life-crippling attempts to make it new and make it whole are not fashionable just now" (675). The United States, Kermode asserts, is the home of those for whom "the books involved are *fully* meaningful," unlike a post-Movement England where Joyce is frowned upon and the totalizing projects of high modernism are as dated as Jimmy Porter's "good, brave causes." For Kermode, writing in 1959, the moment of modernism is sufficiently past to be seen as a coherent, bounded period: the era of Viconian system-builders and Poundian innovators can be identified as such because it is effectively over.

That much is already implicit at the start of the book that most clearly signals Joyce's entrance into the American academy, Harry Levin's *James Joyce: A Critical Introduction* (1941). Levin's study, avers Geert Lernout, made Joyce "academically respectable" and "also inaugurated the shift away from Paris to the United States, where the center of the Joyce industry has remained ever since" (1990: 22). It appeared as the first volume of the "Makers of Modern Literature" series and was issued by Faber in Britain a year later. The book won great respect. In 1959 Richard Ellmann declared that Levin had "laid the foundation of Joyce scholarship" (1982: ix); in 1964 Robert Scholes asserted that every discussion of "epiphany" was derived from it (1992: 60); and in 1970 Robert H. Deming considered Levin's study still the best general work on Joyce (1970: 29). In the late 1980s Morton P. Levitt reckoned that "my entire generation of students of Joyce—thus, the teachers of the next—is . . . indebted to Harry Levin, in ways that we cannot always calculate or even perceive" (1991: 96). Levin had originally expected the commission to be some way off, but once his subject was dead he was fit to be discussed (1960: 13). The book's genesis makes it a somber parable of the delayed academic response to modernism, which could begin to generate exegesis and scholarly respectability once the life had finally gone out of it. Already in the first preface Levin had written that "Meanwhile, in the wider world, the pace of events has so accelerated that we have already begun to look back upon his work as upon the legacy of an earlier period," and that this made it "the proper occasion for a full critical appraisal" (9). "The pace of events" seems an oblique reference to the onset, since the publication of Joyce's last work, of World War II; in a later preface Levin again somewhat coyly mentions "circumstances of general distraction which—as I see now—have left their imprint upon these pages" (13). Joyce's reception in the American academy thus begins with the sense of an ending. The war, among its other and more significant effects, calls a final halt to the era of modernism, which is at last ready for wholesale recuperation. In Levin's words, "Now that [Joyce's] work is completed, we must try to understand its significance" (9).

Bernard McGinley's claim that "With the Second World War, International Modernism lost whatever coherence it had had" (1996: 17) is therefore a half-truth. While the writers themselves—notably the "Men of 1914"—were indeed depleted and scattered at this point, at another level International Modernism only *gained* its coherence at midcentury. In his 1960 essay "What Was Modernism?" Levin echoes this paradox: "[W]e live at least in the afterglow of the Moderns. Insofar as they were ahead of their time, we can even claim to be nearer to them" (1966: 282). Levin's book is both emblematic and aware of a movement "from Bohemia to Academe" (1960: 14), and this journey is aided by his own literary accomplishment. Control, balance, and aesthetic achievement are qualities that he both discerns in Joyce and displays in his own text. Like *Ulysses,* the book is structured around blocks of three chapters: the final section, "Richness," answers the first, "Reality." Levin's well-weighed sentences partake of the same drive toward elegant balance, conspicuously measuring and offsetting clauses: "Since Joyce lived to write, though he never wrote for a living, he went on writing to please himself, with an almost paranoid disregard of any other reader" (145). Chiasmus and ironic inversion flow thick and fast: "Bloom is an exile in Dublin, as Stephen is a Dubliner in exile" (79); "Stephen starts as an individual and becomes a type. Bloom starts as a type and becomes an individual" (80). Well-wrought form speaks as eloquently as its content: Levin's cool, wryly detached discourse on Joyce is itself a sign of the work's arrival at respectability. The texture of Levin's book is eloquent to the second power, ceaselessly proclaiming over and above its actual content that Joyce and the academy hold no fears for one another.

Levin's approach is unmistakably cosmopolitan. A scholar whose interests ranged from the Renaissance to modern French fiction, he gives Joyce a strongly European context. The density of reference in the following lines is not unusual: "A novelist, like Dostoyevsky, or a dramatist, like Ibsen, was hailed as a saviour or damned as a charlatan. A poet, like Victor Hugo, was a *mage effaré*. Consequently, rather than trouble with form, the most influential writers set up as lay preachers—Carlyle, Emerson, Nietzsche" (1960: 177). One effect of this was sought by most other defenders of Joyce: the legitimation of his work by its placement in a tradition. More specifically, Levin follows Edmund Wilson, who had viewed his modernists as the heirs to French Symbolism and affirmed that "the work of these writers is the result of a literary revolution which occurred outside English literature" (1961: 25). Levin indeed opens with a reprise of Wilson's theory of modernism, reflecting on the bifurcation of Symbolism and Naturalism and their potential to combine. Hence his play on the idea of the "two keys" to *Ulysses*—the *Odyssey* and *Thom's Dublin Directory*—to supply "its epic symbolism and its naturalistic atmosphere . . . the myth-making fantasy of literary tradition . . . [and] a literal-minded itinerary of daily business" (1960: 65). "Like Wilson," notes Hugh Kenner, "[Levin] read a European novel" (1987b: 170). Levin, Kenner adds elsewhere, "saw accurately how Joyce belonged rather in the conceptual spaces commanded by Flaubert and Turgenev than in a box with Thackeray and Jane Austen, where he only made trouble" (1987a: xi). Levin's final judgment on *Finnegans Wake* aligns it with "the most serious and percipient of modern writers": Dostoyevsky, Tolstoy, Ibsen, Zola, Gide, Eliot, and Mann (1960: 170). This is indeed "comparative literature," the subject of the chair that Levin held at Harvard. In 1953 he amplified the analysis of Joyce as a citizen of the world in an address he gave in Paris entitled "James Joyce et l'Idée de la Littérature Mondiale" (1963: 269–86). The very fact of this French performance is telling: Levin signals his comparative and cosmopolitan approach in the act, as well as the content, of enunciation. He thus confirms that internationalization of Joyce previously observed in such mutually antagonistic figures as Ezra Pound, Eugene Jolas, and F. R. Leavis. Indeed, the book begins by emphasizing Joyce's extrication from an Irish context: "[H]is books could not and cannot be published or sold in his native country. They are of Irishmen and by an Irishman, but not for Irishmen; and their exclusion was Joyce's loss as well as Ireland's" (1960: 21). Ireland has a place in Levin's study, but never for very long: its national politics turn up as part of the meaning of *Finnegans Wake*, but fizzle out inconclusively (147, 167–69). Levin's tone is wryly detached, lending its own sense of distance to its image of Joyce. With its sidelong references to air-raid sirens (69) and its mood of global crisis, the book hints at a comparison it never makes explicit, namely that amid the perils of 1941 the ructions of 1916 look like small beer. Historically and geographically, Levin gazes at Dublin through the wrong end of a telescope.

Levin's Joyce is emphatically modern—but in two divergent modes. On the one hand, Joyce's work offers "[an] eclectic *Summa* of its age: the *montage* of the cinema, impressionism in painting, *leitmotif* in music, the free association of psychoanalysis, and vitalism in philosophy. Take of these elements all that is fusible ... and you have the style of *Ulysses*" (1960: 82–83). Joyce's writing articulates the themes and forms of the twentieth century: Leopold Bloom's mind is "a motion picture, which has been ingeniously cut and carefully edited to emphasize the close-ups and fade-outs of flickering emotion, the angles of observation and the flashbacks of reminiscence. In its intimacy and in its continuity, *Ulysses* has more in common with the cinema than with other fiction" (82). Yet the work cannot be taken as a celebration of the modern. The twentieth century for Levin is an epoch of anomie, alienation, and "cultural disintegration" (30), embodying "the parched life of the metropolitan *Waste Land*" (38). Where several of Joyce's early reviewers found him a prophet of doom, Levin sees an anatomist of contemporary melancholy: his *Ulysses* is more tragic than comic. Bloom is "this apologetic little man," a "thoroughly uninteresting" misfit (101, 102). "Ithaca," where the characters are contemplated "from the scope of planetary distances" (108), marks the true emotional center of the book. "Further wanderings can only bring further sufferings": the seventeenth of June promises a paralyzing repetition of this book "totally lacking in the epic virtues of love, friendship, and magnanimity" (115, 114). All of this elaborates upon Levin's central dialectic: "Joyce's most protean variations are played upon two obsessive themes—the city and the artist. The connection between these themes is all the more poignant because it is so slight. It is as tenuous and strained as the connection between life and art in our time. The modern metropolis is lacking in beauty; the contemporary writer is without a community" (31).

This is not New Criticism. It is a mode of historicism, and part of the general dialectic of modern literature that Levin stakes out in his final section. He once declared his hope for a criticism that "while analyzing the formal and aesthetic qualities of a work of art, will fit them into the cultural and social pattern to which it belongs" (Levitt 1991: 103), and his book attempts to account for the historical deadlock it describes. Joyce's "brooding" fiction is generated by a specific historical situation:

Levin quotes the Marxist Plekhanov as observing that aestheticism arose "when discord had developed between the writer and his environment" (1960: 177), and with the world wars "[Joyce's] life enters history, and his work converges with the main stream of European culture" (182). Levin should not, therefore, be mistaken for a stereotypical midcentury "formalist." Yet his sense of history in this work remains general, a matter of broad strokes rather than local details. For all his sociological seriousness, he partly enacts the move from particular to general that we have already observed. His claim that Joyce "rediscovered in ancient myth an archetype for modern man" (67) suffers from one archetype too many: "modern man," thus broadly conceived, is as abstract as the myth that is supposed to give him weight. Here is the second mode of modernity in Levin: the Eliotic aesthetic of abstraction, subordinating locality and texture to planetary distance and allegorical structure. Kinesis loses out, once again, to stasis. In *Ulysses* "Joyce, even in the heat of practical experiments, remains true to his classical theories. His sense of movement is all on the surface. His underlying purpose is to call a halt, to achieve a stasis, to set up an immovable object against the irresistible forces of the city" (113). Even *Finnegans Wake* leads to a similar conclusion: "It was Joyce's lifelong endeavor, when all is said and done, to escape from the nightmare of history, to conceive the totality of human experience on a simultaneous plane, to synchronize past, present, and future in the timelessness of a millennium" (165).

Midcentury criticism has been charged with depoliticizing literature to fit a cold war agenda. In Alan Sinfield's account, a modernist art washed up on American shores was put to work legitimating an "international" aesthetic compatible with the global ambitions of the United States. The diverse politics of modernism were homogenized and neutralized into the expression of anguish at a notional "modern condition," which was "the special contribution of Modernism to Free World ideology" (1989: 182–92). One can see that Levin, a comparativist and literary historian, is a far more complex case than this. Yet even his reading partakes of a characteristic midcentury modernism in which art strives for stillness in a world that shuns it.

Levin's book fired an opening shot in what Charles Newman has called the "second revolution," a "revolution in pedagogy and criticism which interpreted, canonized and capitalized the Modernist industry" (1985: 27). American scholars writing after the Second World War were central to this canonizing process, and nowhere more so than with Joyce. For decades now it has been taken for granted that the bulk of serious work on him has gone West, and farther than Galway. By 1950 Oliver Gogarty was calling the United States "the chief infirmary for Joyceans" (1970: 765), while nine years later Anthony Cronin stressed the disparity between Joyce's English and American reputations (1959: 669). Anthony Burgess's foreword to *A Shorter "Finnegans Wake"* mentions that "Joyce scholarship has become a major industry in some American universities" (1965: 5), while in *Joysprick* he nods at the main linguistic work being done on the writer, "inevitably in the United States" (1973: 10). However, recollections of the 1930s and 1940s show American universities only gradually getting the hang of Joyce. William York Tindall's *Finnegans Wake* reading group, founded at Columbia in 1940 (1969: 24), was notably early. A. Walton Litz recalls studying *Ulysses* at Princeton as "an unusual thing for the late 1940s" (1986: 220). In a memoir of Richard Ellmann, his former collaborator Ellsworth Mason recalls the absence of twentieth-century literature at Yale in the early 1940s: Ellmann himself was forced to introduce it in a postgraduate group, which appropriated W. K. Wimsatt's rooms once a week, and also to reassure Mason that he would one day be able to make sense of Eliot. "Joyce, like Dante," Mason remembers, "was considered a great genius, but despite all the copies of *Ulysses* slipped into the United States illegally in the 1920s and its liberation in the 1934 Random House edition, nobody really read it.... Nobody knew how to read it" (1989: 5). A breakthrough was eventually made: "Ellmann's dissertation on Yeats in 1947," Mason eagerly stresses, "was the first ever accepted on a twentieth-century subject, and mine on Joyce in 1948 was the second" (5). Even then Joyce was a dubious field of study: Richard Ellmann, of all people, had written to Mason on Armistice Day 1946 to warn that Joyce was "fine as a hobby but not dissertation material" (10).

On Mason's account, the 1940s seem as barren a period for Joyce studies in the United States as they were in Leavisite Britain, which failed to produce a single book on the writer during that decade. Hugh Kenner has similar memories of Canada: "In 1946 the University of Toronto's Chancellor ... was offering me kindly advice: did I really mean to squander my talents on someone like Joyce? Yes, I stubbornly meant to, though I had to go elsewhere to do it. The Toronto library did possess a copy of *Ulysses,* but to inspect it one was required to produce two letters, one from a doctor, one from a clergyman" (1987a: ix–x). It is thus unsurprising that the editors of Ellmann's memorial volume should laud this generation for its revolutionary forays into unknown literary territory: "They launched themselves into a systematic exploration of the texts of high modernism with an audacity which must, at times, have unnerved not just their teachers but also themselves. Almost like monks of some unproven new religion, they undertook exegesis of seemingly impenetrable works with no certainty that the wider world would concur that these texts were sacred" (Dick et al. 1989: xiii–xiv). In fact, important discussions and exegeses of Joyce had already appeared by 1940—not least the "authorized" interpretations that the present chapter has examined. What Harry Levin terms Joyce's "quick transit from the *avant-garde* to the academy" (1960: 198) thus produces a paradox. On the one hand, Joyce is made strange all over again: by the standards of university curricula in the 1940s, the twenty-year-old *Ulysses* suddenly becomes a dangerously new text, as it had been in the 1920s. Yet the academy simultaneously has an opposite effect for which it is more notorious, namely, the institutionalization and "taming" of modernism's subversive energies. As Levin puts it, "For his original readers Joyce was a heretic, for many of them an emancipating force. The shift of values at mid-century has recast him in a priestly role, the patriarch of a neo-orthodox cult" (198).

It has become commonplace to distrust the "domestication" that institutions have effected on formerly subversive texts. Levin himself could rue Joyce's destiny as "a happy hunting ground for doctoral candidates" and the sight of poets "domesticated by institutions of learning" (1966: 278, 279). As Michael Bérubé argues, such "anti-professionalist" thinking may even be endemic to the field of literary studies due to the discipline's uncertain place "between its ideals of post-Kantian, Romantic autonomy and its ideals of professional social service" (1992: 25). Nonetheless, a sense of Joyce's canonization by the American academy has become central to his reputation. There are a number of reasons for this development.

I have already examined a negative one: F. R. Leavis's symbolic expulsion of Joyce from the English canon. The way was thus made clearer for American critics to appropriate—or rescue—Joyce and construct the dominant image of him in the postwar period. This makes prophetic William Carlos Williams's 1929 judgment that "English criticism" could not handle Joyce: "And this is the opportunity of America! To see large, larger than England can. . . . This American thing it is that would better fit the Irish of Joyce" (1961: 180–81). The historical sympathy of Americans for colonial Ireland has also been adduced as a factor in America's embrace of Joyce (Herr 1996: 208). More ingeniously, Declan Kiberd has argued that Irish writing—Yeats and Joyce above all—served as a salve for humanist American critics after the Second World War had cast traditional values in doubt. The enclave of Ireland, neutral in the "Emergency," offered an unexpected reprise of cultural holism to a critic like Richard Ellmann (Kiberd 1998). I shall examine Ellmann's organicist and humanist treatment of Joyce in the next chapter.

The institutional context also demands attention. The funds of American universities have been decisive in securing archives of drafts, letters, diaries, and other documents. By the end of the 1950s, the manuscripts of Joyce's Epiphanies were ensconced at the University of Buffalo, along with Joyce's own library and a set of *Ulysses* drafts. The manuscript of *Ulysses* was at Philadelphia, Cornell had acquired an extensive set of correspondence, and parts of the text of *Stephen Hero* had found their way into Cornell, Harvard, and Yale. Such collections rapidly generated further texts cataloguing and anthologizing the archives. *Stephen Hero* was edited by Theodore Spencer in 1944, and the conveyor belt was still in motion in 1965, with Richard M. Kain and Robert Scholes's edition of the Epiphanies and other *Portrait* drafts as *The Workshop of Daedalus*. An exorbitant, all-consuming logic is at work here, as apparently mundane matter—*Thom's Directory, The Evening Telegraph*—is absorbed into the archives. The archive even has a self-fulfilling capacity to create its own new material, as the record of Richard Ellmann's research into the collection now becomes a collection for research in its own right. By 1960 Harry Levin himself felt a little queasy at the scattering of Joycean material into the libraries of the Ivy League, but he concluded that it was sufficiently true to the writer: "[T]he disposition of Joyce's effects was bound to reflect the hazards and ironies of his uprooted career. We can imagine him being consoled by the parallel of the several cities that vied in claiming the vagrant Homer after his death" (1960: 187).

The universities' stockpiling of Joycean material coincided with a massive expansion of higher education in the United States. Gerald Graff records that the proportion of the eligible population going to college rose from 14 percent in 1940 to 40 percent in 1964, and for the study of literature these were indeed the years of growth (1987: 155). Twentieth-century literature, Graff adds, dramatically increased its share of undergraduate attention after the War (196–97). Observers have been quick to argue that this pedagogical inflation had a theoretical correlative in the New Criticism, a movement, Hugh Kenner has written, whose thrust "was toward facilitating classroom discussion, and [whose] procedures tended to move into prominence chiefly those poets whom they rendered lengthily discussable" (1976: 43). In turn, it is frequently proposed that New Criticism is the critical counterpart of a modernism newly acceptable to the academy. Michael Bérubé proposes that the ascendancy of what John Crowe Ransom called "Criticism, Inc." "begins with the rise, in the 1940s and 1950s, of a series of related phenomena: the maturity of the New Criticism, the assumption that the business of criticism is interpretation, and the transmission of modern literature and modernist ideologies into university curricula" (1992: 38). For Bruce Robbins, too, "the professionalization of literary criticism was largely accomplished by the New Critics," and "the profession of literary criticism was born as a modernist institution" (1993: 66, 64). Robbins points to one reason for left-wing hostility to the canonization of modernism: the simultaneous *professionalization* of criticism and *autonomization* of literature. If the former seems to integrate art within a capitalist economy, of which the United States is seen as the apogee, the latter removes that art's teeth, rendering it harmlessly ahistorical.

One thus returns to the alleged ideological pact between a formalist criticism and the recent literature upon which it could feed. According to Sinfield, critical formalism "was congenial to Cold War ideology, since it discouraged political, economic and social ideas among writers and critics. . . . This formalism developed the strand in Modernism that imagined the poetic text as autonomous, drawing upon Modernist critical suggestions" (1989: 188). Although this account is suggestive, it has been shown to be inadequate for Levin's influential book, and in Joyce's case it needs to be qualified. Eliot and Pound were the supposed inspirations of New Criticism, but given their enthusiasm for Joyce's work, that movement's role in Joyce studies is surprisingly slight. The major New Critics themselves—Ransom, Tate, Warren, Brooks—published little on Joyce; as Jeffrey Segall has observed, aspects of Joyce's writing were always difficult to insert within these critics' paradigm (1993: 124). Terry Eagleton partially "explains" New Criticism in terms of practical exigency: "Distributing a brief poem for students to be perceptive about was less cumbersome than launching a Great Novels of the World course" (1983: 50). But the cumbersome *Ulysses* indeed found itself on a Great Novels of the World course: Harry Levin's Proust-Joyce-Mann lecture series (Mason 1989: 5, 441).

If Levin fails to fit a New Critical template, so do two other notable American works of the 1940s that take the interpretation of Joyce in opposite directions: Joseph Campbell and Henry Morton Robinson's *Skeleton Key to "Finnegans Wake"* (1944) and Richard M. Kain's *Fabulous Voyager* (1947). The former is a lavishly mythological exegesis that reads Joyce as a panhistorical universalist: "Wherever Joyce looks in history or human life, he discovers the operation of these basic polarities. Under the seeming aspect of diversity—in the individual, the family, the state, the atom, or the cosmos—these constants remain unchanged. . . . James Joyce presents . . . nothing more nor less than the eternal dynamic implicit in birth, conflict, death, and resurrection" (Campbell and Robinson 1944: 21). Kain, by contrast, extends Levin's approach in his empirical study of *Ulysses* as a document of "the inherent contradictions and shortcomings of modern civilization" (1947: 10). His mapping of events in the novel onto the real *Evening Telegraph* for 16 June 1904 (55–61) is a distant ancestor of the detailed historical work that would begin to occupy radical critics some four decades later. Biographical archives, mythopoeia, sociological speculation: work on Joyce as he entered the modernist canon cannot easily be reduced to "New Criticism." To see what actually happened, let us look more closely at the two critics who came to dominate the Joyce Industry between World War II and the 1980s.

3

The Men of 1946
Tales Told of Dick and Hugh

> Joyce's theme in *Ulysses* was simple.
>   Richard Ellmann, preface to *Ulysses*

> This is not simple, and nothing in *Ulysses* is simpler.
>   Hugh Kenner, *Dublin's Joyce*

"Once it could somehow read *Ulysses*," recalled Hugh Kenner in 1987, "the critical community took the bit in its teeth" (1987a: xv). He and Richard Ellmann represent what became of Joyce when the first hurdles had been cleared, the fate of a criticism that—even, increasingly, in the case of *Finnegans Wake*—no longer had to spend its time identifying and explicating the story from behind a veil of signs. The result was a fresh bifurcation, a departure from hard-won consensus into new ways to disagree. Both men have occasionally been accused of over-elaboration, the decadence of a literary criticism that has lost sight of its explanatory function. While Ellmann's elaboration has been mocked by Stan Gébler Davies (1975: 197) and Bruce Arnold (1991: 91–92), the ostentatious erudition of Kenner's early work *Dublin's Joyce* appeared excessive even to more unashamedly intellectual readers. Harry Levin protested that by the mid-fifties "the actual sense of the narrative seems to be generally understood; and subsequent interpretations, such as Hugh Kenner's in *Dublin's Joyce,* tend to become capricious and doctrinaire through their very effort to discover novel readings" (1960: 193). Even Samuel Beckett, no stranger to the mind's infinite capacity for permutations, commented in 1958 that Kenner's book was "very brilliant and erudite but dementedly over-explicative." He qualified this with what was becoming a familiar judgment: "though admittedly Joyce invites such herrdoktoring as much as any writer ever" (Knowlson 1996: 454).

Ronald Bush has remarked that for a subsequent generation of scholars "it seemed that Kenner and Ellmann shared as much as they disputed" (1996: 523). Both aspects—the relative stability of knowledge and opinion about Joyce and the concomitant desire to complicate and (as Kenner puts it in *The Stoic Comedians*) do "something utterly unforeseen tomorrow" (1962: 107)—are part of the postwar picture. But the retrospective gaze at a given period is liable to homogenize it—"Romanticism," "Modernism," "American liberal humanism"—so in what follows I shall emphasize the important differences between Ellmann and Kenner, the leading Joyceans before the arrival of theory.

Ellmann's importance is in little doubt: his 1959 biography, revised in 1982, is the best-known of all books on Joyce and has been indispensable to Joyceans for over four decades. Until his death in 1987, writes Bruce Arnold, "Ellmann was regarded as the leading Joyce scholar of the day," a critic who had "assumed a dominance in Joyce scholarship" since the 1950s (1991: 106, 92). The biography would have been sufficient for this, but Ellmann also introduced Stanislaus Joyce's memoir *My Brother's Keeper* (1958), coedited (with Ellsworth Mason) the *Critical Writings* (1964), produced three volumes of *Letters* (1966, 1975), and catalogued Joyce's Trieste library (*The Consciousness of Joyce*, 1977). Kenner, like Ellmann, has ranged well beyond Joyce, his weightiest work being *The Pound Era* (1972). Yet Harold Bloom has dubbed him "pope of the alternative tradition to that of Ellmann in Joyce studies" (1986: ix), and at the 1984 Joyce Symposium in Frankfurt, Kenner, not Ellmann, was awarded the first Thomas Gear Gold Medal for outstanding services to Joyce scholarship (McGinley 1996: 21). "Ellmann . . . has stood for the last three decades as Kenner's principal adversary," writes Jeffrey Segall (1993: 179), testifying to the prevailing relationship between the two critics.

How can the distinction between the two best be characterized? A. Walton Litz sees them as the postwar embodiment of a fundamental duality in the reading of Joyce. Drawing on Arnold Goldman's description of a "fact/myth ambiguity" in *Ulysses,* Litz claims that these key terms can be traced as critical emphases all the way from Joyce's divided loyalties to Defoe and Blake, through Pound and Eliot's contrasting construals of *Ulysses,* into subsequent critical work on the text. This polarity resembles the one offered by Edmund Wilson in his account of *Ulysses* as a marriage of Naturalism and Symbolism; Frank Budgen and Stuart Gilbert's respective stresses on the work's "Bloomian" and Homeric dimensions offer another notable enactment of this persistent dialectic. "In our own time," writes Litz, "Hugh Kenner and Richard Ellmann have been the most prominent inheritors" of this split tradition (1974: 16). Jeri Johnson endorses Litz's line: "Henceforth [from the early 1920s] Joyce critics would steer a course between the Scylla of novelistic realism and hard facts and the Charybdis of myth, symbol and form for its own sake. . . . Richard Ellmann . . . and Hugh Kenner . . . took up (respectively) the Gilbert and Budgen, Eliot and Pound, lines once again" (1993: xviii).

One might extrapolate from this that Kenner, addicted to the empirical, represents an incorrigibly "realist" mode of reading Joyce, whereas Ellmann, enamored as he is of totalizing structures and universal narratives, has a greater affinity with high modernism. There is some basis for Litz's claims. Ellmann was indeed given to grand gestures and high-flown readings: his *Ulysses on the Liffey* even commences with the promise of "a new myth for *Ulysses*" (1972: xii). Kenner, a longtime friend and influential critic of Pound, begins his first book on Joyce by explicitly aligning himself with that poet's essay on *Ulysses* (1987a: xvii). And his subsequent work on Joyce does reveal a fascination with such concrete matters as the hour at which Bloom's watch stopped (1978: 113–16) or the fate of Conan Doyle's *Stark-Munro Letters,* standing overdue on Eccles Street's fictional bookshelves in 1904 and declared missing by the real Capel Street library two years later (1987b: 143). But "fact" for Kenner tends to be not some positivist building-block but the disruptive "awkward fact" or ironic anomaly, like his record of Bloomsday encounters with the word "Bloom" (1987b: 156). It is actually Ellmann, of course, who has assembled more facts than any other writer on Joyce; among his greatest contributions to *Ulysses* criticism is his search for the real-life models for every main character. Litz's, then, is an inadequate account of Ellmann and Kenner. This chapter will offer a different account of what divides them.

Cataloguing the Unfacts: The Ellmann Era

Academic criticism of Joyce has become an increasingly self-sufficient sphere, with its own journals, conferences, and lines of communication. Many names instantly recognizable in this small world—Bernard Benstock, Clive Hart, Fritz Senn—have much less currency outside, in the alternative circuits devoted to other writers or in the academy at large. It is thus ironic, and a sign of changing times, that the two most important postwar Joyceans spent much of their professional careers working on other writers. Richard Ellmann came to Joyce via W. B. Yeats, whose work he researched in Dublin in the mid-1940s. His access to the archives of the poet's widow George Yeats led Ellmann to publish his first book, *Yeats: The Man and His Masks* (1948). The preface to *James Joyce* informs us that it began to germinate when Ellmann was first shown Yeats's unpublished account of his first meeting with Joyce (1982: vii). Ellmann was already well aware of Joyce in the 1940s—not least through Ellsworth Mason, who wrote his Yale dissertation on the writer in 1948. Ellmann's visit to Sylvia Beach's Shakespeare and Company shortly after the German surrender of Paris (Fitch 1985: 407) was surely prompted by Joyce's prominent association with the bookshop.

It was with Joyce's name that Ellmann, in his turn, came to be most closely associated. The posthumous essay collection *a long the riverrun* gives Joyce priority as the writer "for whom Ellmann performed so many services" (Ellmann 1989: viii). Robert Scholes suggested that Ellmann's presence as coeditor of the Viking Press *Portrait* (1964) was invoked "ritualistically, for the sake of his prestige in matters Joycean" (1992: 54). The word "Ellmann" itself, like "Bloom" or "Weaver," has an instant significance for anyone concerned with Joyce, usually functioning as shorthand for a reference to the 1959 biography. As Bernard McGinley remarks, the phrase "It's in Ellmann" has come to serve as a kind of guarantee of authenticity—"epistemologically final, the last word"—for all kinds of claims about the writer (1996: 31). This reflects not only Ellmann's biographical skills but the cultural and academic significance of the genre in which he did his most extensive and admired work. The status that his name carries could only have been attained by a biographer; the plainly entitled *James Joyce* retains its centrality amid the welter of other identically titled books partly because of its generic difference from works of pure literary criticism. A literary biography is more likely than a critical work to be seen as achieving a kind of identity with its subject, a fit correspondence between text and individual. Such congruity may also be taken to imply that other works are superfluous by comparison, that only the biography is finally necessary—as in Patrick Parrinder's assertion that "In all the vast secondary literature on Joyce, one work (and one only) stands out as essential and indispensable reading. This is Richard Ellmann's biography *James Joyce*" (1984: 255).

Ellmann's biography, with its relentless stockpiling of what—*pace* Litz—look like hard facts, has indeed become a metatext for all other commentaries on the writer, a reference point almost as unavoidable as Joyce's fiction itself. As Joseph Kelly has pointed out (1998: 173), Ellmann's biography is the only text not written by Joyce to be granted its own standard abbreviation by the *James Joyce Quarterly*. At some point all commentators on Ellmann, however critical, remark on the Joycean community's debt to him. Phillip Herring pictures Ellmann's critics "like a few small mice nibbling around a royal wedding cake" (1989: 126); Bernard McGinley describes "our debt and our gratitude to Ellmann" (1996: 37); Hugh Kenner himself calls the book "the best Joyce biography we are likely to see," adding that Ellmann has "earned our gratitude for all he has preserved" (1982b: 1384). Ellmann gained the status of a tribal elder, a chronicler and curator to whom one can always refer when necessary. Yet Ellmann's biography remains a version: the facts—and these, as we shall see, are not wholly stable—are molded into a narrative. The notion of biography as a "scientific" practice, a valiantly neutral record of data devoid of artifice and interference, would find few supporters today (Nadel 1991: 87–88). Indeed, as Laura Marcus has shown, an acceptance of the artistic, fabulatory character of the genre reaches at least as far back as the moment of modernism itself. Virginia Woolf argued that the biographer "chooses; he synthesizes; in short, he has ceased to be the chronicler, he has become an artist" (Marcus 1995: 92). As Marcus comments, "A focus on the subjective nature of the interpretation of the 'facts' about an individual, and on the necessary shaping and selection that goes into biographical portraiture, led to an emphasis on the aesthetic dimensions of biography and the increasing similarity between the novel and biography" (92). In his inaugural lecture at Oxford in 1971, Ellmann himself remarked that "The form of biography ... is countenancing experiments comparable to those of the novel and poem" (1973: 15).

Melvin J. Friedman finds the resources of a novelist in Ellmann (1991: 139), and the narrative character of biography is significant. Leon Edel, Henry James's biographer, claimed that Ellmann's biography adhered to "the old-fashioned Victorian chronological manner" (Friedman 1991: 134), and Ellmann himself conceded that biography "must retain a chronological pattern, though not necessarily a simple one" (1973: 15). The contemporary quickening of interest in biography may partly stem from a public desire for the linearity and coherence that twentieth-century fiction has put in question, which the record of a life can still hope to achieve. When the biographical subject is an artistic innovator like Joyce, an ironic disparity can result, with the modernist being reclaimed by the kind of "transparent" language and chronological narration against which he had set himself. Through biography, the most radically avant-garde and antilinear figure can be reclaimed for sequential time and the consolations of storytelling. Even the life of Joyce, in Ellmann's version, does not end in midsentence but with the resounding declaration that his intense commitment to art "raised his life to dignity and high dedication" (1982: 744). Biography can thus effect a certain recuperation of difficult, challenging artists, as the reassuring unity of a life is discovered behind the fragments of the work. It has often been argued that major modernist writers sought in art a formal stability they could not find in the mess of real history and everyday life. But in the case of biography this model can be inverted, as the fragmentation and intransigent alterity of avant-garde art is explained by and recuperated into the retrospective unity of a completed life. The modernist's "I cannot make it cohere" is met with the reassuring "it coheres all right" of the biographer. In its ability to reassert the lived, continuous selfhood of a Joyce against or beyond his disruptive productions, biography is thus a quintessential genre of humanism.

Ellmann's unique position in Joyce studies is also due to his success in conquering the biographical field. Joyce had already had one biographer.

But Herbert Gorman's *James Joyce* (1939) has an exceedingly poor reputation among Joyceans. Hugh Kenner recalls "struggling to extract even rudimentary chronology from Gorman" (1987b: 171); Nora Joyce's biographer, Brenda Maddox, finds Gorman's book "uninformative, obsequious and lifeless" (1988: 510); and Stan Gébler Davies brusquely labels it "more or less worthless, being distinguished chiefly by its omissions and evasions, and its presentation of James Joyce as a plaster saint" (1975: 7). "Though Gorman worked throughout the 1930s," writes Bernard McGinley, "the Joycean world-picture that emerged was not very recognisable.... The published book was abandoned rather than completed, and inadequate to its task" (1996: 11–12). Gorman's work is now considered part of the long publicity campaign that also included Gilbert, Budgen, and the *Exagmination*. Ellmann's biography promised to break this incestuous relationship, with Joyce at last unable to exert any direct influence over his chronicler.

Ellmann could thus lay claim to being Joyce's first proper biographer; the surprise is that he has also been virtually the last. If Gorman's book is seen as a mouthpiece for Joyce, Stan Gébler Davies's *James Joyce: A Portrait of the Artist* (1975), though a good example of the popular—even populist—tendencies of biography, is rarely cited. ("Brisk, hearty, superficial" was Kenner's assessment [1987b: 176].) Meanwhile, other books such as Kevin Sullivan's *Joyce Among the Jesuits* (1958) or Peter Costello's *James Joyce: The Years of Growth* (1992) do not attempt to cover the writer's whole life. This unusual situation is due, in part, to the constraints imposed by the Joyce estate in the name of family privacy. Bernard McGinley makes the case for a new full biography but admits that "in the light of the combative behaviour of the Estate regarding quotation and copyright, one seems unlikely to be forthcoming for many years" (1996: 37). But there is another reason why Ellmann's biography would be difficult to supplant. It is "the most comprehensive biography we are likely to get," remarks Hugh Kenner, "so many sources having vanished since Ellmann was making his inquiries. People have died, Dublin and Paris have changed; most subtly, witnesses to events long gone now know, thanks to Ellmann, what it is they remember" (1987b: 171–72). The moment of Ellmann's research, the wealth of firsthand evidence available to him (many of his notes record "Interview"), are unrepeatable. Although Peter Costello has recently demonstrated the potential of archival sources for enriching the picture, many of the voices of Joyce's own time are now only available to us through Ellmann's mediation.

Ellmann's book has been held in high esteem for over forty years. A recent volume on the teaching of *Ulysses* reports that "When questioned about biographical reading for themselves and for their students, most teachers mentioned Ellmann's *James Joyce*, which they often characterized as 'monumental'" (McCormick and Steinberg 1993: 5). The same word is used by Steven Connor (1996: 104), while Gébler Davies, in the course of justifying his own effort, also complained that Ellmann's book had "too much of the monument about it" (1975: 7). (Derek Attridge, in a slight variation on the theme, calls the book "magisterial" [1990: 292], while Bernard McGinley goes one better and refers to "Ellmann's magisterial monument to Joyce" [1996: 19].) The persistence of this term probably refers to the book's sheer size as well as its contents: over eight hundred pages long, it comfortably outweighs *Ulysses* and *Finnegans Wake*. This still leaves the book only half the size of Leon Edel's *Life of Henry James*, the kind of work that—heroically published over a period of twenty years, beginning in the early 1950s—threatens to overturn altogether the relations between literature and the scholarly texts that supplement it. If Ellmann's book was bigger than *Finnegans Wake*, at least it hadn't been quite so long in the writing. But such prolixity is in itself something of a guarantor of authority, bespeaking a level of research that needs this many pages to document; Ellmann's notes, implicit insurance for the reliability of his narrative, occupy fully sixty pages of small print at the end of the book. As Attridge says, the "massive labour to which the weighty volume testified" (2000: 3) had a powerful effect in its own right.

Anthony Cronin, anonymously assessing Ellmann's book for the *Times Literary Supplement*, was, if anything, affronted by the size of Ellmann's undertaking, remarking that "much of the difficulty with Mr. Ellmann's book is in seeing the wood for the trees. It has been twelve years in the writing, which has been aided by the bounty and blessing of no fewer than five American organizations.... He has interviewed scores of people; has crossed the Atlantic at least three times; has read every scrap of the published matter and all the voluminous unpublished material, most of which has gravitated to American collections over the years" (1959: 670). But how reliable was the appearance of pedantic authority that Cronin found so off-putting? In "The Impertinence of Being Definitive," a review of the second edition of Ellmann's biography, Kenner writes that "reviews of Mark I ('definitive,' 'masterly') made it seem that what Ellmann had asserted of Joyce was *so*" (1982b: 1384). Two years earlier Kenner claimed that "the biography overwhelmed" on its publication, though "After twenty years it is easy to see that *James Joyce* is by no means what it still tends to get called, definitive" (1987b: 171). Kenner slightly exaggerates the original acclaim for Ellmann's book. Stuart Gilbert really did call it "a biography that we are justified on every count in regarding as definitive," adding that it was "a masterpiece of scholarly objectivity and exact research, in which the facts are marshalled and set forth with fine lucidity, and the imposing mass of detail never clogs the analysis" (1959: 43). Robert H. Deming also incautiously referred to "a definitive biography" (1970: 29), and Frank Kermode found the biography "superlatively good . . . 800 pages of remarkable authority" (1959: 675). But Anthony Cronin challenged Ellmann on matters of fact, provoking the biographer to reply in the *TLS*; and in the *New Statesman* William Empson balked at Ellmann's system of notes and indexing ("like climbing a ten-foot wall with broken bottles on it"), complaining that the forbidding format of documentation obscured the contentiousness of some of Ellmann's choice tales. "[T]he immense machine is often reporting gossip," writes Empson, demonstrating that a story about Joyce leaving Nora in a London park had been embellished by Joyce's sister Eva four decades after the event. "This," Empson concludes, "is not really a scientific way to write biography" (1959: 585).

The definitive character of Ellmann's facts was thus never quite as secure as Kenner implies; and over the decades other lacunae, confusions, and omissions have been teased out. Ira Nadel (1991) and Bernard McGinley (1996) have assembled a wealth of these, including erroneous claims about Joyce's place of birth and Ireland's nonexistent ban on *Ulysses*. The revised edition of 1982—"more accurately merely the same anew," comments McGinley, "the fuller or more idiosyncratic edition" (1996: 34)—seems to have spurred rather than assuaged the doubters, with existing errors uncorrected and a growing sense among Joyce scholars of the biographer's fallibility. Ronald Bush suggests that the 1982 edition, rather than shoring up Ellmann's authority, in fact "provided an occasion to think about how the 1959 original, for all its virtues, might have hindered the ongoing process of coming to terms with Joyce." Bush considers Kenner's essay "The Impertinence of Being Definitive" as "probably the document that most of us remember from that moment" (1996: 523); and, indeed, Kenner's review remains one of the most damagingly dogged assaults on Ellmann's methods. Kenner takes particular care over the demolition of Ellmann's discovery of "P. J. D'Arcy" as the model for Bartell D'Arcy in "The Dead." An interview with John Joyce, glossed by Ellmann as a key piece of evidence, may have been fabricated by Flann O'Brien, while the whole story is backed up by a Dubliner who was telling Kenner tall tales as far back as the mid-1950s (Kenner 1982b: 1384).

The status of this or that individual fact is not the central issue here. What is damaging to the book's "definitive" reputation is the sense that Kenner induces of the tenuousness of these tales, the speculation and fabulation necessary to keep the narrative moving. A major aspect of this is Ellmann's tendency to mingle biographical and literary evidence. This is a particular problem in the early part of the book, where firsthand documentation is scarcer. For instance, while fleshing out Joyce's ancestors Ellmann introduces his granduncle William O'Connell: "His grandnephew described William as 'a hale old man with a well tanned skin, rugged features, and white side whiskers,' who was still good for a ten- or twelve-mile constitutional, and smoked a pipeful of vile-smelling tobacco every morning in a backyard shack, with his hair carefully greased and his tall hat perched on his head" (1982: 13). From the way these details are framed, they would seem to come from the reminiscences that emerged from one of Ellmann's interviews, or perhaps from a memoir or letter. The passage is actually based on a few memorable pages of *A Portrait of the Artist as a Young Man*, which describe "Uncle Charles." Kenner (1978) has used this figure as an example of the slipperiness of Joyce's style, in which words are infected with characters' idioms. Ellmann elects to reinterpret Uncle Charles's words: Joyce's "reeking outhouse" (1992a: 62) becomes Ellmann's "backyard shack," but without alerting us to the shifting nuances that were a significant part of Joyce's narrative. A more blatant example of this tendency in Ellmann is his account of Joyce's arrival at Clongowes Wood in 1888: "His tearful mother begged him not to speak to the rough boys; his father reminded him that

John O'Connell, his great-grandfather, had presented an address to the Liberator at Clongowes fifty years before. He gave him two five-shilling pieces, and told him never to peach on another boy. Then his parents went off, and James was plunged into the life of Clongowes" (1982: 27).

The scene sounds familiar. Ellmann's note refers us to a page of the *Portrait* where we can read: "[H]is father had told him that he would be no stranger there because his granduncle had presented an address to the liberator there fifty years before" (1992a: 24). The other details—rough boys, ten shillings, peaching—are from a paragraph several pages earlier than the one Ellmann refers to: "His mother had told him not to speak with the rough boys in the college.... And his father had given him two fiveshilling pieces for pocket money. And his father had told him if he wanted anything to write home to him and, whatever he did, never to peach on a fellow.... [A]nd the car had driven off with his father and mother on it" (5–6). The free-indirect subjectivism with which Joyce has Stephen reflecting on his mother's tears—"But he had pretended not to see that she was going to cry. She was a nice mother but she was not so nice when she cried"—becomes in Ellmann's text the succinct subject "His tearful mother." But given Ellmann's evidently heavy, even exclusive reliance on the *Portrait* for this passage, his alterations and elisions appear somewhat arbitrary. Joyce's modernist text has been filtered and translated back into a reliably representational mode, Stephen's childish staccato easily made over into the succinct plain-speaking of a man reporting the life behind the art.

This strategy of Ellmann's is the more surprising because he sometimes shows that art diverges sharply from life. To take one striking example: on the same page as his description of Joyce's entry to Clongowes, he informs us that "His immediate response to Clongowes is less clear than one would expect; his brother Stanislaus ... remembers him as happy and well there, while *A Portrait* represents him as unhappy and unwell" (1982: 27). As Bernard McGinley remarks, "a reading of the life through the texts [can] distort both, while simultaneously oversimplifying the connexions between them" (1996: 20). During the composition of the biography, Ellsworth Mason worried at Ellmann's "tendency to identify the plausible with the actual," warning that "if you are weaving both the works and the non-works into a single, supposedly factual, fabric, it is a serious flaw" (Kelly 1998: 152, 153). Why, then, beyond sheer convenience, does Ellmann tend to conflate the two? The question leads us to the overall picture of Joyce that emerges from his work.

Kenner's 1982 review suggests that the conflation of life and work is in line with one of the principles of Ellmann's portrait, namely that Joyce "put down little he'd not actually seen and heard: indeed possessed so little imagination that 'imaginative' becomes a word of courtesy" (1982b: 1384). Ellmann's deployment of literary sources as evidence, in other words, subtly slants things against Joyce; it also creates a circular effect whereby once this impression of Joyce has been established, anything that appears in the fiction *must* have happened to him—which makes Ellmann's job that much easier. "If one's man was a writer with little imagination," Kenner summarizes, "then testimony however shaky to an event that turns up in his writing acquires high plausibility" (1384). On this view, Ellmann's tendency to blur fact and fiction subtly denigrates Joyce. But the deeper effect is the opposite of what Kenner proposes. The fundamental principle of Ellmann's Joyce, the watchword all the way from the biography through to his later critical discussions, is unity. Ellmann's search is always for a life that can be read as a coherent narrative, a systematic intellectual program of tirelessly propounded values, a continuity between experience and art. Ellmann's holism emerged with particular clarity in 1975 when the *Times Literary Supplement* asked him to review Clive Hart and David Hayman's collection of essays on *Ulysses*. "The assumption on which *James Joyce's 'Ulysses'* rests," Ellmann's review begins, "is that *Ulysses,* because it contains eighteen episodes, can profitably be discussed piecemeal by eighteen different critics. Whatever merit attaches to particular essays . . . the effect of splitting the novel up this way is to lose sight of the 'wholeness, harmony and radiance' that Joyce intended it should manifest." Future critics, Ellmann concludes, "will pull the book together rather than apart" (1975: 1118). And what goes for the work goes equally for its relation to the life. In *The Consciousness of Joyce* Ellmann writes that "truth," for Joyce, "required that there should be between the writer's life and his work an umbilical relation. . . . The more genuine the urge to expression, the more it had to do with accessible feelings" (1977: 74). In the introduction to the biography he expands on this principle: "The life of an artist, but particularly that of Joyce, differs from the lives of other persons in that its events are becoming artistic sources even as they command his present attention. . . . [H]e shapes again the experiences which have shaped him. . . . In turn the process of reshaping experience becomes a part of his life, another of its recurrent events like rising or sleeping" (1982: 3). The hypnotic language, itself full of "recurrent" terms, lulls us into a sense of plenitude, of a constant organic reciprocity between life and letters; the emergent totality of "James Joyce" is enacted by Ellmann's even, assured tone. Ellmann also shares with Harry Levin a stylistic gift, a way with neat paradox and elegant summary: "Before Ibsen's letter Joyce was an Irishman; after it he was a European" (75); "Joyce has been derided as more mimic than creator, which charge, being untrue, is the greatest praise of all" (363). This syntactical shapeliness achieves in style what Ellmann consistently sought: an effect of unity. I have suggested that the organic coherence that seems to be the property of an individual life can make biography a definitively humanist mode. Ellmann's biography exemplifies this principle, producing and responding to an understanding of Joyce that is fundamentally harmonious.

This is not Ellmann's only voice. *James Joyce* in fact represents its subject in two modes that are distinct—even seemingly opposed. One is the heroic tone we have just seen: this rises to the surface when Ellmann celebrates Joyce's dedication to his radiant art. In *Ulysses*, writes Ellmann, Joyce "expressed his only piety, a rejection, in humanity's name and comedy's method, of fear and cruelty" (1982: 379). Grand generalities and big words predominate here. Discussing the *Portrait*, Ellmann develops an image of art as embryonic gestation: "[T]he soul discovers the goal towards which it has been mysteriously proceeding—the goal of life. It must swim no more but emerge into air, the new metaphor being flight" (297). Art, Life, the Soul—we are decidedly departing the literature of the latrine. In a moment of peculiar vapidity, Ellmann records that Joyce "stated once and for all his lifelong conviction that literature was the affirmation of the human spirit" (96). The uncritical uplift here is unusually empty. Yet while this manner defines Ellmann's ultimate view of the work, he narrates the life in a different voice, one that is urbane and amused. Joyce's first departure for the Continent offers a good example: "Having decided that medical school in Dublin did not suit him, Joyce rather illogically resolved to try medical school in Paris. Of course he wanted to go to Paris anyway, but he always presented his caprices as reasoned plans. Whether a Paris degree would be of any use to him in Ireland he did not investigate, and he did not bother his head over other questions he might have asked himself, such as how he could hope to pass chemistry in French when he could not do so in English" (106).

Ellmann is equally wry on the relation to Ireland implied by Joyce's move: "Joyce needed exile as a reproach to others and a justification of himself. . . . [L]ike other revolutionaries, he fattened on opposition and grew thin and pale when treated with indulgence. Whenever his relations with his native land were in danger of improving, he was to find a new incident to solidify his intransigence and to reaffirm the rightness of his voluntary absence" (1982: 109). In passages like these—and many of Ellmann's judgments share this mood—Joyce is ostentatiously ironized. The seriousness of his motives dissolves into display: his avowed pain becomes a public performance. Ellmann himself plays a part: he gazes with paternal indulgence at the antics of the young man (and even, later on, the middle-aged man), patiently mocking yet never withdrawing his tolerance.

There is wisdom in Ellmann's view of Joyce. His eye for the ridiculous is matched by the grace of his sentences, in which the subject's disorderly life is brought into shape. Yet one must also notice the effect of this treatment. If the heroic mode exalts the artist, the ironic note makes the man's life a more cheerful spectacle, however grim the evidence. (The two modes seem to meet in the claim, at once grand and bathetic, that Joyce managed "to mother and father himself, to become, by the superhuman effort of the creative process, no one but James Joyce" [1982: 299].) Like Harry Levin before him, Ellmann seems to look at Joyce from a distance—a figural and, perhaps behind that, a geographical one. The art wins undying respect: the history amid which it unfolds is over with, no ground for any further anxiety. It might be harsh, or generous, to say that in this life of Joyce there is no longer really anything to worry about—whether the concern be the writer's demands on others, the literary challenge that he posed to so many readers, or the turbulent world in which these unfolded. William Empson complained that Ellmann had taken Joyce's politics altogether too lightly, failing to appreciate that "socialism" might be more than another adolescent caprice (1959: 585). Ellmann, like Levin, does historicize Joyce—but with a transatlantic detachment that can become Olympian. Unlike Levin's, his vision is fundamentally genial: whether ironized or lionized, Ellmann's Joyce ultimately says yes to life. This, as much as any of Ellmann's more specific claims, would be decisive.

If Ellmann's thought is humanist in its assertion of a continual identity and its satisfying artistic expression, it is also humanist in an evaluative sense, reading Joyce as the democratic champion of everyday folk. Here Ellmann develops the reading laid down by Frank Budgen in the 1930s. At the start of his biography he informs us that "Joyce's discovery, so humanistic that he would have been embarrassed to disclose it out of context, was that the ordinary is the extraordinary" (1982: 5). His analysis of *Ulysses* naturally supports this view. "The divine part of Bloom," we learn, "is simply his humanity—his assumption of a bond between himself and other created beings" (362). Joyce "give[s] Bloom the power that he has himself, to infuse common things with uncommonness" (362); in the temporary union of Bloom and Dedalus "Joyce affirms his perception of community" (372). Finally, "The theme of *Ulysses* is simple. . . . Casual kindness overcomes unconscionable power. . . . In Joyce's work the soul—a word which he never renounced—carries off the victory" (379). The rhetoric is stirring, and has rung out powerfully for generations of readers. The process that Emer Nolan has characterized as "Joyce's canonization as the most congenial of early twentieth-century writers, 'the saving humanist of English language modernism'" (1995: 1) has as one of its central events Ellmann's powerfully affirmative reading of Joyce in the late 1950s. The critical studies influenced by Ellmann's humanism include C. H. Peake's *James Joyce: The Citizen and the Artist* (1977), John Gross's *Modern Masters* volume (1970), and Patrick Parrinder's *James Joyce* (1984). But a list of critics indebted to Ellmann could run for pages and remain incomplete. In one way or another he has influenced most Joyceans since the end of the 1950s. An unusually vivid example is Marilyn French's interpretation of *Ulysses, The Book as World* (1976), with its conclusion that "there remain the small, shining, stubborn seeds of human decency, human suffering, human aspiration—the nobility that is the other face of ignominy, the significance contained in a mass of trivia, the godliness shining in a handful of slime. If you can see that godliness, it is your own you are seeing" (1982: 268).

Even this kind of secularized grace seems modest beside Ellmann's own later work. The reading of *Ulysses* adumbrated in *James Joyce* is expanded in *Ulysses on the Liffey* (1972), a book that takes Joycean affirmation to new heights. In one of the most ambitious exegeses since Stuart Gilbert's forty years earlier, Ellmann seeks to show that *Ulysses* is governed by deep structural rhythms only hinted at by the Linati and Gorman-Gilbert schemata. Ellmann divides the novel into six triads of three chapters apiece, each enacting a dialectical conflict resolved in the third chapter of the triad. "I shall propose," he explains early on, "that in every group of three chapters the first defers to space, the second has time in the ascendant, and the third blends (or expunges) the two. Space has priority because in each triad the external world has to be posited before it can be countered or undermined" (1972: 19). The evidence adduced for such theories can be tenuous. "Stephen's refusal to swim," writes Ellmann, "is in part a refusal to yield to the blandishments of space, which may also be regarded as the diversions of hell" (20). The appearance at the end of "Proteus" of the *Rosevean* "seals the marriage of form and matter, of body and soul, of space and time, at which Aristotle had officiated" (26). Such observations serve to support the general metaphysical propositions that punctuate the book, like the following: "[M]ale and female elements—world without and world within, agent and reagent—copulate to form by spirit from what once was flesh the word which is fleshed spirit" (90). Confronted by such material, it is not surprising that A. Walton Litz described Ellmann as the era's foremost "mythical" reader of Joyce. Litz viewed Ellmann as the descendant of T. S. Eliot, but in the ambitious cosmic architecture of *Ulysses on the Liffey* one can also see the trace of Ellmann's first great literary interest, W. B. Yeats. Indeed, we are explicitly told that "the harsh geometry of [Yeats's] *A Vision* bore extraordinary resemblances to the equally harsh geometry which formed the marrow of *Ulysses*" (57). The literary company Joyce is asked to keep is always revealing, and Ellmann's "return to Yeats" in this book contrasts tellingly with the canon proposed by Kenner.

Ulysses on the Liffey represents the high point, even the decadence, of the symbolic readings of Joyce initiated by Gilbert. Pattern after encrusted pattern is listed in Ellmann's expanded schema, as the book yields to him everything he hopes to find; the symbol-hunting for which Oliver Gogarty had scorned Americans (1970: 764–65) is visible here in its most intoxicated state. Ellmann's is also a profoundly totalizing reading. Where *James Joyce* reconstituted the organic oneness of the writer's life, the later book finds this unity and harmony running throughout his work. The rhetoric of the book constantly seeks such closure: "Birth-death and death-birth join like land and water. . . . Beyond these circles, Joyce established a larger enclosing circle of Bloom and Stephen" (Ellmann 1972: 55–56). Joyce "conceived of his entire book as a silent, unspoken portrayal of an archetypal man . . . whose body would slowly materialize as the book progressed" (73). Or again: "God the creator has fused with man the creator . . . both producing, by intercourse of contraries, life from death, generation from corruption, art from dialectic" (88–89); "None of the principal figures is complete in himself, but together they sum up what is affirmable" (167). In one sense this drive for organic fullness is a traditional emphasis, demonstrating, among other things, the enduring influence of Ellmann's New Critical tutelage under Wimsatt. At the same time the book's method oddly chimes with its own moment. Narrative as a rigidly organized working through of key motifs and preoccupations; contradictions set up and efficiently resolved; the whole affair mappable onto the austere space of a grid; in retrospect *Ulysses on the Liffey* looks like an unusually accessible demonstration of the structuralist activity. What makes the resemblance superficial is that Ellmann's focus is not on narrative process as such but on "theme," the voyage and fate of certain key principles, not the technical and discursive mechanisms through which all this takes place. A more authentic encounter between Joyce and structuralism will be discussed in the next chapter.

This newly systematizing Ellmann, then, is finally the same as ever, only more so: his assertive humanism and genial vision of Joyce, far from being tempered by the book's structural paraphernalia, have been amplified over the years. Nor was this process of clarification yet complete. A peculiar feature of Ellmann's writing on Joyce is his tendency to evoke a mysterious spiritual war or emergent metaphysical conflict running through *Ulysses*. The biography had dropped enigmatic hints: "Stephen and Bloom, the mental men, are ranged against Mulligan and Boylan, the burly men, and Joyce's partisanship is clear" (1982: 372); "the soul . . . carries off the victory" (379). *Ulysses on the Liffey* makes this more explicit, with a central summary section entitled "The Battle for Dublin" and a mysterious rhetoric of combat: "The powers of this world and of that other world try to keep this Bloom from blooming. They must be shown to fail" (1972: 61). Pitched at this level, Ellmann's cosmic conflict remains an idiosyncratic extrapolation. His vision of Joyce's world as one of domination and struggle only rejoins the main current with *The Consciousness of Joyce*, where the metaphysical clashes of his earlier criticism are at last transmuted into more concrete political terms. In a final chapter drawing on the political texts contained in Joyce's Trieste library, Ellmann argues that *Ulysses* "constituted a political act . . . a measure against which British State and Catholic Church can be evaluated" (1977: 89, 90). Joyce's rejection of the church is of a piece with the "communal" thrust of his art, his desire "to write for the benefit of his race" (84); his fiction was devoted to the service of an idea, namely socialism.

The politics sketched by Ellmann remain vaguely defined despite the fervor with which he insists upon them. Nonetheless, the political claims of *The Consciousness of Joyce* were in tune with their times, clarifying and redefining Ellmann's long-standing humanistic and ethical view of Joyce at a moment when politics were returning to the critical agenda. Three years later Dominic Manganiello, a student of Ellmann's, published the biographical and scholarly study *Joyce's Politics* (1980), and the enactment of such politics at the level of the Joycean text would become a growing concern. In *Joyce's Anatomy of Culture* the American Marxist critic Cheryl Herr cited Ellmann's and Manganiello's books as among the few texts that had adumbrated a political reading (1986: 7). Yet Ellmann's late-developing emphasis on Joyce's socialism, despite his one bold quotation from Barthes's *Mythologies* (1977: 73), was only in part a radical new turn. I have commented on the 1959 biography's air of detachment from politics, but its generous liberalism and respect for the everyday arguably contained the seeds of Ellmann's later, more explicit pronouncements. If his unstinting humanism and organicism are now old-fashioned features of Ellmann's critical makeup, his progressive tendencies have had a major effect on the perception of Joyce and his relation to the rest of modernism. Emer Nolan notes that Ellmann's biography "did much to create our contemporary estimate of Joyce" (1995: 2), and Ellmann's influence ultimately contributed to the "progressive" reordering of modernism described by Tony Pinkney, in which Joyce and Woolf displaced Pound and Yeats as central figures (1989b: 6–7). When

Frank Kermode claimed that Ellmann had "fixe[d] Joyce's image for a generation" (1959: 675), he underestimated.

Signs on a White Field: Kenner's Counter-Humanism

In an interview in the early 1980s, Ellmann was asked about the politics and conflicts involved in Joyce scholarship. "It's a very hotly contested field," he replied, "and the animosities engendered are considerable. I suppose it's much more full of [pause] . . . it's a much more competitive field than almost any other modern writer. There are modern writers about whom the scholars all seem to be more or less agreed, or at least respectful of each other, whereas Joyce arouses much more frantic passion" (Robertson 1989: 47). It is likely that Ellmann is in part reflecting on his own differences with Kenner. The latter was one of the biography's most assiduous critics, and the unusual hostility of his *TLS* review may in part be read as a retort to Ellmann's broadside in the same weekly seven years earlier. In his review of Hart and Hayman's collection Ellmann goes out of his way to take issue with Kenner, the occasion being the latter's essay on "Circe." Ellmann considers that piece full of "fancies," including Kenner's hypothesis that Stephen Dedalus punches Buck Mulligan at Westland Row station somewhere between "Oxen of the Sun" and "Circe." "Mr Kenner," Ellmann informs us, "has discovered a new way of reading *Ulysses*, by sparking up its plot," but, given Joyce's own distaste for violence, "for Stephen to have taken a swing at Mulligan would be a break with the ideology that informs the book. Mr Kenner's championship brawl must wait for another novel" (1975: 1118). The quarrel, like those in Kenner's critique of Ellmann, appears trivial yet reflects a deeper disagreement.

Digressing to criticize *The Pound Era*, Ellmann belittlingly remarks that "Mr Kenner has been turning Joyce topsy-turvy for many years now, always asserting that Joyce was totally jaundiced towards his leading characters and towards the modern world" (1118). Many readers of Ellmann and Kenner have considered this the fundamental difference between them. Point for point, character by character, much of what Ellmann reads as sincere or affirmative is inverted in Kenner's work, interpreted as black comedy or ironic mockery on Joyce's part. This is particularly true of *Dublin's Joyce* (1956), a book that openly declares its presiding spirits to be Pound and Lewis. The book's description of *Ulysses* as "an inferno whose apotheosis is the debris-crammed brain of hapless Leopold Bloom" (1987a: 230) echoes Pound twice over ("he has done an inferno"; "Bloom very much *is* the mess" [Pound 1967: 198, 251]); and Lewis appears toward the end of the final discussion of *Finnegans Wake*. Calling Lewis's "the most brilliant misreading in modern criticism" (1987a: 362), Kenner proposes that Lewis was correct to spot the messy crassness of *Ulysses*' world and the clichéd banalities of its characters and language, but mistaken in not realizing that Joyce shared his judgment. In Jeffrey Segall's words: "Lewis, Kenner argued, was too engaged in a polemical tug-of-war to notice that Joyce . . . was actually tugging gently and discreetly at Lewis's side of the knot" (1993: 150). If everything that repulsed Lewis about the book is revealed as the object of a subtle social critique, *Ulysses* emerges as an even more caustic book than Harry Levin had suspected. "Dublin," writes Kenner, is "an immense graveyard of buried hopes, heroic promises dead, promised Homeric heroisms shrunken to the fulfilment of a Bloom" (1987a: 210). It is no accident that this indictment is followed by a quotation from "The Fire Sermon": *Dublin's Joyce* is the last great *Waste Land* reading of *Ulysses*, before Ellmann's biography swung the consensus the other way and it became a truism that Eliot had misread the novel in the light of his own concerns. Kenner, according to Segall, was guilty of doing much the same: "Brilliant as his insights are, influential as they have been, his signature is indelibly sketched in his skewed portrait of Joyce in *Dublin's Joyce*" (1993: 148).

Few aspects of *Dublin's Joyce* would come to appear more skewed than its treatment of Leopold Bloom. The unassuming but kosher heroism that Richard Ellmann assigned him in 1959—"a humble vessel elected to bear and transmit unimpeached the best qualities of the mind" (1982: 5)—seems to have become as inseparable from the character as his potato, making Kenner's postwar disdain for him show its age. Kenner's grim assessment of Molly Bloom—"The 'Yes' of consent that kills the soul . . . is the 'Yes' of authority: authority over this animal kingdom of the dead" (1987a: 262)—also appears dated, not least in its mixture of mythical and moralistic language. However, one of Kenner's readings of character has been enduringly influential, namely his treatment of

Stephen Dedalus. "The *Portrait* in Perspective" was first published, in an abridged form, in the *Kenyon Review* in 1947 and again in Seon Givens's *Two Decades of Criticism* (1948). It reappears, reedited, as a chapter in *Dublin's Joyce*, and its influence has been diffused by its being anthologized as much as any Joycean essay of its period. "James Joyce," Kenner recalls, "had somehow to be distinguished from Stephen Dedalus" (xii). One of the chief burdens of "The *Portrait* in Perspective"—which, like much of the rest of the book, is often a rambling, seemingly ill-formed affair—is to achieve such a separation: "He recast Stephen Dedalus as a figure who could not . . . detach himself from Dublin because he had formed himself on a denial of Dublin's values. He is the egocentric rebel become an ultimate. There is no question whatever of his regeneration. . . . The Stephen of the first chapter of *Ulysses* . . . is precisely the priggish humourless Stephen of the last chapter of the *Portrait*" (112).

The "prose surrounding Stephen's flight," Kenner argues, "is not immature prose. . . . Rather, it is a meticulous pastiche of immaturity" (120). Kenner insists that none of Stephen's thoughts or actions can be identified with Joyce, who crafts the whole with the kind of detachment demanded by "Tradition and the Individual Talent." This was novel. Marvin Magalaner and Richard M. Kain record that "Throughout the jazz age all the sad young men took Stephen Dedalus to their hearts" (1956: 259); and by the 1940s the character was still regarded as enjoying the support, for better or worse, of the author. As worldly a critic as Harry Levin read the *Portrait* in 1941 as the epitome of fictionalized autobiography, "based on a literal transcript of the first twenty years of Joyce's life" (1960: 50). Kenner's critical coup has made critics wary of associating Joyce and his character. It has also generated a miniature debate among such readers as Wayne C. Booth (1961: 323–36) and Robert Scholes (1992: 70–81). "My case got overstated, yes," Kenner retrospectively ruminated, "Yet after forty years there's now a pretty wide consensus that Stephen Dedalus is someone to view with such wariness as we accord a Mulligan or a Boylan. . . . On the whole, I was right about Stephen" (1987a: xii).

He did not stop there. Early in *The Pound Era* Kenner also casts a cold eye on "Eveline," concluding that readers have for too long been seduced by Frank's stories of a home waiting in Buenos Aires: "That latter world belongs to fictions of a different order, shopgirls' romances printed in magazines, romances on which Eveline has founded her sense of the possible" (1975: 37). Most critics, Kenner argues, have been as impressed as Eveline by Frank's frankness, though they would not take Gerty MacDowell's word about the quiet gravefaced gentleman on Sandymount Strand. In effect, the flagrant pastiches of Joyce's later fiction are read back into the innocuous-looking *Irish Homestead* tale, and the result—if we are to believe Kenner—is another critical epiphany, a deliverance from credulous faith in the letter of Joyce's narrative to a worldly understanding of its less edifying real implications. Not every reader has been swayed. The naval veteran Richard Ellmann, in his 1975 review, registers a comical protest: "The only evidence adduced is that Eveline's lover is a sailor, and sailors—the critic is convinced—always betray. This is a blanket condemnation of a decent profession which neither Joyce nor Homer, let alone the National Maritime Union, would have countenanced. We shall next be told that the true hero of *War and Peace* is Napoleon" (1975: 1118). The distinction between Ellmann and Kenner is again less between Litz's "myth" and "fact" than between sincerity and irony, sunny optimism and bleak pessimism, the wide-eyed Pollyanna and the hardheaded cynic. This is played out again in the two critics' long-running dispute over *Ulysses'* "word known to all men." Ellmann, writing as critical authority in the Corrected Text of 1986, asserts that "Most readers have supposed that the word known to all men must be love." They are apparently vindicated by Hans Walter Gabler's controversial restoration of a fragment of interior monologue on the subject, "though one critic maintains that it is death, and another that it is synteresis; the latter sounds like the one word unknown to all men" (Ellmann 1986: xii). A good joke, but ("one critic") Kenner's claims are slyly slid in next to it to receive a touch of reflected absurdity. The two critics openly disputed this issue at the 1984 international symposium in Frankfurt: Ellmann, true to form, insisted that *Ulysses* was "an affirmation of love in a world of hate and violence," and that "critics who suggest that it is a cold, misanthropic work are wrong" (Arnold 1991: 146). In *Joyce's Voices* Kenner could still describe Bloom's "Love. I mean the opposite of hatred"—which is central to Ellmann's interpretation—as "perhaps his most fatuous remark of the day" (1978: 34). At its simplest this is the alternative "school" represented by Kenner: a sly and suspicious take on Joyce, reprising the perspectives of the Men of 1914 themselves, as opposed to Ellmann's celebratory version; a portrait of the artist as a cynical satirist, far from the kind of sincere declamations or open political commitments found in *The Consciousness of Joyce*.

This divergence is undoubtedly important. Yet there is more to Kenner's suspicion of Ellmann's humanism than sheer curmudgeonliness. He has retracted a number of his early positions, writing in 1987 that "I was wrong about Bloom . . . not yet understanding the tenacity of his virtues; wrong especially about Molly, misled like everyone else by that list of a 'preceding series' that seemed to make her a habitual and hardened deceiver" (1987a: xii). The assault on the Blooms is already absent from *The Stoic Comedians* (1962), let alone *The Pound Era* ten years later. By *Joyce's Voices*—"We are quick (aren't we?) to recognize the device: Flaubertian Received Ideas, concatenated" (1978: 56)—Kenner seems to be reflecting wryly on his own early belligerence, and in *"Ulysses"* (1980) the circle is complete: "[Bloom's] distinction is to have been fit to live in Ireland without malice, without violence, without hate" (1987b: 1). Kenner's attitudes have not stood still, nor are they reducible to a mere spite toward fictional characters. But persistent themes and tendencies running through his work offer a sophisticated qualification of Ellmannian humanism. I shall call this stance "counter-humanist" to indicate Kenner's idiosyncratic place, his tendency to problematize the humanist reception of Joyce without subscribing to the full-blown theoretical antihumanism more common in subsequent generations. I shall consider three elements of this stance in turn: divinity, technology, and textuality.

Kenner's early work is often classified not as liberal or New Critical, but as religious. Jonathan Culler refers to Kenner's "vivid, Catholic eclecticism" (1988: 28); if Catholic eclecticism is in one sense a tautology, in another it is exemplified in *Dublin's Joyce*, though the book never expressly declares its religious commitments. Jeffrey Segall considers it virtually the founding text of a Catholic school of Joyceans, including Kevin Sullivan and the clergymen Robert Boyle and William T. Noon, whose more buoyant readings stressed Joyce's residual faith and his unending debt to the Jesuits (Segall 1993: 160–69). The critique of Stephen Dedalus condensed above is central here: Joyce's ironization of his alter ego is treated as evidence of a circumspect retraction of his apostasy, and his renewed embrace of Catholic modes of thought. Such a position is not spelled out in *Dublin's Joyce*, but may be read between the lines of its religious and political commentary. Much of the book's disdain for the Dublin of *Ulysses* is directed toward what is perceived as a debasement of the spiritual currency: "The body usurps the room of the soul, theology gives way to associationist psychology, visions become hallucinations, the metaphors of scripture receive bitterly literal realization in matter" (1987a: 230). Shane Leslie, reviewing *Ulysses* in Dublin in 1922, had advised that "the Inquisition can only require its destruction or, at least, its removal from Catholic houses.... [N]o Catholic publicist can even afford to be possessed of a copy of this book, for in its reading lies not only the description but the commission of sin against the Holy Ghost" (1970a: 201). Kenner, redeeming it for the faithful, needed to effect a major transformation in turning Joyce from a condemned sinner into an ironic moralist. But to produce this reading his description of the book's events must retain much of the scornful vehemence of a critic like Leslie. "This Dublin," he explains, "this city... is an immense blasphemy against the New Jerusalem of the faith of Christ" (1987a: 234). Nowhere is Joyce's anatomy of religious corruption more evident than in "Lestrygonians": "In this sensate and appetitive world the Mystical Body has rotted; this transmogrification of an early Christian symbol underlies the evocation in the next paragraph of a rotting fish.... Bloom's innocent associative shift... parallels the descent of Christian culture into a brainless world of associative logic and material conceptions of nutriment.... As fish, once the symbol of Christ, has become the brain-food of folklore, so every religious symbol is devalued" (234). The corollary of all this is a quiet dedication to the church on Joyce's part. This did not escape the militantly atheist eye of William Empson, who branded the attempt to reconvert Joyce "the Kenner smear." According to Empson, "The chief claim of this theory is that Stephen Dedalus is not presented as the author when young (though the book title pretends he is) but as a possible fatal alternative, a young man who has taken some wrong turning or slipped over the edge of some vast drop, so that he can never grow into the wise old author (intensely Christian, though in a mysteriously paradoxical way), who writes the book" (1984: 204).

Empson's attack on the religiosity of post-Eliot criticism lands a convincing blow on Kenner's exculpatory project. What one should note here, however, is the contrast that Kenner's Catholic outlook offers to

Ellmann's humanism. The attack on the corrupt materialism of Joyce's Dublin is made in the name of a higher force; Kenner's contemptuous attitude toward Dublin's citizens is sponsored by a sense of something beyond the human, namely the divine. Ellmann writes of Bloom that "there is god in him. By god Joyce does not intend Christianity. . . . Nor is he concerned with the conception of a personal god. The divine part of Bloom is simply his humanity" (1982: 362). Ellmann employs a notion of the divine to valorize the human; Kenner uses it as a yardstick to measure the human's deficiencies (Bloom is described as "the most inadequate messiah imaginable" [1987a: 256]), and then to beat it with. Kenner's continual maneuvering of Joyce away from Ellmannian humanism is thus powered, first of all, by religion.

Kenner's early position was also enigmatically political. *Dublin's Joyce* argues that Joyce has learned, and repeatedly exposed, the folly of the romantic quest for a life beyond social and religious bonds. This emerges with particular clarity in the discussion of *Exiles*, which is treated as an immanent critique of Ibsen. Joyce's Norwegian master, writes Kenner, "thinks of the State, and by extension all frames of reference for action—religious, moral, aesthetic—as convertible with the police" (1987a: 80); "This skeletal righteousness deprived of all social, political or theological context is in sharp distinction from the sense of collective wisdom that secured Wordsworth . . . a dignified place in the English tradition" (80). Joyce, it emerges, is on the Wordsworthian side of this equation, wisely aware that "the man who abandons the wreckage of the community for the *vidda* above the snow-line comes to a paralysing realization of nakedness" (85), that "The City is not a refuge from the demands of alert living but the context of meaningful life" (90). Joyce, in short, had no time for the rebel who would fly by custom's nets. The politics of *Dublin's Joyce* might be called communitarian, and are thus ambiguous. As Raymond Williams observes, the idea of community is in itself somewhat politically empty, as so few people consider it a bad thing (1989b: 112–13). It is not always easy to distinguish between a socialist concern for reciprocal, supportive relations between individuals and a conservative defense of the finely woven, interpersonal fabric of custom and tradition, the transcendence of which is a revolutionary chimera. Analogously, the political meaning of Kenner's defense of community in *Dublin's Joyce* is hard to decipher; if it apparently allows caustic religious and social satire, it proscribes the desire of a Dedalus—so emphatically supported by Ellmann—to leap beyond theology and ideology in a radical gesture of refusal.

Kenner's assault on modern culture is also unavoidably political. Apropos of "Lestrygonians" Kenner writes that "The hungry sheep look up and are fed tenth-hand thinking, tabloids, pre-processed food, predigested sensational news" (1987a: 235): this is among the more lurid examples of his jeremiad against urban life, mass culture, and technology. "Everything," writes Kenner in the book's most despairing moment, "has become all that it can ever be, the past is exhausted, the passage of time simply crams the museum of history fuller and fuller of Laocoönic tableaus, nothing can be willed away, nothing can change, nothing is of the slightest intrinsic interest, and that is hell" (1987a: 238). Once again a direct line links the cultural politics of Ezra Pound's "Party of Intelligence" (in a world that, Pound remarked, was "largely inhabited by imbeciles" [1967: 115]) to Kenner's fulminations. Critiques of contemporary society are not, of course, the sole preserve of the political Right, but Jeffrey Segall (1993: 167) is correct to view the anti-urban and antimodern politics of *Dublin's Joyce* as part of a familiar conservative tradition.

The rhetoric of *Dublin's Joyce* is rooted in the cultural and social criticism of its era. A notable example is Vance Packard's study *The Hidden Persuaders* (1957): published the year after *Dublin's Joyce*, its compellingly paranoiac analysis of advertising overlaps directly with aspects of Kenner's book. "Large-scale efforts," writes Packard, "are being made, often with impressive success, to channel our unthinking habits, our purchasing decisions, and our thought processes by the use of insights gleaned from psychiatry and the social sciences" (1960: 11). Packard argues that big business deploys behaviorist and psychoanalytic techniques on its consumers, trawling for information about spending habits and lifestyle and feeding this back into a program of collective stimulation and mass hypnosis. In a vivid, digressive section of *Dublin's Joyce* entitled "The Metaphors of Mechanism" Kenner effectively extends a similar analysis back to 1904. "Immediately after World War II we began to hear a great deal about mechanical brains" (1987a: 162), he informs us, before reading this context back into *Ulysses*. From pulp fiction and sales catalogues, Kenner argues, Joyce lifted "whole congeries of metaphoric assumptions: that mind is mechanism, that the Body Politic is wired together, that human relationships, domestic or civic, are reducible to problems in engineering" (162). Amid this "mechanization of the community," in a world dominated by the crudest behaviorist models of the mind, "The market researcher asks the consumer how he wishes to be exploited, and is enabled to exploit him more effectively every time he asks" (165). This sentence could have been penned by Packard; and Joyce is assumed to be mounting a critique of the mass-cultural world that *The Hidden Persuaders* describes. Standardization ("Ithaca"), manipulation ("Aeolus"), the narcotic ("Lotus-Eaters"); the early Kenner rewrites *Ulysses* in the terms of midcentury discourses on the mass media and manipulation.

The inspiration for this apparently eccentric move is not hard to discern: Kenner's old Toronto mentor, Marshall McLuhan. Another maverick Catholic, McLuhan was a modernist scholar before becoming a media guru. His essays on Joyce dating from the early 1950s are strikingly similar to Kenner's work from the same period, mixing literary history, Catholic doctrine, and social criticism. The most distinctive theme that they share, however, is the machine. This is the real significance of the use that *Dublin's Joyce* makes of midcentury thought on the media and social manipulation. In "Joyce, Mallarmé and the Press" (1954) McLuhan presents Joyce as a prophet of modern journalism and electronic communication, which usher in a new aesthetic drawing on the popular arts of "industrial man." McLuhan's Joyce is the great prose poet of the twentieth century thanks to his ability to absorb new technology into the very forms of his writing. By 1900, one of Kenner's essays informs us, "the Machine was all around" (1982a: 5); and by the 1950s it was turning up in his own work. In *Dublin's Joyce, Ulysses* acts as an immanent critique of the mechanized world: "A huge and intricate machine clanking and whirring for eighteen hours—at one level *Ulysses* is just that.... This tesselated mosaic belongs to a world of gears and sidewalks, of bricks laid side by side, of data thrust into a computer and whirled through permutations baffling to the imagination but always traceable by careful reason.... Joyce is mocking the super-brain with a monstrous parody of its workings. If you were to project an auctorial personality behind *Ulysses*, you would find it mechanical and craftsmanlike and unreflective" (1987a: 166–67).

Although this passage is part of Kenner's polemic against the modern world, the insight here adumbrates all his subsequent writing on

Joyce. The argument in *Dublin's Joyce* is essentially *anti*-mechanical: Joyce has satirized a world of behaviorism and rationalization by fashioning a book that mimes that world's logic. Echoing McLuhan's language, Kenner writes that "It is by the insane mechanical meticulousness of that mode of consciousness, the mode of consciousness proper to industrial man, that in *Ulysses* industrial man is judged" (1987a: 167). That mode of consciousness is exaggerated to its apotheosis (its "epiphany," the early Kenner would say) as the Implied Author, "this sardonic impersonal recorder, that constantly glints its photo-electric eyes from behind the chronicle of Bloomsday" (167–68). But this powerfully *inhuman* way of discussing *Ulysses*—inconceivable in Ellmann's writing, though it actually appeared three years before the biography—proves to be a Pandora's box, a notion that, once entertained, starts to refashion literature.

The Stoic Comedians (1962) bears almost no trace of the social and religious polemics of *Dublin's Joyce,* and the antipathy to the machine is gone. This is crucial, for the burden of the book is to isolate a tradition of novelists whose writing is intimately related to the technology with which it is manufactured. "Stoic Comedian" is Kenner's name for the writer who works with Flaubertian fastidiousness, compiling, organizing, and placing rather than simply narrating: "He could not, we know, improvise a tale by the fireside, not to save his life; but he is enough the master of Gutenberg technology to fabricate the traces of a tale out of printed signs" (1962: xviii). *Printed* signs: for one thing that marks out *Ulysses* and *Watt* as exemplars of the mode that Kenner calls the "machine-novel" is their self-consciousness about being bound books mechanically produced. "The demands Joyce makes on the reader," Kenner writes, "would be impossible ones if the reader did not have his hands on the book, in which he can turn to and fro at his pleasure. And more than that: the whole conception of *Ulysses* depends on the existence of something former writers took for granted as simply the envelope for their wares: a printed book whose pages are numbered" (32–34). Kenner is fascinated by the peculiar character of the Joycean text, its relation to the anonymous modes of cataloguing at work in dictionaries and encyclopedias, which break information down into manageable units and remove it from any extended narrative context. "Any book so conceived has broken with narrative," he writes of *Ulysses*. "[T]he text of *Ulysses* is not organized in memory and unfolded in time, but both organized and unfolded in what we may call *technological space:* on printed pages for which it was designed from the beginning" (34–35). The Joycean text, aware that it will be produced on a machine, presciently assumes a "mechanical" form unfamiliar from the mainstream of realist fiction. "To an ever greater degree," Walter Benjamin had written, "the work of art reproduced becomes the work of art designed for reproducibility" (1973: 226); and much of Kenner's work since *The Stoic Comedians* has been an exploration of how this principle affected the course of modernist writing. He would eventually produce a whole book on the subject, *The Mechanic Muse* (1987), in which Joyce again plays a central role. Analyzing, not for the first or last time, the opening page of the *Portrait,* Kenner asks, "If the narrator has disappeared, where is the text coming from?" answering, "Let's agree to say that it's present on a printed page, thanks to the intricate and largely anonymous mechanisms by which that can be made to happen. We look at printed pages all day long without ever reflecting on how so many thousand letters got there. . . . Joyce alone seems to have understood from the first what it can mean to be writing for print. Each stroke of his pen encoded instructions for a print-shop technician, a fact of which he was at all times fully aware" (1987c: 68–70).

In this study—whose title pays homage to McLuhan's *The Mechanical Bride*—Kenner is concerned to explore the otherness of technology, the unexpected disturbances and seismic shifts that it has caused in Western culture and society. The linotype, he tells us, "illustrates two principles: 1) that the way to imitate a human activity is never to replicate the human action; 2) that the resulting pressures on human behavior are apt to elude foresight utterly, and be occulted from most present sight, and leave hindsight flabbergasted" (1987c: 7–8). What McLuhan called the extensions of man—figured in Kenner's tableaulike chapter titles, which find "Pound Typing" and "Joyce Scrivening"—also prove to be disruptions, subtly reordering human practice and habit. Ever since *Dublin's Joyce* Kenner has been fond of quoting Eliot's observation that the internal combustion engine has altered our perception of rhythm. This kind of unpredictable interaction between the human subject (especially the writer) and technology results in a mingling of the two terms, so that aesthetic objects can no longer be seen simply as evidence of human creativity but have something inherently mechanical about them. (Kenner's vision of a mechanical "mind of the text" has had a broader influence through David Hayman's notion of the "Arranger," developed in *"Ulysses": The Mechanics of Meaning* [1970] and refined by Kenner himself a decade later.) The humanism of an Ellmann, for whom even Joyce's works were, in the end, expressions of the writer's character and beliefs, is evidently qualified by such a perspective, losing some of its plausibility rather as Benjamin's work of art is drained of its aura. Flaubert—the first of Kenner's machine-novelists—once declared that the artist was "a monstrosity, an unnatural thing" (1997: 160); but Kenner's modernist writer, accompanied by the mechanic muse, is closer to a cyborg, operating on the borderline between humanity and technology and producing art from a historically original blending of the two.

Kenner's moralistic Catholicism is thus supplanted in his work by a growing emphasis on the role of technology in modernism. Both themes seriously qualify the humanist reading of Joyce developed by Ellmann. But if the machine is for Kenner a sociological fact—the reason that vast crowds can assemble from underground in a matter of minutes—it is also a metaphor for a third counter-humanist theme, namely, textuality itself. What the notion of the machine-novel, or the comparison of *Ulysses* to a newspaper or dictionary, most crucially achieve is a *de-organicization* of the text, a sundering of the book from the living individual and its critical connotations—personality, voice, unity—that are so visible in Ellmann's conflation of life and work. The result is a relative autonomization of the book, a stress on its materiality. James's novel *The Ambassadors*, Kenner remarks, is "a hundred cubic inches of wood pulp" (1975: 28). Kenner has always been one of Joyce's closest readers, with an ear for his *mots justes* ("The felly harshed against the curbstone: stopped."). His attentiveness to style and syntax is one reason for his admiration for the Swiss Joycean Fritz Senn; both men have described each other as Joyce's best reader. But Kenner's approach to Joyce's language is not reducible to "close reading." In an essay on the New Criticism he declares that the movement's achievement, despite its shortcomings, was to "return the study of literature . . . to the central American intellectual concern, which is Language" (1976: 41). In a sense this is also true of his own work, which returns obsessively to modernist literature's linguistic character.

Like technology, this motif has a surprisingly long history in Kenner's work. The prologue to *Dublin's Joyce* finds Joyce "listen[ing] with a fascination he could not explain to the endless talk of Dublin" (1987a: 4). Within a few pages the opening chapter is speculating about the talk that surrounded the young writer: "Nothing there: gossip, question, response, vacuity . . . speech surrounds the citizen from birth" (7). Language is figured as something beyond the individual, an archive of preformed phrases and sedimented social relations to which speakers are unconsciously subject: "[T]hey can speak only in quotations, and despite their consciousness of effort, their thought runs in grooves. . . . Their circumambient language doesn't serve the citizen's thought but directs it. He inherits locutions that were once alive, and shapes his mental processes accordingly. . . . [The Dubliner] speaks the language that is given him, and entertains the corresponding ideas. . . . [H]e acts on the promptings of *idées reçues* and talks in words that have for too long been respoken" (8–10). Already Kenner's Flaubertian scorn for a society of cliché is leading him toward a sense of the formative power of signs. Kenner's maverick intelligence frequently seems to have taken him beyond his time: in seeing individuals as spoken by language rather than the reverse, in viewing social life as discursive—"Dublin's civic reality was contained in its language alone" (18)—and in exploring (as in *The Stoic Comedians*) the relation between as "written" a book as *Ulysses* and the alleged phonocentrism of Ireland.

The shaping effects of style and discourse on experience, and the consequent impossibility of objective metalanguage, is the burden of *Joyce's Voices*, published as poststructuralist theory was arriving in the literary academy: "For nothing is as dependent as Objectivity on language and the rituals of language, Objectivity which had promised to evade rhetoric and make the facts effect their own declaration" (1978: 14). Kenner describes "style" as "a system of limits": "[P]astiche ascribes the system to another person, and invites us to attend to its recirculating habits and its exclusions" (81). Perception, thought, and subjectivity itself come close in this book to being effects of language, for which Joyce's work is a primer: one of its central lessons is that "scrupulous homespun prose, the plain style of narrative fidelity, was a late and temporary invention, affirming the temporary illusion that fact and perception, event and voice, are separable" (94). This had also been a theme of Barthes's

Writing Degree Zero (1953), and it would remain an article of faith through the rise of postmodernism—for instance, in Linda Hutcheon's discussions of how metafiction undermines the belief in a culturally unmediated access to the real. More locally, the assault on "metalanguage" is also central to Colin MacCabe's *James Joyce and the Revolution of the Word* (1979), and it is striking that Kenner, without MacCabe's polemical urgency, had nonchalantly argued a similar stylistic case a year earlier.

The Joycean world for Kenner is one of artifice, quotation, acting. In an essay on "Circe" he suggests that "the ideal reader is meant at this point to reflect how thoroughly congenial is the theatre of roles and surfaces to this author's vision of things" (1974: 341); and elsewhere he extends the metaphor considerably. Things "are done in the world as they are done in the theater, by changing garb and diction" (1978: 52), *Joyce's Voices* tells us; but Gabriel Conroy plays Orpheus unwittingly, as Bloom plays Odysseus: "That is how it is apt to be in the Joyce country. People posture, people play roles, people fit themselves into myths, even venture explications. But the myths of which they are conscious are not the right ones, nor the explications either coherent or applicable" (40). The line of thought here is analogous to the vision of language hazarded in *Dublin's Joyce:* individuals prove to be less in control of their own meanings than they think, their lives mapped out by different scripts from the ones they have learned. Again the metaphor produces a certain displacement of the autonomy and agency of the human subject, which unconsciously mimes a preassigned role or archetype, decentered by "culture" and the narratives available. Narratives, it is commonly supposed, are comforting, offering consoling matrices of sense and shape to human experience. For Kenner things are not so straightforward: multiple stories cluster around a situation and inflect it differently, just as a character like Uncle Charles bends language out of one shape and into another (17). "Eveline" is his major example, "1800 words about intersecting fictions" (1975: 34), "homeomorphic" narratives collaged together about the single event: "an omniscient authority might have plotted its vectors, Frank's and Eveline's and her father's. . . . All these stories are the one story rotated. The version Joyce chose to write maximises her ignorance and her pathos, and emphasizes his earliest and most constant insight, that people live in stories that structure their worlds. Eveline lives in a story . . . a febrile unreal story she got from somewhere" (39). "People live in stories that structure their worlds," not "People structure their worlds with stories": narrative, like language and acting, is in Kenner's hands one more figure for that which is beyond the subject's control, inconspicuously shaping his or her destiny. There is an unsettling alterity about these invisible cultural determinants that—like the image of the machine—makes Joyce's work look less assimilable to humanism than it had appeared.

All of this demonstrates the divergence between Ellmann's and Kenner's work, the way in which Kenner has plotted a different trajectory from Ellmann's humanist recuperation. Some readers have accordingly associated Kenner with the supposed "textualism" of contemporary theory, adducing his rhetorical flourishes on language (Gillespie 1991: 143; Segall 1993: 155). "All is words," *Joyce's Voices* repeatedly asserts, "all the book, the book has been insisting, is words, arranged, rearranged" (1978: 49). Kenner's penchant for paradox, his sense of the simultaneous primacy and slippery inadequacy of language, makes such comparisons understandable. The same can be said of Fritz Senn, who remarks on how a "foreign" reader of Joyce notices "that words are words, the only prime reality in literature" (1984: 44). Christine O'Neill reports that other critics see an affinity between Senn and Derrida (Senn 1995: xi). Yet both Kenner and Senn disavow any connection with contemporary theory. In Senn's words, "if theorists have something of interest to say, to say on Joyce, then in the long run something of this would rub off, something would get around—so that it might even reach the likes of me, the obtuse, pedestrian, naive simple-minded readers. It may happen tomorrow. It hasn't yet" (1995: 2–3). In truth, both Kenner and Senn belong to a generation older than the advent of theory, which looks to them like a distraction from the real challenge of reading Joyce. To treat *Finnegans Wake* as "pure 'text,'" as "a massive vindication of poststructuralist theory," Kenner judges, is "one quick way to make it uninteresting" (1983: 228). Here is a clue to his divergence from previous, as well as subsequent, generations of Joyce's readers. In poststructuralism—pictured, to be sure, in knockabout, caricaturing fashion—Kenner sees a new homogenization, as blind as earlier critics to the quirks and specificities of the Joycean page. Much of the distinctiveness of Kenner's writing consists in its attention to nuance—to particularity, whether textual or historical. It may be in this instinct, rather than in any superficial resemblance to critical theory, that Kenner has most valuably anticipated the future of writing about Joyce.

The key to Kenner is his sense of indebtedness to the modernists. "They had come of age to commence that [aesthetic] revolution," Kenner writes of the Men of 1914, "and been old enough after Europe blew up instead to know what had been lost in that vast amnesia. . . . There was no more Vortex after 1919, and they went each his own way from that common memory" (1975: 553). Patrick Parrinder plausibly describes *The Pound Era*'s retrospective modernist reunion as a piece of "literary mythmaking" (1982: 155). Indeed, the reverent language of myth is the vehicle for Kenner's attitude to the legacy of Joyce's generation. He glosses the image of Pound staring at Joyce's statue in Zurich with a fragment of the *Cantos* about the departure of the gods. But "The gods have never left us": "We read differently now, though the only possible evidence is the way we write. So reading, we have kept the classics alive. . . . The men of the Vortex achieved all that and more. We will never know how much of our minds they prepared" (1975: 554–55). Kenner has dubbed Samuel Beckett the "regretful closer of modernism's gates" (1993: 28), but here the critic himself assumes that role. Much of his work on the modernist canon can be seen as an attempt to fulfill a debt to it, to introduce and explain it to the rest of the world. This is a personal as well as a purely intellectual matter: Kenner has recounted how Pound, whom he first encountered in 1948, told him that "you have an obligation to meet the great men of your own time" (1984: 373), an instruction that led to meetings with Lewis and Eliot and resulted in the epic narrative of *The Pound Era*. The figure most conspicuously absent from this tour was, of course, James Joyce himself, who died when Kenner was only seventeen. But Joyce had been the subject of his doctoral dissertation and, as one of Lewis's Men of 1914, was assured a place in the book's subtitle. He thus became central to the twentieth-century pantheon that Kenner took it upon himself to define.

"What a critic may hope to accomplish in his lifetime," Kenner has suggested, "is no more than a few acts of clarification" (1976: 36). His own major project has been the unending "clarification" of a certain modernist canon, some of whose characteristics he has, in turn, assumed. He does not, of course, echo the notorious political views of some of his heroes, but is affiliated with the conservatism of the *National Review*. Once the social criticism of *Dublin's Joyce* is discarded, the one overtly political outlet in Kenner's work on Joyce becomes Irish nationalism. In *Joyce's Voices* it is trivialized, along with anti-Semitism, as "name-calling" (1978: 55). Discussing the "Cyclops" episode in his *"Ulysses*," Kenner writes of "gaga patriotism," of "fools [who] exult in their own fermenting hatreds" and "the vortex . . . that drew sane men screaming into civil war" (1987b: 98, 93, 96). The abiding sense is of a conservative suspicion of political action as irrational and doubtfully effective. Its direction is opposite to the activist rhetoric of the later Ellmann, and closer to Pound's assessment that "If more people had read *The Portrait* and certain stories in Mr. Joyce's *Dubliners* there might have been less recent trouble in Ireland" (1967: 90).

Kenner's politics remain very different from Pound's. He echoes the Pound generation, though, in his use of language. When Kenner writes that a critic should display "a cunning susceptibility to the procedures of what he is writing about" (1991: xv), he discreetly refers to his own procedures. Kenner's eccentric, digressive style owes much to Pound himself, but Joyce's hand is also discernible. For instance, the frequent subdivisions of *Dublin's Joyce* ("SAD *SUPERBIA* THE KEYNOTE OF RICHARD," "CONTAMINATION OF GENIUS BY POWERHOUSE," "WHO ARE THE CANNIBALS?" [1987a: 82, 168, 232]) give that book some of the rowdily fragmented atmosphere of "Aeolus." Elsewhere Kenner's idiosyncratic arrangements of words, either strikingly economical ("the language Joseph Conrad and Ford Madox Hueffer steeled themselves daily not to write" [1978: 68]) or sprawlingly loose ("That does still have a certain conjecturing feel. . . . Yes, words, a century ago, were newly mysterious" [1993: 23]), not to mention his propensity to pastiche ("and yer young compatriots themselves it is will put out their pennies to make believe yer the voice of the oul' sod itself, mossa" [1983: 70]), represent an indirect tribute to Joyce's stylistic resources. One of Kenner's most outlandishly "literary" moments— "Through a spattered pane wide aristocratic eyes saw in a sudden blazing lightning-flash the shocking pink cover start forth, the five fierce black letters, B L A S T" (1975: 246)—reads like an effort at the disjointed but grammatical syntax of "Wandering Rocks": "Stephen Dedalus watched through the webbed window the lapidary's fingers prove a timedulled chain" (Joyce 1986: 198). His work is also notably resistant to closure. *Dublin's Joyce* descends into a confusion of notes and possible trails, ending not with a conclusion but with a cut-and-paste quartet of obituaries untouched by any explanatory metalanguage. *Joyce's Voices* and *"Ulysses"* wind on through appendixes and quirky, digressive endnotes, and even *The Pound Era* ends with the enigmatic observation that "Thought is a labyrinth" (1975: 561), a sentence that beckons the reader further into uncertainty. In this sense, too, Kenner is the authentically "modernist" critic of modernism, a Joyce to Ellmann's George Eliot. Or, it might be said, he conforms more closely to a version of modernism— as provisional, fragmented, abrasive, and enigmatic rather than holistic and self-certain—that he himself has taught us to read.

For if Ellmann's great project was to record his writers' lives, Kenner's has arguably been a pedagogic one: to make readable the texts that—as he frequently reminds us—the public of a few decades ago found unintelligible. Yet readability can involve remembering unreadability. "At our earliest stages of engagement with Joyce," he writes in *The Mechanic Muse*, "we stare at his page and wonder how to get a purchase on it" (1987c: 72). His own attempt to regain those "early stages" recurs through the decades. As late as 1993, in an essay entitled "Joyce and Modernism," he can be found hammering away at the same theme: "How the big book we're facing came to be written down, moreover with undeniable narrative skill, is a question creators of fiction used not to urge us to confront. For we were to be drawn beyond the printed words into sheer illusion; yet the arranged existence of those words that drew us in remained to be accounted for. . . . 'Modernism'. . . may be described along one of its cross-sections as a coming-to-terms of printed language with print, thus with our consequent problems as readers. . . . Why anything, for instance, a voiceless page of the *Times*, is less impenetrable than it is: that is something truly obscure" (1993: 21–22). Like little Stephen Dedalus pondering the sound of the word "suck," Kenner halts again and again at the level of the signifier, baffled—or seeking to contrive a state of bafflement—at the queerness of words. His own preferred analogy is with the boy in "The Sisters," childishly unable to piece together the fragments of conversation around him; this, with convenient symmetry, is also where readers of *Finnegans Wake* find themselves, "clutching . . . at alphabetic straws" (1993: 30).

It is thus paradoxical that Kenner is regarded as a central player in the "domestication" of Joyce and of modernism generally. Terry Eagleton reviewed Kenner's study of *Ulysses* as "yet another blow-by-blow bluffer's guide," written by the "chief executive of the American branch of the industry" (1980: 21). While *Joyce's Voices* or *"Ulysses"* indeed impart a way of reading Joyce, they also enact a simultaneous process of *un*-reading, confronting received presuppositions and seeking to forget them. The ironic faux naiveté of Kenner's rhetorical gambits is often part of this attempt: "James Joyce, B. A., taught English in Trieste, where he had found something else you could do with an Irish degree" (1983: 144); "Now here is James Joyce, in the first lines of a novel" (1987c: 67). Coming at the same small oeuvre time and again, Kenner ceaselessly searches for a sidelong approach that might happen upon it suddenly and make it new one more time. The wager of his work is that another productive reification of the text will always be possible, giving us not characters and events but the clanking of narrative and signifying machinery, or simply black marks on a white background. His long project of making modernism readable has thus gone hand in hand with an insistence on its strange alterity—or, to be precise, an insistence on its own insistence of alterity, an attempt to estrange estrangement and remind us how shocked we ought to be. During his development into something of a venerable monument himself, Kenner has become not modernism's chief executive but its curator, taking upon himself the paradoxical role of at once familiarizing and defamiliarizing readers with it. The necessary pedagogic transmission of the modernist canon—of which Joyce's work is the paradigm—runs the risk of making it all *too* readable. It must repeatedly subvert itself by a critical feat of active forgetting, returning the grizzled professor to the innocent incomprehension of Baby Tuckoo.

Canonical Consequences

The work of Ellmann and Kenner offers an important dual history. The two men's different emphases have had a lasting effect on how Joyce is read. One can consider their impact by returning to the legacy of

F. R. Leavis in Britain. Leavis's hostile judgment of Joyce weighed heavily in English literary and academic culture, while most work on the writer became the work of American critics. Ellmann's *James Joyce*, with its powerfully humanistic and holistic interpretation, did as much as any other single work to reappraise Joyce's status and make him acceptable (Attridge and Ferrer 1984: 6). I have noted that Ellmann's work created a legacy of such readings, like those by French and Peake in the 1970s. Ellmann's work in effect challenged the Leavisian assessment from the inside: if Joyce's excesses made a certain adjustment of canonical parameters and criteria necessary, he still proved assimilable to the main current of fiction. Though Ellmann himself, whether in the United States or England, was never particularly subject to Leavis's legacy, the humane and benevolent Joyce that he bequeathed was not repugnant to a Leavisian Britain. His biography also did much to establish Joyce's image and reputation outside the academy, and one can hypothesize that a "popular Joyce" will have much in common with the version that Ellmann inherited from Frank Budgen.

Meanwhile, Hugh Kenner was constructing an alternative to this humanist recuperation. What I have called Kenner's counter-humanism has variously focused on religious doctrine, technology, and textuality in a prolonged attempt to preserve something of the disruptive alterity originally possessed by modernist literature—a paradoxical task, since Kenner has also played a major part in the postwar American academy's assimilation of modernism. Yet if Kenner has contributed to Joyce's canonical status, there remains the question of which canon is at stake. *The Pound Era* reinstates Joyce in the matrix of the "Men of 1914"—exactly where Leavis had disdainfully left him in *D. H. Lawrence, Novelist* (1955). In "The Making of the Modernist Canon" Kenner makes explicit his disagreement with Leavis, "from whom was hidden, all his life, the truth that England had become, linguistically speaking, a province" (1984: 370). To be excluded from such a man's canon, Kenner implies, is no calamity.

The Pound Era is one way of narrating the alternatives available, and another is offered by *The Stoic Comedians*. Here Kenner rewrites the history of modernist prose in a manner to which an English reader is likely to be particularly sensitive, for it reroutes the main current of the past century away from the trajectory that Leavis had mapped, in which

Lawrence renews and revitalizes the novel as the central medium of a rooted English language. Kenner's countertradition thoroughly inverts the valences and virtues that English readers had inherited from Leavis—and also marks out a distance from Ellmann—with Lawrence explicitly excluded: "Flaubert and his major successors, Joyce and Beckett, each scorching in turn the earth where his successor would sow his crop, carried forward the novel as Knowing Machine, lifelike, logical, for a hundred years. If during that time there has flourished a different fictional tradition altogether, the tradition of Dostoevski, Tolstoi, George Eliot, D. H. Lawrence, for which the unit is not the sentence but the event, the person not a product but an energy, and the vision not a satire but perhaps an apocalypse, it has flourished thanks in part to the success of the Stoic Comedians in keeping the machine-novel busily at bay" (Kenner 1962: xix). Craft is pitted against spontaneity; language as an intransigent material to be organized ("the sentence") against words giving us life as it really is ("the event"); and the novel is viewed not as bright book of life but as an intricate mechanism of parts, functions, effects. *The Stoic Comedians*, along with Kenner's other work, finds Joyce a new home where his "failings"—formalism, detachment, excess—no longer have to be excused. On the contrary, if Leavis's England is now peripheral, it is Joyce himself who is central. At the start of *Joyce's Voices* Kenner writes that "As the great age of twentieth-century Modernism recedes, it grows increasingly clear that the decisive English-language book of the century was *Ulysses*, the pivotal book in English since *Paradise Lost*" (1978: xii). The affront to Leavisism is double, for Leavis had done much to unsettle Milton's reputation—not least in an article that appeared in the same edition of *Scrutiny* as "Joyce and the 'Revolution of the Word.'" While Ellmann and others, then, were securing Joyce's place in the novelistic canon, Kenner took the slightly different route of devising a new narrative of literary history around him. In this respect Kenner's work from the late 1950s onward powerfully adumbrates the shifts in literary judgment and canon formation that recent decades have witnessed.

Central to this nudging of the canon is an emphasis on the international character of modernism. The twentieth-century map is dominated by the rootless "International Modernism," a movement that Kenner finally enshrined with capital letters in the 1980s: "there was arguably a new center, locatable in books but on no map. English was the language not only of the Three Provinces [England, Ireland, America] but also of several masterpieces best located in a supranational movement called International Modernism" (1984: 367). *Ulysses* thus belongs to no national literature but rather to that cosmopolitan space at which Ezra Pound and *transition* had gestured, and in which Harry Levin's Joyce also dwelled.

The next critical generation might be said to have brought together the separate threads traced in this chapter, drawing both on Ellmann's socialist sympathies and on Kenner's sense of the text as a field of force, his pursuit of aporia and the unassimilable fragment. The two critics themselves represent the most intriguing and longest-running tussle in the history of Joyce's reception, an extended debate that has had a profound effect on our understanding of the writer. One is left with the image, somewhere between the lavatory of "Grace" and the scene of a wake, of two gentlemen standing over a mysterious body of work, and arguing over how to bring it to life.

4

Tout va bien
The Arrival of Theory

> The French have always reasoned about literature far more than the English have.
> Edmund Wilson, *Axel's Castle*

> *Moi, je suis socialiste.*
> *Ulysses*

By the 1960s Joyce had arrived in the American academy. Ellmann's biography gave emphatic notice of Joyce's status as a major figure of the twentieth century: though he warned that to "bestride literature like a colossus" was not Joyce's manner, he also found a "new notion of greatness" in the writer (1982: 7). It is surprising in hindsight to see Ellmann in 1959 considering Joyce's reputation still in flux: "Joyce holds his place of eminence under fire; he is much more assailed than writers who are evidently his inferiors. Though the name of Joyce is as inextricably associated with modern prose as is the name of Eliot with modern verse, or that of Picasso with modern art, it is possible that the current of opinion will swerve, and not-to-like Joyce will become as fashionable tomorrow as not-to-like Picasso is becoming today" (4). Perhaps this guess was intended to defeat itself—to ward off the risk of its actually happening. *James Joyce* itself did more than any other work to make Ellmann's doubts redundant: if it made the life story available to a mass audience, it also sealed Joyce's eminence among the ever-increasing ranks of Ellmann's colleagues.

It is in Ellmann's wake that the Joyce industry really does its work. Scholars approach the oeuvre down every visible avenue. Life and art feed into one another in a process adumbrated by the anecdotes of Budgen. Academic work on Joyce begins to be not merely the travail of lone enthusiasts but a scholarly circuit—even, as the symposia became biannual in the early 1970s, a traveling circus. After 1960 major critics of Joyce were harder to count on one or two hands. They multiplied into a team, a regiment—or that form with which Joyce collated disparate elements, the list. William York Tindall, Adaline Glasheen, James Atherton, Matthew Hodgart, Mabel P. Worthington, Ruth Bauerle, A. Walton Litz, Robert M. Adams, Clive Hart, Morris Beja, Bernard Benstock, Shari Benstock, David Hayman, Zack Bowen, Robert Scholes, Thomas F. Staley, Weldon Thornton, Michael Groden, Phillip F. Herring. All of these critics and more made Joyce studies what it is, not only in their particular projects and insights—Glasheen's *Census* of names in *Finnegans Wake* (1956), Hayman's formulation of the "arranger" (1970), Hart's timetable of "Wandering Rocks" (1974)—but also in their contribution to a collective understanding. The reading of Joyce developed a strong communal emphasis: down to the present day, reading groups and collaborative research are as important as solitary scholarship.

This was true, above all, of *Finnegans Wake*, whose pioneering scholars—many of them initially isolated—recall the early importance of contact and conversation with each other. Much of Glasheen's research for the *Census* was famously epistolary: the Joycean conversation ineluctably spread across space. Glasheen's correspondents, notes Bonnie Kime Scott, soon included Thornton Wilder as well as Atherton and Hodgart: "thus the collaboration already involved a creative writer and scholars from the other side of the Atlantic. . . . Far-flung contributors to later editions included Fritz Senn from Switzerland and Clive Hart from Australia. Two Americans who helped on the first census were perhaps the most famous Joyceans of all, 'Mr Hugh Kenner' and 'Mr Richard Ellmann'" (Scott 1991: 47). Academics of increasing eminence entered ongoing, open-ended collaboration with readers outside the academy. If "Joyce studies" was becoming an industry, it was also an international community that existed beyond ordinary spatial limits. The growing prominence, through the 1990s, of the World Wide Web in Joyce studies would take international connections to new levels of complexity, but it would also build on a network that had existed for decades.

The list of names above contains difference and dissent, divergent backgrounds and ages. But it also points to a critical era, which one can dub the age of humanism in Joyce studies. Not all of these critics would declare Joyce's triumph as resoundingly as Ellmann; many would survive to be senior figures in the late twentieth century and beyond. But they all at least began their major work sometime before the next great intellectual upheaval: the arrival of "theory" in the British and American academy, challenging and transforming the priorities and practices of literary study. "Theory" here is not a precise descriptor but a shorthand. The word gestures at developments in French thought since existentialism—at structuralism, semiotics, and other linguistic models derived from Saussure, as well as at the various strains of critique known as poststructuralism. But it must also take in other horizons—Russian Formalism; neo-Marxism; phenomenology and ethics—that have multiplied as academics have investigated more and more intellectual models. In a sense, what "theory" means, in its very imprecision, is this process of intellectual borrowing, translation, amalgamation, as overtly "foreign" modes of thought and writing are imported into the Anglophone world. It is this use of theoretical discourses by British and American critics, rather than their Continental origins, that will be my primary focus in this chapter.

The critical lexicon registers conceptual change: from symbolism, unity, ambiguity, through textuality, signification, dissemination, to hybridity, heteronomy, deterritorialization. The terms overlap and coexist; there is no absolute break from one epoch to the next. Historical change, as usual, is piecemeal and partial: the new develops from, as much as it displaces, the old. In Joyce studies the emphasis on continuity can be peculiarly strong thanks to the belief that theory is a response to what has been at least latent in Joyce all along (Attridge and Ferrer 1984: 11). A recurrent focus of this chapter will be the dynamic relation between Joyce and theory that results. I am interested not only in "how theory was applied to Joyce" but in how Joyce affected the rise of theory; in the rhetorical alliances posited between the two. In Colin MacCabe's words, "Joyce's concerns with questions of sexuality and cultural identity made him, in the aftermath of the sixties, perhaps the crucial author around whom to re-evaluate the whole impact and force of modernism" (1982: xii). It is to the new meaning and importance of Joyce's writing, at this new historical moment, that I now turn.

Made in U.S.A.: Structuralist Joyce

Two of the earliest attempts to bring Joyce and theory together were made by American critics, both of whom used the term "structuralism" in the early 1970s to describe their method. Robert Scholes's essay "*Ulysses:* A Structuralist Perspective" was delivered as a lecture to mark the fiftieth anniversary of the novel in 1972, and was rapidly published in three places, including Scholes's theoretical introduction *Structuralism in Literature* (1974). This highly iterable essay thus occupies an interesting role, serving as a kind of hinge between the two textual realms of Joyce and the emergent structuralism. In Joycean publications, like the volume *Fifty Years "Ulysses"* (1974), the essay represents an incursion or controlled importation of strange new terms and models into the still humanist main current of Joyce commentary. "Structuralism" is a foreign entity with which Scholes is experimenting, one that may yet lend support to the central task of redescribing and understanding *Ulysses*. In Scholes's introduction to structuralism, on the other hand, Joyce's function is to serve as an example, making the theory more readily comprehensible by means of "practical" demonstration. This double focus will prove to be typical of the ambiguous relations between Joyce and theory: does he explain the theory or does it explain him? If he is a useful example, why is this so?

Scholes explicitly reflects on this question: "In a sense, structuralism is giving to literature with one hand and taking away from it with the other. It has given writers ideas in abundance and I shall be illustrating this in some detail. But this is not, of course, a matter of something called Structuralism coming up to a writer and handing him [ideas].... On the contrary, writers as thinkers have often been in the forefront of this intellectual process. James Joyce became a structuralist long before the word was current" (1974: 168). From the start, the attempt to apply theory to Joyce is viewed as complex, with a strong suspicion that the theory in question may be latent in the fiction itself. Scholes asserts that "Joyce's later work can not only be seen more clearly from a structuralist perspective but that it is structuralist in its outlook and methodology" (1992: 123). The resistance to structuralism, in his view, is closely analogous to the resistance to Joyce. Structuralism "has met with a very understandable resistance—especially in literary studies. . . . I will maintain that the reluctance of many critics to accept the later Joyce (and by this I mean the last chapters of *Ulysses* as well as *Finnegans Wake*) is an aspect of this larger reluctance to accept the structuralist revolution" (118). It will soon become apparent that Scholes is not the only one to draw a parallel between the unsettling forces of Joyce's writing and French theory.

In its deployment of the distinction between paradigmatic and syntagmatic elements of language, Scholes's structuralism is akin to the Jakobsonian literary theory contemporaneously developed by David Lodge, in which prose or "realism" are seen as dependent on the combinatory chains of the syntagmatic, while poetry or "modernism" play on the metaphorical substitutions of the paradigmatic (1977). Indeed, Lodge explicitly uses Joyce as an exemplar for the modernist pole of this model: "*Ulysses* does have a story . . . but this story echoes and parallels another one—the story of Homer's *Odyssey*. . . . The structure of Joyce's novel is therefore essentially metaphorical, based on a similarity between things otherwise widely dissimilar and widely separated in space and time" (1981a: 11). Scholes, too, sees Joyce as addicted to the "metaphorical" axis of meaning: "Often, it is as if he cannot bear to part with many of the paradigmatic possibilities that have occurred to him. He will stop and climb up the paradigmatic chain on all sorts of occasions, such as the various lists in 'Cyclops'. . . in which displaced possibilities are allowed to sport themselves and form syntagmatic chains of their own" (1992: 126). His "structuralist Joyce" is thus partially in tune with the modernism influentially identified by Lodge at this time. Scholes's structuralism also resembles Lodge's in its enthusiastic accommodation of myth. Scholes describes *Ulysses* as a self-regulating system, in which "the Homeric parallels function as a kind of feedback loop, operating to correct imbalance and brake any tendency of the work to run away in the direction of merely random recitations of Bloom's day. . . . Each chapter, in fact, is designed to run down when certain schematic systems are complete and when a certain temporal segment of the Dublin day has been covered. Whereupon the next Homeric parallel is activitated [sic] to provide a diachronic scheme for the following chapter" (1992: 124). Despite its challenging conceptual armory, Scholes's structuralism in some ways offers a confirmation of available conceptions of Joyce. The treatment of myth as an ordering device ("operating to correct imbalance") actually reaches back to T. S. Eliot ("simply a way of controlling" [1975: 177]), while the "ecological" model provides an emphasis on formal unity and autotelic efficiency reminiscent of Ellmann's reading in *Ulysses on the Liffey*—which was first published the same year as Scholes's lecture. If Ellmann's approach to *Ulysses* bore some resemblance to the models offered by an emergent structuralist narratology, the point can be inverted: Scholes's "structuralist Joyce" itself is partially harmonious with existing and influential humanist and mythic readings.

Yet aspects of Scholes's essay point in other directions. His conception of the "structuralist revolution" of which Joyce brings the "good news" uses theological imagery to characterize the radical decentering of humanity that is at stake: "[T]his revolution has put something like God back in the universe—but not a God made in man's image, bursting with individualism and subject to temper tantrums when His will is thwarted. [Rather,] a God who truly 'is not mocked' because It *is* the plan of the universe, the master system which sets the pattern for all others" (1992: 120). This extraordinary image, its rhetoric more absolutist than anything ventured by a William Noon or a Robert Boyle, is Scholes's extrapolation from Gregory Bateson's claim that "man is only a part of larger systems." In the lexicon of French structuralism it roughly corresponds to Claude Lévi-Strauss's assertion that the ultimate goal of the human sciences is not to constitute man but to dissolve him. If Scholes's structuralist Joyce chimes with a certain liberal humanism, it also threatens it through an emphasis on the determining force of the "ecosystem" as a whole. This is confirmed at a literary level by Joyce's advanced approach to characters: "As his career developed, he accepted less and less willingly the notion of characters bounded by their own skins. . . . Unlike Lawrence, for instance, who reacted against 'the old stable ego of the character' simply by giving us characters with unstable egos, Joyce attacked the ego itself" (121). In *Finnegans Wake,* Scholes suggests, this attack amounts to a dissolution of individual subjectivity into its surroundings, a self-pulverizing "acceptance of the ecosystem" (123). This is a major clue to the question, first thrown up by Scholes, of what contemporary theory may have inherited from Joyce. Scholes's answer seems to be that *Ulysses* adumbrates a posthumanist mode of thought and representation in which the solidity and autonomy of an individual identity are progressively eroded, and that structuralism is the scientific self-consciousness of this process.

Scholes hesitates between totalization and dissolution, invoking an "ecological" order that is at once comfortingly stable and disconcertingly inhuman. In this ambiguity of emphasis he is representative of other American attempts to link Joyce and theory in the 1970s, which seem unsure whether the job of theory is to firm up or shake up our understanding of Joyce's fiction. Does "structuralism" represent a sounder footing on which to base the long-standing attempt to fix and understand Joyce, or does it represent an unassimilable challenge to existing practice, whose ultimate effect will be to undermine those certainties that have been achieved? This uncertainty—which echoes pervasively, beyond Joyce, during the initial takeup of theory—is well demonstrated by Margot Norris's study *The Decentred Universe of "Finnegans Wake"* (1974), the first book-length attempt from the English-speaking world to approach Joyce with the new French ideas.

Norris's book, like Scholes's article, looks in two directions at once. On the one hand, it is concerned with the import and explanation of new ideas; on the other hand, it quarrels with the existing critical consensus on Joyce. The motley assembly of theorists on whom Norris draws—Freud, Lacan, Heidegger, Lévi-Strauss, and Derrida—includes only one figure who would now normally be dubbed a structuralist; its subtitle, *A Structuralist Analysis*, indicates the uncertainty of the book's moment, a Heroic Age of experimental and ambitious theoretical combinations. Some of the earlier chapters of the book indeed appear "structuralist" in their eagerness to treat *Finnegans Wake* as a kind of map of human relations, an anthropological fable that reworks the founding myths of social order. Taking advantage of the homologies between different mythical systems, the book "uses Oedipal and Christian myth to plumb the conflict of the individual, confronted by primordial guilt" (Norris 1974: 39). Norris's study thus has a strong tendency to universalism of a Lévi-Straussian kind, an insistence on the fundamentals revealed to us by the family resemblances between different myths. Joyce uses myth, she writes, "as a dramatic and narrative analogue to the psychological conflicts that beset all men at all times" (39). We are told that the family theme in *Finnegans Wake* "serves as the paradigm of a primal social structure" (54), consisting as it does of "a series of oppositions in which the conflicting demands of the society and the individual are expressed" (42). In this vein Norris's book remains the major application of structuralism to Joyce, the most determined attempt to read his fiction as itself an analogue for an anthropological or psychological system. As with Scholes, Norris's insistence on "the suitability of the structuralist approach to Joyce's work" (4) turns out to be based on a partial sleight of hand, a discovery that Joyce himself "was" a structuralist. "[K]nowingly or unknowingly," writes Norris, "he participated in those intellectual currents of early-twentieth-century Europe, whose destructive impact depended on a profound revision of the understanding of language" (2). She also notes that "we find in *Finnegans Wake* that intellectual shift which locates meaning in relationships and structure rather than in content—a shift formalized by Saussure's recognition of the arbitrary nature of the linguistic sign and his focus on the synchronic laws of language" (3). The implication is that Joyce dramatizes or textualizes what Saussure "formalizes," that *Finnegans Wake* performs structuralism at the level of literary discourse.

Yet just as *Dubliners* can, with sufficient effort and hindsight, be "discovered" to contain the seeds of *Finnegans Wake,* so, by the end of Norris's book, structuralism has flowered into its subversion. Halfway through the book Norris is already focusing on aspects of the text that trouble the hermetic mythical economies that she has already identified (64). In particular, the archetypal figure of Anna Livia Plurabelle—and here Norris's approach is itself archetypal for many subsequent feminist readings of Joyce—is seen as a point of disruption for the masculine order: "If law is a structuring, ordering principle governing societal systems, then ALP's gift-giving is unsystematic and archaic. She obeys no such distinctions as those that lie at the foundation of the concept of law, which is based on the orders of preference, and on prohibitions, as is language itself" (68). By the final chapter Norris has unmistakably moved beyond the style of thought that powered her earlier chapters, as Derrida's "Structure, Sign and Play" becomes the key explanatory text. If earlier on Joyce seemed to be the exemplar of the "structuralist revolution" (Scholes 1992: 119), he now becomes one of the authors of the intellectual caesura announced by Derrida in 1966: "The literary heterodoxy of *Finnegans Wake* is the result of Joyce's attack on the traditional concept of structure itself. This attack was not isolated, but belonged to an 'event' or 'rupture' in the history of the concept of structure, which, according to philosopher Jacques Derrida, took place in the history of thought sometime in the late nineteenth and early twentieth centuries.... Among these destructive discourses of the early twentieth century, *Finnegans Wake* served as a literary exemplar, and in doing so inaugurated a new concept of literary structure" (Norris 1974: 121–22). The final chapter of Norris's book is itself an inauguration, of the association between Joyce and poststructuralism that has subsequently become something of a given. At the same time she echoes the rhetoric of *transition*, for which the tenets of classicist modernism were an obstruction to the appreciation of Joyce.

Norris sees *Finnegans Wake* as unsettling the structures of gender—indeed, structure as such. She is accordingly keen to disavow those critical perspectives that have sought to settle the book down. Much *Finnegans Wake* scholarship prior to the 1970s can be viewed as a search for a coherent story amid the book's ostensible chaos. Campbell and Robinson's *Skeleton Key*, which aimed to strip away the "accidental features" obscuring the book's story (1944: 14), is paradigmatic. "What Campbell and Robinson set out to discover," notes Michael H. Begnal, "is a traceable narrative line in the *Wake*, the hint of a plot that may help to codify the chaos" (1991: 36). Norris's book seeks to break with this imperative. She begins by implicitly allying herself with the search for a "radical" interpretation of *Finnegans Wake*, adumbrated in *Our Exagmination* but subsequently obscured by the steady pileup of criticism. This temporal model of the fall from an enlightened beginning—in this case the *transition* milieu—to which the critic recalls us, will be a significant feature of theoretical readings of Joyce.

For Norris, most *Wake* criticism belongs squarely in the "conservative" camp: "[T]he conservative critics, who have dominated *Wake* criticism for the last thirty years, possess a small but scholarly arsenal: the stylistic and thematic conservatism of the early manuscript drafts, the inclusion of traditional, even arcane, literary material in the work.... Even the recently published *A Conceptual Guide to 'Finnegans Wake'*

[1974], which aims at a comprehensive study of the work, embraces this conservative tradition by approaching the work as a novel: 'along with the problem for the reader of deciphering Joyce's language goes the stumbling block of figuring out the narrative or the plot'" (1974: 1–2). The primacy of plot is among Norris's main targets. She protests against the "novelistic fallacy," the erroneous mode of reading that Harry Levin characterized as "putting critical emphasis on the 'story' and brusquely attempting to extract a quintessential content from the morass of form in which it lies embedded" (Norris 1974: 10). One source of this error, Norris suggests, is a transferral of reading strategies from *Ulysses* to the later book. Thus "The Ulyssean plan is anchored on a naturalistic narrative line, Bloom's day in Dublin. A corresponding literal line, a day in the life of Dublin pubkeeper H. C. Earwicker, serves as the primary point of reference both in Campbell and Robinson's *Skeleton Key to 'Finnegans Wake'* and Clive Hart's *Structure and Motif in 'Finnegans Wake'* [1962]" (23–24). To Norris's examples one can add the approach of Anthony Burgess, whose edition of *A Shorter "Finnegans Wake"* (1966) promises "the gist of the book" and acknowledges Campbell and Robinson as his model, "the first major breakthrough in the hard task of cutting to the narrative line" (1965: 5, 6). The result, notes Michael H. Begnal, is "an unfolding narrative whose basis is essentially cause and effect" (1991: 38), peopled by rounded figures like Campbell and Robinson's description of HCE: "a well-defined and sympathetic character, the sorely harrowed victim of a relentless fate" (1944: 6). On this view, as Begnal put it in 1980, Joyce "remains at heart a traditionalist, working with the basic components of novel construction" (1992: 122).

Norris, however, refuses to read *Finnegans Wake* as an extension of the realist tradition. Joyce's book, she claims, "fails to support . . . novelistic premises and, indeed, there is ample evidence to suggest that the work is designed precisely to refute the realist epistemology that has dominated prose fiction since the eighteenth century. The narrative technique of *Finnegans Wake* challenges the primacy of subjective individual experience in several ways. The singularity of individual experience—its uniqueness—is undermined by the replication of events and the instability of characters. The causal relationship of events in novelistic narration is replaced in *Finnegans Wake* by contiguous associations on the order of psychoanalytic free associations" (1974: 11). To these innovations she adds that the novel's self-reflexive insistence on "the mediation of events by language" contradicts the realist novel's habitual faith in an unproblematic correspondence between word and world. These "departures . . . from the traditional novel," Norris concludes, "signify a critique of the novel form itself, and, consequently, a critique of the literary and intellectual traditions that have sustained it" (15). Norris thus significantly downplays narrative in Joyce. She treats novelistic narrative as reliant on a consistent logic of causality, a recountable sequence in which one event can be said to produce the next. For this emphasis on explanation *Finnegans Wake* substitutes a model based on association. The inexorable linear chain of narrative is broken by an alternative axis of textual proliferation in which proximities at the level of the word override the progress of events. As Norris comments, "[T]he linear narrative line and the poetic forms embedded in it work at cross-purposes to one another. It is the function of the labyrinthian prose to lead the hearer astray, to reduce the issue at hand to confusion, to digress until the main point of the narrative is lost" (100). In fact, it is the very status and existence of that "linear narrative line" that is at issue, for Norris finds not only the "naturalistic" reading but also the Viconian approach offered by Beckett excessively one-directional, and "[s]uch evolutional progress is difficult to discern in the *Wake*" (24). What Norris posits instead is a galaxy of micronarratives that resemble one another in complex and overlapping ways. The eschewal of a single story still allows for a swathe of individual stories; but the principle of relation between these is one of replication rather than succession. Simultaneity, rather than sequence, is the rule.

In emphasizing how *Finnegans Wake* breaks with the novel form, Norris echoes the anxiety about genre provoked by Joyce's earlier works. Eliot, one should remember, had proclaimed the novel dead in the course of describing a *Ulysses* purged of content. As Paul Sheehan (2002) has demonstrated, a suspicion of narrative is one of the chief bridges between modernism and poststructuralism. In both cases narrative tends to imply a dubious unity, a principle of continuity that is held to be suspect—not least, as Sheehan shows, because this continuity is believed to buttress an ideology of the human that comes under increasing strain in the twentieth century. Norris's treatment of Joyce is in keeping with this development. If Pound and Eliot displaced the novel by invoking, respectively, the encyclopedia and the epic, Norris's Wakean alternative is the dream, "in which the systems of cause and effect governing actions in the waking world no longer apply" (Norris 1974: 13). The dream is a figure for the emerging new postgenre of the "text," which Jennifer Levine describes as "a web, a tissue, a signifying field, or even a process of signification, rather than a self-contained entity" (1990: 146). For Levine, a "textual" reading of *Ulysses* supplants not only a "novelistic" one but also a "poetic" approach, in which "sequence is less important than a synchronic and spatial mapping based on repetition: allusions, echoes, symbols, and archetypal patterns all being, essentially, modes of repetition which forestall the onward moving logic of narrative" (141). This is, in effect, a "postmodern" view of a "modernist" mode of reading—variously exemplified by Eliot, the New Critics, and Joseph Frank's theory of spatial form. In fact, the "poetic" approach bears a resemblance to Norris's radical reading of *Finnegans Wake*—which again demonstrates the continuity between the two moments.

Against this, Norris herself, in a retrospect on the "postmodernization" of the *Wake*, argues that poststructuralism rescued the book from the misprisions of the New Criticism: "[F]rom the forties to the sixties, the avant-gardism of *Finnegans Wake* was put on hold, as it were, deferred while the text was rerouted through the formalistic requirements of an American criticism inspired by New Critical dicta that demanded a poetic intelligibility, a formal logic, of texts. . . . Like Eliot years earlier confronting the seeming chaos of *Ulysses*, American criticism sought a hidden key, method or monomyth in *Finnegans Wake* that would validate aesthetic assumptions about its internal logical coherence" (1992: 344). In 1992 Norris identified as "New Critical" the hegemonic readings of the *Wake* that, twenty years earlier, she had rejected for their overemphasis on novelistic narrative and naturalistic characterization: hardly staples of New Critical method, which is more commonly accused of "unwriting" prose into poetry (Eagleton 1983: 50–51; Connor 1997: 123–29). The ambiguity here gives us an insight into the shifts in perspective brought by the intervening years. Norris has rewritten the erstwhile "naturalist" readers of *Finnegans Wake* as high modernist New Critics, against which a "postmodern" interpretation reacted. In fact, however, one can see a *continuity* between her own poststructuralist reading of Joyce—which reacted against a "realist" approach and aimed to "resume the radical viewpoints of the early critics" (Norris 1974: 2)—and an earlier modernist one. Norris's "novelistic fallacy" (10) echoes Eliot's dismissal of the "narrative method" (1975: 178); the emerging model of the "text" both replaces and in some ways resembles the modernist model of the "poem." The break into new thinking includes a return to origins. But the new emphasis that does gradually emerge, from Levine's "poem" to her "text," is one of instability and textual dynamism. Both modes are inhospitable to narrative; but the move from the age of Eliot to the age of theory is a move from stasis to kinesis. This becomes clear when one considers theoretical developments on the other side of the Atlantic.

Vent d'est: Paris–London–Cambridge

It is unsurprising that American critics like Scholes and Norris should have made such early progress, given the dominance that the United States had already achieved in Joyce studies. But the challenge of theory was also taken up in Europe, often with a more polemical edge. The center of the ferment was, of course, Paris itself. Geert Lernout (1990) has offered a history of Joyce's French reception, which need not be rehearsed here. But it is worth emphasizing that the encounter of Joyce and theory did not begin with Anglo-American critics adapting French ideas to writing in English. Joyce already had an important place in the literary canons of major theorists—notably Derrida, Lacan, Cixous, and Kristeva. Theory did not need to be brought to Joyce from France, as it did with several other major names in the English canon. Rather, the arrival of theory seemed to bring Joyce with it, remade in its own image. In turn, it emerged that Joyce's writing had helped to make the theory that remade it. Jacques Derrida is the best example. His first sustained encounter with Joyce took place not in Paris but at Harvard in the 1950s—a Harvard where Harry Levin was teaching (Hillis Miller 1982: 4; Derrida 1984: 148). One can trace a connection from Joyce (in Ireland and Europe) to Levin (reconstructing modernism for the United States) to Derrida (back in France) and finally to the deconstructive readings of Joyce produced almost routinely in the Anglophone world during the last twenty years. In a final circularity, the trail will lead back to Dublin itself, as postcolonial critics like Richard Kearney and Declan Kiberd import theory to redescribe their own national literature.

Derrida's engagement with *Finnegans Wake* played a subtle but central role in bringing Joyce's work to the attention of the theoretical avant-garde. The key text here is Derrida's first publication, his 1962 introduction to Husserl's *Origin of Geometry*. In the course of a sustained analysis of Husserl, Derrida dramatically announces a choice of two approaches to language and culture. To Husserl's practice of a reduction or impoverishment of language to "the univocal and translatable" Derrida counterposes Joyce's writing, which recaptures "all equivocation itself" and "circulates throughout all languages at once"; a writing that, "rather than put it out of play with quotation marks, rather than 'reduce' it . . . settles itself *within* the *labyrinthian* field of culture 'bound' by its own equivocations, in order to travel through and explore the vastest possible historical distance that is now at all possible" (1978: 102). Like the structuralist work discussed earlier, Derrida's divergence looks in two directions. It simultaneously installs Joyce as an exemplary potential (or potential exemplar) at the very start of Derrida's project and hands Joyce's readers the hint of a new descriptive vocabulary. Derrida appropriates Joyce, but in the same gesture he makes himself appropriable by Joyceans. According to Patrick Ffrench, it was these pages by Derrida that brought him into the *Tel Quel* circle: "[Philippe] Sollers refers to his enthusiasm on reading a passage in this book where Derrida mentions Joyce. . . . The writing Derrida describes . . . offered *Tel Quel* the vision of writing as an envelopment of the languages of science and philosophy and hinted at writing as a concept that could unhinge metaphysics and institute a generalized critique of the Western ideology of presence. Literature, celebrated equivocation, would eventually become the privileged locus of such an unhinging. The possibilities of Derrida's vision, visited on Sollers, were extremely promising" (1995: 16–17).

Tel Quel was at the heart of avant-garde thought during the intellectual and political ferment of the late 1960s. By the end of the decade, as Christine van Boheemen-Saaf explains, Joyce had become central to the journal's aesthetic: "[T]he name of Joyce, seen as a major representative of a revolutionary, international modernist style rather than as a national author, had by the time of the revolution of 1968, become synonymous with, and an emblem of, the notion of writing prevalent in *Tel Quel* which seems closely identified with that revolution" (1998: 249). In the 1970s, as Ffrench records, Joyce came even more firmly to epitomize the

Tel Quel aesthetic (1995: 250). Several of the bigger names of poststructuralism—Derrida, Barthes, Kristeva—published pieces in the journal. So did many lesser-known writers, including Stephen Heath. The latter recalls the Parisian situation as follows: "[N]o one, of course, seemed to have read *Finnegans Wake*, to have any particular idea of what to do with it.... At which point Sollers said to me something along the lines of 'Joyce has got to be important, we need something in *Tel Quel*, write it.' So surrounded by the writing going on, the theoretical work being produced, I read and re-read in Joyce's work, especially *Finnegans Wake* of which I'd only read this or that brief run of pages before and which had clearly now become an available contemporary text in a way it hadn't previously been, and everything came together" (Tredell 1994: 185). Heath indicates that the *Wake* was *becoming* readable at this time, made "available" by new historical circumstances. His own status as a native speaker of English was evidently his distinctive qualification in Sollers's eyes, allowing him to bridge different national contexts. But the primary novelty was the range of theoretical vocabularies that could now be applied to Joyce: Saussure, Lévi-Strauss, Barthes, Foucault, Derrida, and Kristeva all feature in "Ambiviolences," the major essay that Heath produced in 1972. It was at this point that the British poststructuralist reading of Joyce commenced.

"Cultural change," proposes Alan Sinfield, "occurs in long-term, general and uneven ways, but it is manifested through a multitude of individual decisions" (1989: 192). Certain "well-placed individuals," Sinfield submits, can have a crucial role in the advancement or consolidation of intellectual movements. This offers a useful way of seeing the work of MacCabe and Heath in the late 1960s and early 1970s. The pair were clearly among the most important "conductors" of new French theory into Britain during this period, a result of the kind of complex of personal and institutional factors to which Sinfield alludes. Both were affiliated to the political Left; Heath had been influenced by the teaching of Raymond Williams and Terry Eagleton at Cambridge (Heath 1972: 12; Tredell 1994: 179), and MacCabe was a member of the Communist Party. This much was soon evident from the character of the film journal *Screen*, whose editorial board both critics joined in 1973. Both also had crucial firsthand experience of Paris itself. Heath studied with

Roland Barthes at the École Pratique des Hautes Études (1968–69) on the course that led to *S/Z*, and worked with Philippe Sollers and the *Tel Quel* group in Paris well into the 1970s. Heath's work at this time was written in French and then translated into English, in a Beckettian displacement that offered "the possibility of thinking differently and also of feeling at home" (Tredell 1994: 180). MacCabe's commitment to France was less pronounced, but he had spent much time in Paris the year before starting his degree at Cambridge (1966–67), and had encountered the teaching of Derrida and Althusser there in the early 1970s. In MacCabe and Heath, then, one finds a theoretical channel tunnel often dominated by Joycean traffic. Having considered the beginnings of the American and French versions of "theoretical Joyce," I will now look closely at the British experience.

Colin MacCabe's approach to Joyce in the 1970s is crystallized in an article he wrote for the *Cambridge Review* in June 1972. "Uneasiness in Culture" is MacCabe's long and scathing review of Richard Ellmann's *Ulysses on the Liffey*, along with two classics of Joyce criticism (Budgen and *Our Exagmination*) that he rates more highly. MacCabe convicts Ellmann of a constant reduction of Joyce's work to its "content," an inability to confront it as writing: "[L]ittle attention is paid to language throughout the book. Rather, difficulty in writing is seen by Ellmann as the difficulty of getting the substantial content (the myth) into the form" (1972: 174). The effect of Ellmann's reading method is to "ignore the reality of the language with which one is presented, and to once again turn it into an instrument used by the author-subject to convey his message" (176). Ellmann's is an idealist faith in pure meanings beyond the defiles of the signifier—meanings that are located in Joyce's head, in a naive conception of authorship: "[T]he aim is to fix the meaning of *Ulysses*, to tell us what Joyce really meant to say. . . . [W]e move behind the text to create the individual subject producing it, to find and found a fixed source of fixed meanings" (174, 176). MacCabe effectively charges Ellmann with inventing the author and claiming to have discovered him, seeing as a truth what he has forgotten is his own illusion.

Ellmann is an emblematic target for MacCabe's wrath. As we have seen, his tendency was to refer the difficulties and fissures of Joyce's texts back to a reassuringly stable source. Ellmann's achievement as a chronicler of Joyce's life sits comfortably with his unceasing emphasis on the unity of Joyce's work, conceived both at the level of totalizing myth and that of authorial "message." The message of *Ulysses*, according to Ellmann's study, is itself a hypnotically unifying one: "That we are all members of the one body, and of the one spirit" (175). The thrust of MacCabe's polemic is precisely against such motifs of authorial intention, organic unity, and underlying messages. In place of these he offers the activity of writing, which displaces the author, fractures imaginary unities, and will not be effaced by its "content." He envisions "a radical experience of language in which both the writing and the reading subjects find themselves dissolved in a writing concerned not with an instrumental giving of sense to a fixed 'world,' but rather with an investigation of the processes of the production of sense" (174).

Several key features of the "theoretical revolution" are luminously evident in this brief article. There is the focus on language, especially in written form—an emphasis that both echoes and upends F. R. Leavis's complaint about Joyce's enthrallment to the printed word. Along with this goes MacCabe's relative lack of interest in the author, his refusal to view "the individual subject [as] a fixed source of fixed meanings" (176). Like a number of themes in MacCabe's review, this suspicion of authorship echoes Stephen Heath's "Ambiviolences," which insists that "The texts should not be read as the spiritual biography of a full sourceful subject (the Author) but as a network of paragrammatic interrelations" (Heath 1984: 34). For Heath, as for MacCabe, what Foucault dubbed the "author-function" is predominantly a ruse of unity, a strategy for regulating a torrent of words rather than recognizing its true dispersion; hence Heath's disavowal of "the pressure of a criticism founded on continuity and identity (grasped above all in the construction of the Author-source)" (33). Ellmann's search for unity in Joyce is thus revoked along with faith in the author: "[W]riting" is a force that "breaks and shatters the very concepts of language and the author on which English literary criticism depends" (MacCabe 1972: 174), a dissolving agent threatening to the integrity of author and reader alike. For Chris Baldick this triple emphasis describes the thematics of theory: "the primacy of Language, the dethronement of the 'subject,' and the dissolution of 'unity'" (1996: 162). Jennifer Levine, describing the "new Joyce" emerging in the 1970s, offers a similar tripartite focus. The major themes she identifies include the precariousness of subjectivity ("The subject is no longer 'there,' a given, which language struggles to represent, but is itself the product of a particular discourse"); the valorization of discontinuity over totality ("instead of an aesthetics of harmony and consistency, a text is to be valued precisely for its code-breaking activity, and for its refusal of a center . . . which might fix the text . . . in some privileged way"); and an "insistence on language as a mode of production . . . in which discourse is grasped not as an identity . . . but as an activity" (1978: 19, 20, 24). MacCabe's polemical review is thus exemplary—not least in the way that Joyce himself is, for MacCabe, the exemplar.

MacCabe's article also chimes with Geert Lernout's and Anthony Easthope's view of the politicized character of British poststructuralism, both in the generational anger toward Ellmann (a contrast with Norris's polite disagreement with certain *Wake* scholars) and in the gestures it makes toward Joyce's true significance in cultural politics. MacCabe begins by stating that "Today in England, 50 years after the publication of *Ulysses* and over 30 since the appearance of *Finnegans Wake,* the texts of James Joyce occupy an uneasy position in our culture." Joyce's challenge to English criticism is such that "the history of the criticism of Joyce's work in this country is a history of recuperation" (1972: 174). Joyce is unassimilable by the English, unless processed and managed in such a fashion as to neutralize his dangerousness. The "uneasiness" of Mac-Cabe's title turns out to be a good thing, a valuable negativity: the ultimate aim is to make Joyce's position "yet more uneasy. Perhaps for the first time in 50 years Joyce's texts have a chance to be disengaged from the recuperative force of our institutions (once the law, now the universities)" (177). There is an odd slippage in this last parenthesis: the law is indicted for paranoiacally keeping Joyce out, the academy for clubbably inviting him in, but subject to its own protocols. The exact connotations of MacCabe's term "recuperative" become evident in his review of Jonathan Culler's *Structuralist Poetics* published in the same journal three years later: "One of the central concepts developed by the Tel Quel critics during the sixties was that of recuperation—the explanation of a new literary practice within an already existing theory instead of constructing the theory of the new practice. . . . [T]raditional bourgeois culture had refused to try to read modernism on its own terms but had attempted to explain and praise it from early nineteenth century positions" (1975:

186). The one path acceptable to MacCabe's steely ultra-leftism is for Joyce to enter English culture, but on his own terms—which will permit the full disruptiveness of his writing. The quest, then, is for the means to achieve this, a style of reading that would be true to Joyce and sacrifice none of the threat he poses. MacCabe closes by informing us of the one contemporary text that seems to possess this potential: Heath's "Ambiviolences," which "will almost certainly be published in France and in French" (1972: 177).

"France" has a crucial role in the structure of feeling articulated by MacCabe. It is from France, and inspired by a specifically French milieu, that Heath's reading of Joyce comes, and in MacCabe's scheme of things the immigration of such theory to Britain appears to echo and replay that of Joyce's own work. The texts with the potential to undermine English culture—*Ulysses*, *Finnegans Wake*, "Ambiviolences"—emanate from self-exiled native English speakers based in Paris, and hence threaten Englishness from within and without simultaneously. Heath's work will only belatedly cross the channel and penetrate a sluggish English criticism (which MacCabe, in his Culler review, casually describes as "backward" [1975: 185]), just like the Bodley Head *Ulysses*, which took twelve years. (As it happened, the lag between the first French appearance of "Ambiviolences" and its British dissemination in the anthology *Post-Structuralist Joyce* was identical.) A similar retarding process applies to French theory in general. In the pages of the *Cambridge Review*, MacCabe's "Uneasiness in Culture" is immediately preceded by Christopher Prendergast's review of Barthes's *Mythologies*, which sees the fifteen-year absence of a translation as evidence of "a certain resistance in England to this vital growing-point of contemporary research" (1972: 170). England is thus a reluctant, shuffling importer. Either it finds foreign work incomprehensible—as Heath's essay, like Joyce's work before it, will be literally unreadable to much of the Anglophone world—or it "recuperates" it, channeling and rewriting the alien text so as to neutralize it. This dual strategy had been outlined by Barthes in *Mythologies* itself: "The petit-bourgeois is a man unable to imagine the Other. If he comes face to face with him, he blinds himself, ignores and denies him, or else transforms him into himself. . . . [A]ny otherness is reduced to sameness" (1973: 151).

MacCabe accuses English criticism of both strategies in its dealings not only with Joyce but also with French theory. In his review of *Structuralist Poetics* he argues that Culler's procedure "is to select the most unfruitful area of contemporary French theoretical inquiries (grouped in England under the name of 'structuralism') and to subsume all the most interesting and exciting work within this reductive model. Not surprisingly we find as a result of this process that structuralism has very little to offer us" (1975: 185). Heath's "Ambiviolences" opens with its own statement of the "rejection or recuperation" thesis, on which MacCabe probably drew in writing "Uneasiness in Culture." Stating that "Reading Joyce remains a problem," Heath describes "two rigorously complementary poles of critical reaction" to *Finnegans Wake*: "[T]he first, faced with the specific practice of writing in Joyce's text and thus with the impossibility of converting that text into a critical object, rejects it as 'aberration'; the second, seeking to preserve Joyce's text for criticism, finds itself obliged to that end to 'reduce' its writing to the simple carrier of a message (a meaning) that it will be the critic's task to 'extract from its enigmatic envelope'" (1984: 31). (The degree of consensus between Heath and MacCabe is demonstrated by their shared disdain for John Gross's rejection [1976: 89] of the "aberration" of *Finnegans Wake*.) In another *Cambridge Review* piece, introducing a series of articles on French theory in 1974, MacCabe gives this analysis an illuminatingly specific context. The work of I. A. Richards, he claims, has harmed our reading of the novel genre by presenting a misleading view of novels as "the expression of a particular point of view and the representation of a fixed reality." He continues: "Perhaps the most telling example of this are [*sic*] the attitudes to Lawrence and Joyce in Cambridge. Lawrence was hailed as the great example of a modern novelist because his novels, at least at one level, could be read as the expression of a personal experience. Joyce's novels, which in their endless investigation of language as articulation and structure refuse any reduction to some authorial point of view, were for many years dismissed totally and if, more recently, his name has begun to appear in the lecture lists, there is still a tendency to vindicate Joyce by rescuing, at the cost of the most partial readings, an author and a meaning that can be discerned behind the text" (1974: 89).

In addition to providing an exemplary instance of the theory of "recuperation"—Joyce is either rejected or "rescued" by the Cambridge faculty—this passage crystallizes much of what is at stake in MacCabe's approach to Joyce in the 1970s. The poststructuralist motifs are here again: the rhetorical sublimity of Joyce's "endless" investigation and utter refusal to be reduced; the diminution of the author as a centering presence or principle; and the privileging of language as "articulation and structure" over literature as "expression." All of this is made easier for the English reader of the *Cambridge Review* by means of an explicit contrast with D. H. Lawrence. The Leavisian binary opposition of "Joyce or Lawrence?," so starkly stated in *D. H. Lawrence, Novelist* (1955), is thus intact but inverted. Where S. L. Goldberg's study *The Classical Temper* (1961) had attempted to rescue Joyce for the Leavisian canon by applying "Lawrentian" terms to him, MacCabe retains Leavis's descriptions of both Joyce and Lawrence but attaches opposite valences to them. It is now the autonomous word, branded "a dead end" in *The Great Tradition* (Leavis 1962a: 36), that represents the future, and the "expression of a personal experience" that belongs, so MacCabe flamboyantly suggests, to the early nineteenth century at best.

The location of MacCabe's polemics is evidently of prime importance. He had arrived at Cambridge as an undergraduate in 1967, and at the time of these articles was working there on the doctoral thesis which would become *James Joyce and the Revolution of the Word* (1979), spending a year at the École Normale Supérieure in Paris. In 1976 MacCabe took up a post as assistant lecturer at Emmanuel College, Cambridge, before leaving in 1981 amid a celebrated controversy. Heath's trajectory was not too dissimilar. He taught at Jesus College and was already lecturing on the modern novel when MacCabe was still an undergraduate. Despite moving to Paris after graduating, he likewise continued to teach at Cambridge through the 1990s. In short, both critics were formed from the simultaneous, contradictory experiences of the home of Leavisism and the hotbed of poststructuralism. With unusual force, their work on Joyce can be seen as engaging with both milieus, deploying then obscure and little-understood French ideas and terms to perform a revaluation of Joyce—a gesture which was all the more forceful for being made just where Leavis's uncompromising exclusion had taken place.

MacCabe's later reflections on the period confirm this analysis. In the preface to his edited collection *James Joyce: New Perspectives*, he writes that the introduction of Joyce as a special subject option on the

Cambridge English degree "was perhaps more significant than it would have been in any other department of English in Great Britain or the United States. It was in Cambridge, around *Scrutiny* magazine and finding particular force in the writings of F. R. Leavis, that a certain canon of modernist writing had been constituted which included T. S. Eliot, D. H. Lawrence and certain of the early poems of Yeats but which deliberately excluded Joyce" (1982: xi). In a later retrospective essay, MacCabe reemphasizes his sense of the Cambridge norm: "The engagement with modernism had frozen literary development at Lawrence. . . . [M]odern literature seemed to begin and end with Lawrence and Eliot . . . [for] the Leavisite account was, by and large, the Cambridge account" (1985: 20, 21). Heath has echoed this judgment: "Leavis, though in some senses marginal, and certainly dependent for his self-presentation on an idea of marginality, was in fact dominantly influential in what the study of English was and what it was about. . . . [T]here was agreement as to what was to be studied and as to the values it embodied" (Tredell 1994: 190).

All this made it possible for the turn to Joyce to acquire an unusual cultural and political weight. The association of Joyce with Paris—already present in Leavis's "Revolution of the Word" essay, in the lurking rivalry between *Scrutiny*'s and *transition*'s versions of modernism—allows him to stand as an emblem of the unassimilable, a symptom of England's exclusions and the incendiary possibilities lying just beyond its borders. An equation thus becomes possible—even necessary—between Joyce and the new French thought that is even more unacceptable to Cambridge. MacCabe makes this explicit in his 1974 article: "The effort required to read Joyce is exactly the effort of realising one's own languages as a particular and specific articulation. It is this effort which perhaps best characterises the most interesting contemporary work in France" (1974: 89). For Heath and MacCabe, the intersection of Joyce and theory was a holy alliance against the entrenched Englishness that had rejected both.

Ultimately the emphasis on Joyce's kinship with Continental theory served greatly to improve his standing in the United Kingdom. Unlike the United States, Britain had not developed a coherent response to Joyce, still less an "industry." Heath and MacCabe changed this situation. Heath's study *The Nouveau Roman* (1972) offers a sustained critique of novelistic realism. The "realistic," Heath argues, is not a given but a construct, "a process of significant 'fictions'" (1972: 20). A "healthy" aesthetic would be one that refused to collude in the collective misrecognition of realism, and instead set out to probe and expose the *vraisemblable* or dominant sense of the real. The "natural attitude" (Husserl's term) is replaced by what Brecht called the "critical attitude" (1964: 185). Such a move marks a shift on the part of the intellectual Left from socialist or historical realism to a "political modernism" or avant-garde practice more concerned to demystify and unsettle. It is here that Joyce finds a new place. Indeed, Heath soon turns to *Finnegans Wake* to elucidate his notion of a "practice of writing," in which "The series of forms of realist writing, naturalized as writing 'without thickness,' as non-formal, miming 'Reality' as its direct expression, is now deconstructed, grasped as production" (1972: 23). The *Wake*, Heath proposes, "offers the *space* of a work always '*in progress*,' the scene of a play of language . . . and not, as in realist writing, the (intended) linear progression of a process of notation" (26). Hence "The situation of the *nouveau roman* is post-Joyce . . . that work of textual reactivation in which the work of Joyce represents so important a stage" (29).

Heath's book exemplifies the recruitment of Joyce to an antirealist program heavily informed by French theory and with ideological demystification, if not political emancipation, as its declared goal. The influence of such work is evident in a book like Rosalind Coward and John Ellis's *Language and Materialism* (1977), whose ambitious politicotheoretical synthesis is typical of the period. In the wake of Heath and MacCabe, Coward and Ellis are prepared to read Joyce alongside Brecht as the type of the revolutionary writer. *Ulysses* is described as a "radical text" that "dramatise[s] the production of positions in language, showing them to be woven of multiple contradictions" (1977: 38, 51), while *Finnegans Wake* is treated in Kristevan fashion alongside Mallarmé and Artaud as a text that "cannot by any contortion be referred to a narrative structure or any other such system" and "dissolves the identity of signifier and signified upon which the whole of Western discourse is ultimately based" (1977: 43). This typifies one of the major routes taken by theory on its arrival in Britain, as Chris Baldick skeptically notes: "The partisans of 'Theory'. . . tended to encourage an easy equation between cultural and political radicalisms, contrasting the 'closed' literary text of the nineteenth century, say, with the 'open' work of twentieth-century modernism" (1996: 165). Baldick cites *Finnegans Wake* as one of the approved texts of this "politicized formalism" (155). Joyce was regularly invoked by critics seeking to make theory practical. Thus John Sturrock, explicating Barthes's notion of "Text" in the volume *Structuralism and Since*, writes that "[t]he nearest we have to a genuine Text is James Joyce's *Finnegans Wake*, a book that has known a small vogue in France as a result of Barthes' theorizing" (1979: 69). Terence Hawkes's *Structuralism and Semiotics* also invokes Joyce as exemplar of the Barthesian *écrivain*, "taking the activity of writing as its subject, and obviously trying, by experimental methods, to establish a new 'writerly' status for the writer" (1977: 113). Raman Selden's *Reader's Guide to Contemporary Literary Theory* (1985), looking to illustrate the proximity of *jouissance* and boredom in Barthes's study *The Pleasure of the Text*, would incautiously ask: "How many blissful readers of Joyce's *Finnegans Wake* have there been?" (1993: 133). In student handbooks as well as advanced treatises, the association of Joyce with new theory was repeatedly made.

Joyce's centrality to "politicized formalism" was enhanced by *Screen*, the prime conduit for Heath and MacCabe's impact in the 1970s. Film studies constituted a major route for the entry of theory to Britain: "a vanguard discipline," in David Bordwell's words, "a place where people keen on theory could work more freely than in other fields" (1989: 96). Many commentators (Belsey 1980: 69; Sutherland 1985: 137; Easthope 1988: 134) testify to the journal's centrality to the avant-garde aesthetics of the time: a "'political modernist' position," as Peter Wollen puts it, whose core was "the idea that politics in art concerned the signifier rather than the signified . . . a line of argument that could lead to presenting James Joyce as the key revolutionary artist" (1982: 208). In MacCabe's own immodest estimate, *Screen* was where "the most important consistent attempts to discuss and analyse the relation between culture and signification took place" (1985: 4). If Kristeva's Joyce was the missing link between Mallarmé and Artaud, *Screen*'s Joyce might be described as the fictional complement not only of Brecht but also of his cinematic successor, Jean-Luc Godard, who was regarded as the major revolutionary artist of this period. Wollen's own essay of 1972 on Godard's "counter-cinema" sketches an oppositional aesthetic close to that of MacCabe's reading of Joyce (1982: 79–91), and MacCabe himself produced a study of Godard in 1980.

MacCabe's "Realism and the Cinema: Notes on Some Brechtian Theses" (1974) was one of *Screen*'s most influential and contentious attacks on realism (Docker 1994: 65). The chief burden of MacCabe's essay is to argue the ideological function of so-called classic realism. Such art works to contain the clash of points of view that it depicts within the harmonizing field of a metalanguage. Rather than reveal its own status *as* a discourse, this "dominant discourse" effaces its means of signification and effectively becomes invisible, naturalized into the semblance of a neutral gaze at the world (MacCabe 1985: 39). MacCabe's example of such a mode in literature is *Middlemarch*, a choice that has provoked a good deal of skepticism about the validity of the "classic realist" designation (Lodge 1981b). But if, as John Docker graphically complains, "MacCabe's argument rested on a Manichaean combine of binary oppositions, with the classic realist text on the dark side" (1994: 72), what was on the bright side? One answer is James Joyce. This much is made clear in *James Joyce and the Revolution of the Word*, whose second chapter reprints much of the "Realism" essay and expands the controversial discussion of George Eliot to ten pages. Given the fact that MacCabe's doctoral thesis was well underway by the time of "Realism and the Cinema," one can assume that Joyce occupied this crucial conceptual place from the start. Indeed, Joyce is eventually proffered in the essay as the sole example of a writer able to "develop the possibility of articulating contradiction" (MacCabe 1985: 50). It is thus possible to see the central dialectic of "*Screen* theory"—or of Easthope's "British post-structuralism" in general—as having always already included Joyce, of being propelled at its very origin by a reading of his textual politics.

The direct product of this was MacCabe's *James Joyce and the Revolution of the Word* itself. Before *Ulysses*, writes Hugh Kenner, Ireland strained to bring forth what Yeats hopefully called a "Sacred Book of the Arts" (1983: 198). The belated appearance of MacCabe's study at the end of the 1970s earns it that messianic role in the story of Joyce and early British poststructuralism. It was MacCabe's book that most publicly thrust the collocation of Joyce and theory into the English literary-critical world, sharing something of the popularizing and propagandizing project then being undertaken by critics like Terence Hawkes (1977),

Catherine Belsey (1980), and Terry Eagleton (1976b, 1983). Although MacCabe's book differs from the work of those critics in its defiant recourse to abstraction—"such a hard read," as Anthony Easthope humbly complains (1988: 140)—it remains the major British instance of the cocktail of Joyce, high theory, and revolutionary politics that had marked the previous decade. All the familiar themes resurface here. Politically and culturally, the ultra-leftist rhetoric of MacCabe's and Heath's essays of the early 1970s is intact, along with the double bind of "rejection or recuperation" for existing criticism. According to MacCabe, "Literary criticism—and there is no shortage of books devoted to Joyce—preserves him as unread. . . . [T]he situation has been aggravated by the persistent refusal of commentators to engage with the radical novelty of Joyce's work. Instead Joyce's texts are transformed into complicated crossword puzzles whose solution is the banal liberal humanism of the critic" (1979: 3). MacCabe goes back to zero. In the face of the still growing mountain of commentary on Joyce's texts, he implicitly claims to be the first critic ever to have understood them: "The aim of this work is not to provide the meaning of Joyce's work but to allow it to be read" (3).

This withering contempt for existing Joyce studies also signifies a return to origins, as Lacan and Althusser had "returned" to Freud and Marx, respectively. Malcolm Bowie describes Lacan's self-appointed task as "disinterring Freud's ideas from the litter of banalizing glosses and explanations which later writers have heaped upon them," for those later writers "have lost all the weight, the perplexingness and the innovative power of Freud's ideas as they were first formulated by him" (1979: 117). Substitute Joyce's name for Freud's here, and one could sum up MacCabe's project: an approach more profound than the transient misprisions of an Ellmann or Kenner, which will at last, even as the author's centenary approaches, allow reading to begin. MacCabe thus picks up the recurring theme of Joyce's anticipation of theory, in the sense that it is only after theory that Joyce has become legible. Indeed, "*Finnegans Wake* would be a primer" for that "new discipline" that would "concern itself with the changing relation of the body to language (more exactly, of the body in language) through time" (MacCabe 1979: 2). MacCabe, like many others, sees "application" as an inappropriate model for Joyce's relation to theory: "[I]t will never be a question of *applying* linguistic theories to the *Wake*. Rather it is a question of using Joyce's experiments to elaborate methods for the analysis of discourse" (137). Joyce's practice, therefore, "remains in excess of any theoretical development. Here Joyce is still writing in our future" (148).

MacCabe's account of Joyce's writing is another attempt to delineate the new, postnovelistic genre of the "text" adumbrated by Barthes and Kristeva, as well as Norris and Levine. MacCabe's Joyce undermines the very idea of "representation"; indeed, the later Joyce is "concerned not with representing experience through language but with experiencing language through a destruction of representation" (4). MacCabe is even more hostile than Norris to the concept of narrative. Narrative is understood as a falsely harmonizing, ideological process that perniciously guarantees patriarchal sexual relations (54) and autonomous subjectivity: "It is the coherence of narration that grants us a position outside language and to dissolve that position is to subvert narrative" (44). Joyce's writing accomplishes "a destruction of any possibility of a story which, in its narration, would efface the system of language" (44). It does this by "dissolving narrative into discourse instead of fixing discourse in terms of narrative" (62).

MacCabe's Joyce is thus programmatically antirealist, incinerating representation and narration as part of an unprecedentedly avant-garde project. As for what replaces the consolations of realism, MacCabe closely follows Julia Kristeva in his view of avant-garde textuality. For the Kristeva of *Revolution in Poetic Language* (1974) the text is less story or argument than experience and process, a "dangerous and violent crucible" (1984: 104) in which the reader comes undone: "Going through the experience of this crucible exposes the subject to impossible dangers: relinquishing his identity in rhythm, dissolving the buffer of reality in a mobile discontinuity, leaving the shelter of the family, the state, or religion. The commotion the practice creates spares nothing: it destroys all constancy to produce another and then destroys that one as well" (104). Similarly, for MacCabe the significance of Joyce's fiction lies not, as for so many commentators before him, in symbolic meaning or naturalistic detail but in its effect on the reader. He aims to replace literary criticism with "the study of the positions offered to the subject within language and of how literature confirms and subverts those possibilities" (1979: 2). In reading Joyce, he explains, "we are continually forced to work on our discourses in an unceasing transformation of both them and ourselves." If reading realist fiction, like Barthes's *lisible* text, is "passive consumption," with Joyce "it becomes an active metamorphosis, a constant displacement in language" (2). Joyce's writings "disrupt the normal position assigned to a reader in a text and thus alter the reader's relation to his or her discourses" (4–5): "[A]s the covers of the book dissolve, so we, too, lose our definite limits and the bodies of discourse which we are, become evidently open to a continuous re-articulation" (85). Joyce's writing, in short, is presented as having *effects* on the reader, producing ruptures and "shatterings" (Kristeva) of a well-nigh bodily kind. Hence the surprising frequency in MacCabe's book of a term more readily associated with Leavisism, "experience," to describe the subjective convulsions wrought by the text. As Philippe Sollers put it, "Read—and see if you hold your own, if you stay, he or she, the same" (1978: 112).

Such an account of Joyce's writing is oddly familiar. For its early readers, as for MacCabe, *Ulysses* would produce effects on the body. Recall the protests of "Aramis"—"I have no stomach for *Ulysses*.... [It is] enough to make a Hottentot sick" (1970: 192–94)—and Holbrook Jackson, "becalmed ... bored, drowsed, bewildered" (1970: 199), as well as Arnold Bennett's proto-Kristevan claim that "The code is smashed to bits. Many persons could not continue reading *Ulysses;* they would be obliged, by mere shock, to drop it" (1970: 221). I have dubbed such accounts of *Ulysses* "kinetic." This might also be an appropriate term for the Joyce read by Kristeva and MacCabe, a text that produces not aesthetic stasis but convulsions and dissolutions within the reader. In this sense the wheel has come full circle. MacCabe's attempt to make Joyce "readable" reinstates the terms of his original "unreadability," in the ultimate return to origins—one reaching back before even Pound and Eliot's canonical reviews of *Ulysses*. MacCabe's "Uneasiness in Culture" had aimed to make Joyce's cultural place *more*, not less, uneasy, reinstating his original threat to the law and the academy. The return of "modernism" in the age of theory, accordingly, sees the clock being turned back to rediscover the explosive force that Joyce had for his first readers. Indeed, Kristeva's frequent recourse to the imagery of combustion and detonation—"exploding the subject and his ideological limits" (1984: 15)—is close to John Middleton Murry's hyperbolic description of Joyce in April 1922: "He is the man with the bomb who would blow what remains of Europe into the sky. . . . His intention, so far as he has any social intention, is completely anarchic" (1970: 196). More than once Joyce was accused of "literary Bolshevism" (Mais 1970: 191; Leslie 1970b: 207; Noyes 1970: 275). The reclamation of Joyce for literary Bolshevism would not be a bad description of the project of his "political modernist" critics in the 1970s.

In 1980 MacCabe encountered some local trouble. A series of committees, spearheaded by Christopher Ricks, surprisingly refused to create a permanent lectureship for MacCabe, ultimately forcing him to leave Cambridge. The "MacCabe Affair" was a high-water mark for the public visibility of critical theory, attracting unusual coverage in the mainstream media. According to Fred Inglis, *James Joyce and the Revolution of the Word*, while enhancing Joyce's status in a changing academy, also played its part in MacCabe's downfall: "On 22 May the Faculty Board meets, as somebody said, in 'an atmosphere of hatred and anger.'. . . Extracts from MacCabe's book on Joyce are read out aloud and scoffed at by Mike Long. Ribald laughter from two stout parties. . . . Much is made of the notion of 'distinction.' 'Does this work show distinction?' 'What kind of distinction?' 'Well, true distinction. Distinction of intelligence. Of scholarship. Originality of mind. Distinction in the quality of prose.' Laughter. Uproar" (Inglis 1995: 281). In a subsequent meeting, Inglis reports, Christopher Ricks flatly asserted that "Dr MacCabe's book is a bad book," and Michael Long gave "a twenty-minute malediction" over it (282). In the still rarefied sphere of Cambridge English (Williams 1984: 177–211; Kermode 1997: 254–58), MacCabe's attempt to make Joyce unsafe appears to have been all too successful.

Le gai savoir: Deconstruction Industry

Joyce's higher status in British academic debates, however, was unmistakable. Key anthologies published in Britain included MacCabe's collection *James Joyce: New Perspectives* (1982); W. J. McCormack and Alistair Stead's *James Joyce and Modern Literature*, which pronounced a "re-birth" of Joyce and "renewal of interest in Joycean modernism among the New Left" (1982: 1); and Derek Attridge and Daniel Ferrer's *Post-Structuralist Joyce: Essays from the French* (1984), which further abetted the sense of a reverse colonization from Paris. Indeed, in the early

1980s Attridge arguably took over from Heath and MacCabe as the most significant "conductor" of theory. In Attridge's *Joyce Effects* (2000), essays written through the 1980s and 1990s form a peculiarly clear narrative—personal and theoretical—of this period. The international Joyce symposia, as Attridge notes, tell their own story. The 1975 symposium in Paris "included a good deal of French theoretical discussion," with contributions from Lacan, Sollers, and Cixous, but a dichotomy remained between Francophone and Anglophone approaches, enshrined in the two markedly separate volumes of conference proceedings. The 1982 symposium, held in Dublin, found Attridge alongside other young critics (Maud Ellmann and Colin MacCabe among them) on a panel that approached "Sirens" with the inspiration of French ideas (Beja et al. 1986: 57–92). This "thin wedge" (Attridge 2000: 8) of theory had grown a good deal broader at the event that most dramatically marked the entry of theory into the Joyce industry, namely, the 1984 symposium in Frankfurt, where Derrida and Kristeva gave major addresses (Benstock 1988). It was in Frankfurt, Attridge recalls, that his collaboration with Derrida commenced (2000: 9); he would go on to edit the full version of Derrida's "*Ulysses* Gramophone" in the collection *Acts of Literature* (1992). Indeed, Derrida's "Two Words for Joyce," a reflection on *Finnegans Wake* and on Joyce's long-standing importance to him, had already appeared in *Post-Structuralist Joyce*. Few critics in the 1980s and 1990s did more than Attridge to draw Continental theory and the study of Joyce closer together. He was able to fulfill this role thanks not only to an unusual combination of theoretical acuity and Joycean scholarship but also less specialized virtues. His ability to perform detailed readings of Joyce's texts has given theory plausibility (his discussion of onomatopoeia in "Sirens" [Attridge 1988: 136–57] is an outstanding example); and the careful clarity of his writing has made theory—and Joyce—more accessible than they are in other hands. Kevin Dettmar plausibly describes him as "discovering the direction in which Joyce criticism must go, and leading the way" (1996a: xiii).

In one sense Attridge, as a South African who arrived in Britain in 1966, was an outsider. But, as we have seen, the increasingly international character of the field makes any inside/outside division unreliable: notable Joyceans were already hailing from Switzerland (Senn) or Australia (Hart, Goldberg), not to mention the United States. In this sense Attridge was more exemplary than exceptional. He recalls South African literary studies as a home from home for Cambridge English: "[T]he powerful Lawrentian/Leavisian model, premised on a moral earnestness and an attachment to organicism that left little room for playful ingenuity or the foregrounding of linguistic and literary conventions, left little room for effects of the Joycean kind" (2000: 2). In becoming a student at Cambridge itself, Attridge went from frying pan to fire. His intellectual trajectory was thus analogous to that of Heath and MacCabe, confirming again the relation between the valuation of Joyce and the move beyond Cambridge's old critical models: "[T]he pleasure I took in Joyce's works . . . stemmed in large part from their *resistance* to the model of literary appreciation I had been schooled in" (4). Attridge's own contributions to Joyce studies would never claim the revolutionary urgency of the theoretical manifestos of the 1970s. But he echoes them in consistently finding strong affinities between Joyce and theory. Attridge recalls teaching a year-long course on *Finnegans Wake*, not merely for its own sake but also as "a way of developing my own, and encouraging my students', interest in the intellectual opportunities offered by the new modes of thought." Happily, "the *Wake* turned out to be the perfect instrument by means of which to shake inherited assumptions about literature and criticism" (5–6).

Yet Attridge offers an important, characteristic caveat: "Our work in the classroom was not a matter of 'applying' theories derived from philosophers or psychoanalysts, however; it was a process of trying to develop ways of reading that seemed to do justice to Joyce's writing, and thus to enhance our pleasure in it. It was certainly helpful to be reading Derrida, Kristeva, and Barthes at the same time; but *this* reading also required the breaking of old habits, and the *Wake* in turn proved helpful in making headway with the peculiar difficulties of the French writers with whom we were grappling" (5–6). A theme that has recurred throughout this chapter surfaces again here, and throughout Attridge's writing on the subject. There is no question of the "application" of theory to Joyce: criticism cannot approach him from a securely metalinguistic position. This becomes clear partly because Joyce and theory are themselves critiques of metalanguage. Primary and secondary texts work simultaneously to destabilize precisely the hierarchy of primary and secondary: literature and criticism shift roles, or level the playing field between them. To read Joyce (and, above all, *Finnegans Wake*) is to generate "theory," to develop "ways of reading" that can "do justice to it." And to read Derrida is not merely to pick up theory: it is itself a "literary" experience, a challenge to reading analogous to that posed by Joyce. Joyce and theory allegorize and echo one another.

The implications of this are ambiguous. On the one hand, Joyce lends status to theory. New methods of reading and writing, still academically marginal in the early 1980s, gain credence from the claim that they respond sensitively to a major, if difficult, writer. The stronger claim, indeed, is that theory responds more appropriately to Joyce than any earlier critical paradigm; as MacCabe had avowed, it was only after Derrida and Lacan that Joyce became readable. In that sense theory is "Joycean": it offers modes of reading that give us a truer Joyce than we had known before. It becomes even more Joycean in the still stronger claim that theory actually derives in part from Joyce's writing: that poststructuralism was a delayed response to modernism, and to Joyce above all. Numerous critics of various persuasions have made this observation (Young 1981: 189; Bloom 1986: 4; Friedman 1993: 3; Currie 1998); and its historical basis is attested in Derrida's "Two Words for Joyce." The assertion of such a strong link gives theory a striking new hermeneutic status. If deconstructionists can in some sense claim to be Joyce's heirs, then their readings of Joyce can, in turn, claim a peculiar authority—becoming something like authorized versions. (In fact, the metaphorical line of descent from Joyce through Derrida produces a generous alternative to the literal genealogy of the notoriously exclusive Joyce estate.) At the very least, the view (prevalent around various writers in the 1980s, notably Shakespeare) that theoretical readings of Joyce are wildly willful—obscurantist violations of a great artist, performed with foreign tools irrelevant to him—is stripped of its power.

Theory, then, borrows some glamour from Joyce. But in the same gesture, it signs away its own authority to him. Theory cedes its metalinguistic status, admitting that it is on a par with literature—or more than this, it admits the *priority* of literature. "Literature, for us," Attridge remarks of the "Sirens" panel of 1982, "was not the merely passive object of theorizing, but a discourse preempting and exceeding all theories" (2000: 8). In a sense this is a deeply traditional claim: readers from Eliot to Ellmann would have admitted that *Ulysses* held more mysteries than their merely critical discourses could suggest. But in the historical moment of deconstruction, Joyce's preemptive power swells. Derrida himself makes this case, notably in "*Ulysses* Gramophone": "Everything we can say about *Ulysses*, for example, has already been anticipated, including, as we have seen, the scene about academic competence and the ingenuity of metadiscourse. We are caught in this net. All the gestures made in the attempt to take the initiative of a movement are found to be already announced in an overpotentialized text that will remind you, at a given moment, that you are captive in a network of language, writing, knowledge, and *even narration*" (1992: 281). Attridge echoes this view in his own contribution to the Frankfurt symposium (2000: 22–29), whose theme is the two-way relation that should obtain between Joyce and a truly deconstructive criticism. "What," he wonders, "if the critical text should find itself addressed by the writing on which it comments, perhaps even given life and sustained by it[?]" (23). "The deconstructive criticism of Joyce" must be understood as "*Joyce*'s deconstruction of the critic's text as much as the critic's deconstruction of Joyce's text: the critical text would have been made possible by Joyce's text, by the specificity, the uniqueness, of Joyce's writing" (26–27). Any criticism of Joyce's text will "offer itself to be read by the Joycean text, which constitutes a far more comprehensible and tightly bunched gathering of cultural threads than any foreseeable criticism" (27); indeed, "we may regard the Joyce industry itself as nothing more than a vast extension of the Joycean text" (28). A similar case is made by Christine van Boheemen (1988), who delights in Derrida's revelation of the "preemptive all-inclusiveness" with which Joyce achieves "mastership," and who draws an increasingly familiar conclusion about the invalidity of metalanguage demonstrated by both writers.

Unmistakable here is the double gesture I have identified. On the one hand, Joyce's quality of anticipation offers criticism a guarantee of relevance: Attridge's account implicitly shrinks the possibility of a deconstructive reading of Joyce ever being mistaken. On the other hand, Joyce is credited with superhuman powers: criticism, in effect, abases itself before him. One apparent implication of the Derridean pronouncements on Joyce is that Joyce knows everything and can never be wrong. (Strictly, the Derridean claim refers to the operation of Joyce's writing, not the man himself: but this makes little practical difference.) The moment of theory sees great homage paid to Joyce—far greater than that of Levin, who complained about the failures of "Sirens" and "Oxen of the Sun" (1960: 88–95), or Ellmann, who gently mocked Joyce as well as making him a hero. And the rhetoric of reciprocity means that theory, in offering Joyce such lavish tribute, also gives credit to itself. "Theory," writes David Trotter, "no longer implicit but announced, hypostatized, would in turn announce and hypostatize Modernism's newness.... Postmodernist theory and Modernist practice have legitimated each other's claims to avant-garde status" (1992: 191, 192). "A poststructuralist Joyce," Trotter ruefully concludes, "has always seemed inevitable" (194).

Undoubtedly, a major factor in this apparent inevitability was the harsh treatment that aspects of Joyce's writing had received first time around. The new valuation of Joyce in the age of theory is, in part, an attempt to right old wrongs by inverting the aesthetics of the past. Heath, MacCabe, and Attridge have all discussed their reaction against Cambridge's dominant response to Joyce. Even for those critics for whom Leavisism itself was never a major issue, the turn to Joyce is a pointed refusal of organicism, realism, and "the illusion of immediate representation" (Attridge 2000: 4). In the age of theory, the Joyce industry powerfully achieved this reversal. One instance of this is a revaluation within Joyce's oeuvre itself. In an essay on Joyce and history Attridge points out that Fredric Jameson's criticism is powered not merely by objective fact but by narrative tropes. But it is equally striking how readily his response to Jameson itself falls into a narrative mold, in which Joyce's works become progressively more self-conscious about the rhetorical character of history. After developing this case through the *Portrait* and *Ulysses*, Attridge continues: "It is only in *Finnegans Wake* that Joyce fully resists the linear, progressive, subsuming structure" (2000: 83) in which later developments supersede yet preserve earlier ones. The argument is against narratives of progress, but takes the form of a narrative of progress. A similar teleology is at work in several of Attridge's other essays. One reads that "with each successive work Joyce increased the openness of his writing" (32); or that *Ulysses* "leave[s] the conventional concept of history as the union of events and language intact, if somewhat shaken. It is *Finnegans Wake* that breaks decisively with that concept, refusing all the attempts made by its readers to bring it back to the recognizable configurations of history" (87). Similarly, in "The Ideology of Character"

Attridge describes the means by which *Ulysses* plays with proper names, before moving beyond it: "[W]hat remains in *Ulysses* an occasional reminder of the frangibility of the word becomes in *Finnegans Wake* a generative principle" (57). It is thus not too surprising when Attridge elsewhere asserts that "contrary to the common view that Joyce's work becomes less politically engaged as it becomes more formally innovative, the later writings emerge as the most politically committed of all. In particular, *Finnegans Wake*..." (Cheng 1995: xiii). Repeatedly what is glimpsed in *Dubliners* flowers in the *Wake*, with the other two major works as staging posts on the way to the last book's full realization of the materiality of language, the instability of the subject, and the foregrounding of narrativity (Attridge 2000: 131). Arguably, Joyce's corpus lends itself peculiarly well to such a teleological model—which is itself the inversion of the earlier narrative in which Joyce declines, through the last chapters of *Ulysses* and *Finnegans Wake*, into mechanism and self-indulgence. For many readers (Dettmar [1996a] is a brave exception) the new narrative offers a convincing way of understanding what they find most rewarding about Joyce. But we may note its convenience: for it clearly justifies and vindicates Joyce (who was not, as earlier readers thought, increasingly headed down a dead end) and theory (which finds Joyce heading steadily toward a performance of its own tenets).

Attridge's most daring gesture is to enshrine *Finnegans Wake* not merely as the zenith of Joyce's career but as the center of the literary canon. What seems most marginal about Joyce, he proposes, is what is most central about him: the book that once seemed an eccentric jape is in fact the most intensive of all instances of the literary. In *Peculiar Language* (1988) Attridge examines a series of literary modes that seem to digress from linguistic norms: in Derridean fashion, his suggestion is that the relation between norm and digression, center and margin, cannot hold. The book concludes by sketching "the worrying possibility that *Finnegans Wake* may be not an aberration of the literary but an unusually thoroughgoing *exemplification* of the literary ... namely, the impossibility of ever being limited by originating intention, or external reference, or constraining context" (1988: 232). Attridge thus imagines an alternate universe in which *Finnegans Wake* is at the center of the canon, and all other texts—which have less thoroughly sought to go beyond intention, reference, and contextual constraint—are marginal. The aim is not to devalue such texts, however: as Attridge affirms, "the project of centering *Finnegans Wake*" would show "that such [Joycean] enjoyment of writing's proliferating energies extends to all texts; any work of literature can be seen to possess these qualities to some degree, to partake of the modes of textuality which have been variously described in terms of *écriture*, genotext, *signifiance*, heteroglossia, dissemination, rhetoricity, performativity, *scriptibilité*" (236). Literature, in other words, would find itself best described by the terms of theory, as well as exemplified by Joyce. Attridge presents this as a whim, a thought experiment. But elsewhere, too, he has suggested that "the *Wake* represents an extreme of the literary that reveals with particular clarity the characteristic models of literature's functioning" (2000: 131), and that "*Finnegans Wake* is the most typical and the most revealing of literary texts" (160). Certainly this remains an eccentric view in public culture, literary or otherwise; to that extent Attridge's thought is indeed utopian. But in an academic context it is not so far-fetched. It is, in fact, one way of describing changes that really have occurred in the age of theory. Joyce has become canonically central, and Attridge offers a theoretical justification for this, which echoes (and extends, rather than supplants) the reordering of the canon sketched by Hugh Kenner.

Attridge is too canny and conscientious a critic to have no qualms about this situation. By the end of the millennium the question that confronts him is whether things have gotten out of hand. In his essay "Judging Joyce" he admits that all his work on the writer presupposes a prior approval—"the unquestioned assumption that Joyce's writing is to be enjoyed, admired, and learned from rather than weighed in evaluative scales and pronounced good, bad, or a mixture of the two" (2000: 163). As Attridge acknowledges, this is not just a personal quirk, but the situation of almost all writing on Joyce today. The rhetorical justifications proposed during the rise of theory, added to Joyce's existing status and given material support by the International James Joyce Foundation, the symposia, and a string of periodicals, have issued in a situation where Joyce appears virtually unassailable—at least from within the sphere of Joyce studies, which has become simultaneously larger and more semi-autonomous than ever before. For that matter, Attridge has written of Joyce's real influence going far beyond the literary academy. "Far more people read Joyce than are aware of it," he asserts, meaning that the

"Joycean" has become diffused through literature and popular culture: "Even those who read very few novels encounter the effects of Joyce's revolution every week, if not every day" (1990: 1). On the face of it, Joyce—after all the bans and doubts—has achieved some kind of triumph. Even Attridge's valiant attempt to call the whole enterprise into question finally founders on the thought that, whatever happens, "it is hard to imagine that Joyce won't, once again, have the last laugh" (2000: 188). Given the self-confirming Joyce industry that he describes, Attridge must surely suspect that the laughter will be canned.

Masculin féminin: Difficult Conjunctions

Yet other stories can be told about reading Joyce in the age of theory. What looks from one angle like self-perpetuating theoretical proliferation—in which, as Attridge remarks, "much-vaunted 'new approaches' succeed one another, each proclaiming their superiority to earlier approaches, each destined to give way to the next wave of intellectual fashion" (2000: 13)—might also be a process in which long-ignored voices get a belated hearing. This is most evidently true of feminism, which has made a particularly strong impact on Joyce studies. In the century's final decades, a new generation of American critics emerged who were Joyceans, feminists, and, in different ways, theorists too. In addition to Margot Norris one could mention, among others, Bonnie Kime Scott, Suzette A. Henke, Karen Lawrence, Cheryl Herr, and Vicki Mahaffey. Their ascendancy within the American academy and the Joyce industry is in itself a notable event in the narrative I have been tracing. For the first time—Beach and Weaver notwithstanding—women have played a visibly important role in directing the reading of Joyce.

To read the first major feminist works on Joyce is to find not an endless conveyor belt of theoretical models, but rather a political urgency that demands that new questions be asked and perhaps even answered. The central text of this moment is Bonnie Kime Scott's *Joyce and Feminism* (1984), which stakes out ground with the dogged determination of the pioneer. The range of contexts sketched demonstrates how much work there was to be done, and the difficulty of knowing in advance which approaches would prove most fruitful. Scott, writing in the early 1980s, simply loads everything in: prehistoric Irish mythology;

Mariolatry; female republicanism; the position of women as students in late-nineteenth-century Dublin; Ibsen and Hauptmann; Joyce's letters to his mother; Lucia Joyce's career as a dancer; the "free women" of "Odéonia"; the prehistory of feminist criticism from Djuna Barnes to Colin MacCabe—in addition to close analyses of three major female characters from the fiction. The book is marked by its necessary inclusiveness, the genre-hopping manner in which it incorporates anything that might prove useful in the future: there is a strong sense that it is intended as a kind of database for later feminists. In fact, the book's rangy eclecticism is reminiscent of some of the earliest and most important works on Joyce—such as Ellmann's biography, in which room must be found for any decent anecdote, or Kenner's *Dublin's Joyce*, which leaps aboard each passing train of thought to prevent it going unused. The date of Scott's assemblage indicates how long the challenge of gender had been ignored while Joyce's relation to numerous other topics was pursued. Yet in a sense her discoveries are not new, as she herself notes late in the book. *Joyce and Feminism* "does not invent or substitute a subject, but reclaims one that was there, too little recognized and worked, from the start" (1984: 201–2). The task of the feminist critic at this stage is a salvage operation: "[R]eclamation work is one of the core definitions of feminist criticism; it needs to be done early to prepare for new visions" (201–2). Feminists can build on the work of "the androcentric critical establishment" but should "follow the female strands of Joyce's experience farther, ask different questions, and assemble patterns that are organized by female experience" (6). A good deal of Scott's book is spent collating facts about the existences and activities of women whose lives touched Joyce's but otherwise risk falling into obscurity: Gretta Cousins (who barely registers in Ellmann's biography), Josephine Murray, and Harriet Shaw Weaver, who is reread as Joyce's most creative correspondent (93–94). The work is thus a revisionist account of Joyce's career that gives it new parameters and emphases.

In offering a revaluation of women in Joyce, Scott also raises the possibility of a revaluation of Joyce himself. This, in fact, is her book's greatest challenge. A history of the women Joyce knew can be viewed as a supplement to Ellmann; but the more radical implication of this new history is that Joyce himself may be up for judgment. Should feminists be writing about Joyce at all? Purists, Scott notes, "might argue that

James Joyce is disqualified by his gender . . . or that he has received far too much attention from the male establishment to require any compensatory effort from a feminist critic" (3). An interest in Joyce needs justification, given the abundance of women writers who have received insufficient attention. A similar anxiety manifests itself in Scott's next book on Joyce, in which she anticipates the objections of "feminist separatists": "Joyce has become the central star in a constellation of male modernists, a literary movement largely defined by men such as Ezra Pound, T. S. Eliot, Wyndham Lewis, and their male successors in academe. Joyce's difficulty and the remote critical discourses that have responded to it are offputting to advocates of an accessible, egalitarian feminism" (1987: 1–2). Karen R. Lawrence (2001: 164–65) recalls that feminist critics in the 1980s were divided between those who viewed Joyce as an ally and those for whom he epitomized modernist misogyny. The American critics Sandra Gilbert and Susan Gubar led the attack in the 1980s, viewing Joyce as the inaugurator of "a new patrilinguistic epoch" and casting suspicion on "feminist re-Joyceings" (1985: 535, 519). In this context, "Joyce and Feminism" names not a congruence but a hostility. This would be Lawrence's starting point in her essay of the same name for the *Cambridge Companion to James Joyce:* "Joyce and feminism—a difficult conjunction, a seemingly forced connection between a man who is quoted as saying, 'I hate women who know anything' and a movement that applauds women's intellects and rights. Perhaps the 'and' conjoins opposites, such as black and white?" (1990: 237).

Like Scott, Lawrence starts with a problem. By 1990, in fact, it would prove less arduous to bring Joyce and feminism together. But the very difficulty created by Joyce's feminist detractors created a productive tension in early feminist readings of him. In Scott's *Joyce and Feminism* Joyce is still under suspicion; and this distinguishes her work from other readings published in the same period. At the outset she announces that she expects her own readership to include "some who have little experience with Joyce but are interested in the female contributions to his literary and social climate—backgrounds that transcend Joyce in their significance" (1984: 2). *Backgrounds that transcend Joyce:* an unfamiliar idea, within a Joyce industry that Richard Brown, in the same period, found marked by "a partly autonomous language and field of reference" (1985: 2). In offering her study to different readerships—feminist as well as

Joycean—Scott achieves a certain decentering of Joyce himself. "Biographers and memoir-writers have noted Joyce's contacts with women," she writes, "but they have paid more attention to what the women did for Joyce than to the women themselves and their intellectual powers" (1984: 7). Perhaps, this suggests, what they did for themselves was as interesting as what they did for him. This emerges particularly strongly in Scott's discussion of Irish feminists, whose political thought and activism Scott shows as going well beyond what is suggested in *Stephen Hero* and the *Portrait*. Joyce's writing, she asserts, "only hints" at the independent and purposeful Irishwomen of his generation (44–45). Reflecting on Joyce's sisters (among whom Ellmann had glibly declared that "the personalities were less distinct" than among the males of the family [1982: 44]), Scott similarly finds that "the experiences of the working mother and the woman outside the home, especially in the workplace, are never depicted in Joyce's works" (1984: 61). All of this is unremarkable—until one compares it with Derrida's vision of Joyce, proclaimed in the same year as Scott's book, as an all-knowing intelligence that has anticipated anything we might say about it. Just as deconstruction was sealing its pact of mutual omniscience with Joyce, Scott's revisionist history was demonstrating how much Joyce—as a historically situated individual—did not know, or knew but did not find a place for in his art. The prospect is visible, here, of a particularizing attention that might offer us a different Joyce from Derrida's abstract intelligence or the icon of the critical industry.

The feminist criticism of the 1980s, however, was also much involved with European theory. In *James Joyce* Scott describes her own trajectory from an "Anglo-American tendency" focused on "the real women around Joyce" to an encounter with French feminist theory, "inevitable for a Joycean of my generation" (1987: xvi). Already visible is a movement beyond *Joyce and Feminism*, which becomes identified as a primarily "Anglo-American" book, while Scott's 1987 volume shows an increased focus on "French" themes, culminating in a reading of *Finnegans Wake* as feminine writing. In this respect it typifies trends that Lawrence sees as following from the Frankfurt symposium (2001: 167–68). The book is indeed a sign of the times. As an introductory volume, it participates in the popularization of feminist criticism (not least for an undergraduate audience). With peculiar directness, it uses a matrix to delineate the relations between Joyce and feminist criticism: Marxist feminists, Scott indicates, are prone to focus on the "realist" Joyce of *Dubliners* or the first half of *Ulysses*, while feminist mythographers and proponents of *écriture féminine* are aligned with *Finnegans Wake*. The chart graphically demonstrates the increasing professionalization and specialization of theoretical models. Theory can now be assigned and bracketed: its plurality is recognized and appropriately dispersed, rather than synthesized into the kind of unwieldy fusion typical of the 1970s. This is not a situation distinctive to feminist criticism, but rather a general condition of the more codified and streamlined entity that theory was becoming by the late 1980s.

Sixty years earlier, as Scott notes (1987: 104–5), Wyndham Lewis had aligned Joyce with the feminine and undermined his claim to classicism. We have now reached the point where that maneuver ceases to be an insult, and becomes a source of value. For Lawrence, writing at the end of the 1980s, the task is to wrest Joyce away from residual classicism or accusations of misogyny, and establish a more productive vision of him after a century of feminism. For Lawrence, as for Heath and MacCabe, Joyce's formal revolution has political point: "[A] catalogue of misogynistic images or female stereotypes in Joyce's work fails to account for his undermining of the grounds of representation" (1990: 240). Specifically, she finds in Joyce an analogy between the feminine and writing, which undercuts his less admirable lapses: "[T]he deconstruction of presences poses a relationship between the metaphor of woman and a writing practice that disrupts patriarchal signature and conventions. . . . [W]oman becomes the figure for illegitimacy, errancy, and forgery" (240–41). This, for Lawrence, is a good thing: for theory, of course, has effected an axiological inversion in which the errant, forged, or fictive become more trustworthy than their stolid opposites. Lawrence's repeated equation of the feminine with these forms of disruption (analogous, in fact, to Attridge's list of the qualities of the literary) clearly risks placing women in a familiar, ultimately demeaning role as that which escapes univocality and rationality. She recognizes that "the undecidability that characterizes 'feminine' writing might appear to reinscribe Woman in her old stereotypes," but believes that Joyce's late work defeats this problem in the play of its language (245). As with Attridge, a tacitly teleological evaluation of Joyce's works is present here. In the early fiction "the staging of the rebellion against the patriarchy exists still within some of its more dominant myths" (245). According to Lawrence, "[I]t was not until *Finnegans Wake* that Joyce wrote a whole book in which he tried to represent what could not be thought or possessed. . . . [a] book that so radically blurs the boundaries between inside and outside as well as the binary oppositions of male and female" (254). A theoretically informed feminism thus comes to offer another framework in which the *Wake* can be celebrated. Theory once more finds itself in Joyce.

This is true on a larger scale in Suzette A. Henke's *James Joyce and the Politics of Desire* (1990). The book confirms the emerging movement from "Anglo-American" to "French" modes of feminist thought, in which Joyce's later writing can be valorized as equivalent to *écriture féminine*. Like Scott and Lawrence, Henke sets her project against the view of Joyce as "a chauvinist author singularly devoted to projects of male linguistic mastery" (1990: 1), stressing Joyce's divergence from the classicist canon of the Men of 1914. Like *transition,* poststructuralism finds in Joyce a countermodernism: the stasis promoted by Eliot, Gilbert, and Levin is dissolved into mobility and kinesis. Henke disavows any "defence of Joyce as 'protofeminist'" (9), but her book is primarily an affirmation of his writing's ability to cross and confound gender identities: among her declared purposes is "to show how Joyce, in the course of his career, became such a revolutionary writer, forging new psychosexual subject-positions in a controversial discourse of desire" (10). Theory has great prominence in this project—not merely as an informing background, but as a constant presence in the text. Henke's evidence is taken as often from theory as from Joyce: the two discourses coexist in a continuum of reference. Thus, while discussing Molly Bloom, Henke writes: "Yearning for the metaphysical presence of (M)Other love, Molly transfers intra-psychic desire to the male penis/phallus/progenitor and seeks a 'substitutable signifier' for mammary/umbilical connection. Locked in oral fixation, she wants to ingest and assimilate the phallic presence that substitutes for a maternal breast. But the aetiology of such hysterical, all-consuming desire is melancholic—a regression from object-cathexis to the narcissistic oral phase of the libido" (131). This is only at the start of a whole page that continues in similar vein without citation from *Ulysses* itself. The details of Henke's interpretation, like any other, are debatable, but one may notice the way that theoretical writing and literary analysis have been collapsed together, to the benefit of the former. Theory is gradually becoming a semi-autonomous discourse that generates its own authority: it serves as an interpretive guarantee without the need of reference to Joyce's own writing. "Theory" here means a multitude of vocabularies and models: the psychoanalytic axis of Freud, Lacan, Cixous, and Kristeva, but also Derrida, Bakhtin, and Foucault as appropriate. The eclecticism and heavy bursts of theoretical artillery make for similarities with MacCabe's *Revolution of the Word*—though in a different political moment, with the shadow of Ronald Reagan replacing the memory of 1968, feminism has thoroughly displaced Leninism.

"A female story," Henke ultimately affirms, "dialogically emerges from Joyce's master narrative, appropriates its textual authority, and gradually deconstructs the linguistic codes essential to the logocentric and phallocentric discourse not only of 'dear dirty Dublin' but of western patriarchal culture" (212). Her book represents perhaps the apotheosis of its mode: the feminist appropriation of Joyce, performed with poststructuralist and psychoanalytic tools. Yet the work's theoretical ambition also makes it peculiarly abstract. What the approach conspicuously lacks is an account of the cultural particularity of gender in and around the times and places of Joyce's work. The intermittent attempt to sketch this background only emphasizes its absence. Henke's description of "a spiritually desiccated Ireland" (25) is almost impossible to substantiate; her references to "[p]ower relations, culturally inscribed in Edwardian consciousness" and "the psychosexual scripts that dominate 1904 Dublin" (110) provide little insight into the actual character of power relations or gender roles in turn-of-the-century Ireland. "Nineteenth-century Irish Catholicism" is mentioned but goes unexamined (71), and a colonial context is invoked through large gestures—"arrogant foreigners who ruthlessly exploit Mother Ireland and dupe her vulnerable farrow" (24)—that mimic, rather than analyze, the rhetoric at stake. In a word, history is thin. Close attention to style, voice, and tone is also displaced by the translation of plot and character into theoretical terms. As theory allegorizes Joyce, the cultural and textual particularities of his writing are obscured. Fritz Senn, as close a reader as Joyce has had, has commented on this development. An older "Anglo-Saxon" criticism, he notes, failed to engage with Joyce's language. In the age of theory "language, though given generous lip service, tends to be bypassed now for different reasons. At first it was not seen at all. Now that it has become Language (or its upstart twin, Discourse), it is abstracted out of our focus again" (1991: 87). Theory, left to its own devices, can produce a Joyce more abstract than Eliot's.

Yet other possibilities existed. One of the most proleptic works of the 1980s was Cheryl Herr's *Joyce's Anatomy of Culture* (1986), which drew not only on contemporary theory but also on extensive empirical research into the history of Irish newspapers, sermons, and popular entertainment. Herr argues for the sociality of Joyce's writing, its insistence on the construction of identity and the collective generation of meaning. Her analysis of "Circe" as the dramatization of this theme makes more systematic Kenner's insight into the pre-scripted character of the Joycean self, even as she builds on Ellmann's late claims for Joyce's politics. Herr's analysis seeks to restore concrete cultural reference; it also implies a certain displacement of Joyce himself in relation to the discourses of his time. "Joyce told his contemporaries nothing that was new," she insists: his writing's novelty lay in its "combination of coded elements" (1986: 84–85). The writer is decentered into a history whose voices he manipulates, but did not invent.

Herr's study suggested the beginning of a new kind of attention to historical detail. Much of her subsequent work falls under the rubric of cultural studies, and that discipline's influence can be discerned in the fin-de-millennium output of the Joyce industry. A collection like *Molly Blooms: A Polylogue on "Penelope" and Cultural Studies* (1994) represents a multivocal attempt to respond to the cultural density of Joyce's text: theory (Baudrillard, Benjamin, Bhabha) is combined with research into advertising and consumption. Of course, there is an ambiguity about each new contextualization: does it respond to Joyce, or reinvent him? Does the field of cultural studies resituate Joyce in his time, or remake him for our time? In practice the two may be inseparable. Several American critics have been increasingly candid about the "presentism" of their perspective: running discussions of Joyce into Don DeLillo (Herr 1994: 76–77) or Laurie Anderson (Dettmar 1996b); illustrating the politics of "Telemachus" with a *Doonesbury* cartoon (Cheng 1995: 163); concluding a discussion of "Penelope" with a report on greeting cards in 1990s New York (Leonard 1994: 229–31). One witnesses a loosening of context: an apparent willingness to juxtapose Joyce with any cultural instance, in the confidence that his work will respond by providing links to it. The electronic metaphor is pertinent, for the proliferation of contexts for Joyce has accompanied, and been encouraged by, the infinity of new imaginary spaces on the World Wide Web. Derrida's coinage "joyceware" (1984: 148) was prescient. Another cause of the increasingly open sense of context is pedagogical: for many lecturers, the resituation of Joyce alongside contemporary literature and popular culture has proved an effective way of stimulating student interest (Newman 1996). The very title of Florida University's annual conference, "Miami J'yce," is an instance of an increasingly relaxed attitude to Joyce, in which U.S.-based scholars freely translate him into an American idiom. Vicki Mahaffey writes that "Joyce is finely attuned to the way the diurnal rhythm of nightfall and sunrise is repeated in the names for the seasons, 'fall' and 'spring'" (1995: xv), seemingly unconcerned that Britain and Ireland share an un-American name for "Fall." More playfully, she likens the Odyssean trajectory to baseball, in which "victory can only be attained by coming home against resistance, by strenuous play coupled with cool-headed strategy" (xvi). When she notes the irony that the *Odyssey* was "penned by a man named 'homer,'" the main disappointment is that *The Simpsons* goes unmentioned.

This process of translation and recontextualization is part of what culture means—at least today, in a moment of unprecedented global connection and intellectual itinerancy. When Steven Connor writes that the name "James Joyce" signifies "a peripatetic global institution, a whole hermeneutic culture, a vast and ever-expanding enterprise of exposition and interpretation" (1996: 2), one may add that the greater part of this enterprise runs on American capital. In the second half of the twentieth century, the United States progressively became the paradigm for the global. In the same period it has also become the center of Joyce studies, to the point where American readers can use Joyce's work as the occasion for talking about their own culture. In an important sense, Joyce has become an American institution. Nor is he the first Irish emigré to whom this has happened. But the Irish in America, as Fintan O'Toole (1997) reminds us, have repeatedly returned to Ireland in a variety of ways. And at the turn of the millennium it was Ireland that once again came to claim the attention of Joyce's readers. With theory and the Joyce industry at the height of their powers, a sense has grown that the internationalization of Joyce—from Pound and Jolas to Kenner and Derrida—may have left something behind. Joyce, asserts Vincent Cheng, has been "canonized by an Academy that has chosen to construct a sanitized 'Joyce' whose contributions are now to be measured only by the standards of canonical High Modernism" (1995: 3). Emer Nolan is more specific: "The modernity to which Joyce responds . . . is not transnational or universal, and the major trends in Joyce criticism have occluded the particularity of Irish historical experience as it determines and is reflected in his fiction" (1995: xii).

The relation of theory to this state of affairs is ambiguous. Has it abetted a premature cosmopolitanization of Joyce's reputation, or does it provide the tools with which to interrogate just this depoliticizing view? In Andrew Gibson's view, the "re-historicization" of Joyce parts company with "the grandiosities of humanism and the abstractions of theory alike" (1997: 2). There is no necessary consensus in Ireland itself about the value of theory. But there is a powerful sense both in and beyond Ireland that the dialectic of national culture and international modernism has not yet been completed. The final chapter will reconsider the shifting status of Joyce in Ireland, which has recently culminated in a complex homecoming.

5

When He's at Home
Joyce's Reception in Ireland

> I thought I'd be better off here. I managed to sneak across in a small freighter. Thank God I can still pass for an Irishman.
> "James Joyce," in Flann O'Brien, *The Dalkey Archive*

In 1928 W. B. Yeats reported on the redesign of the Irish currency that he had overseen: "We might have chosen figures from the history of Ireland, saints or national leaders, but a decision of the Executive Council excluded modern men" (1964: 250). Seventy years later things had changed, and modernist, if no longer quite modern, men were evidently welcome on the Irish Republic's paper money. From September 1993 to the Republic's entry into the Eurozone on 1 January 2002, a portrait of James Joyce adorned the ten-pound note.

How are we to read this? A precedent is set by Graham Holderness, who has analyzed the image of Shakespeare that adorned the English twenty-pound note in the 1980s. The "currency of Shakespeare as a cultural token," Holderness proposes, "enhances the material worth of the promissory note; while the high value of the note itself confers a corresponding richness on the symbol of high art and national culture. . . . The fortunate holder of a Shakespearean banknote possesses both monetary wealth and aesthetic richness" (1988: xi–xii). In the case of Shakespeare, one can see the cultural materialist's point: culture is being used to legitimate capital, and as a way of signifying the kind of value into which the note may be translated. Joyce has, to be sure, inspired his own critical industry, which the Modern Language Association has frequently declared second only to Shakespeare's (Bérubé 1992: 323), and Colin MacCabe is just one among many to have called him "the major writer in English since Shakespeare" (1979: 3). But what is most provoking about the comparison is the thought of Joyce occupying a similar role in Ireland's historical imagery—even its contemporary self-image—to that of Shakespeare in England. A few decades earlier, the image of Joyce on the banknotes would have been unthinkable, a bad joke. In this chapter I want to pursue what has changed, and how that banknote became possible, since Joyce left Ireland behind. I shall conclude by considering the important critical work that has also—with very different aims—recently urged us to think of Joyce and Ireland in the same frame.

Certainly Ireland, and Dublin in particular, have loomed large for Joyce's readers. When Robert Nicholson, the director of Joyce's Tower in Sandycove, declares that "The city of Dublin, perhaps more than any scholarly work of reference, is the most valuable document we have to help us appreciate the intricate craftsmanship of *Ulysses*" (1988: vii), he speaks for a respected critical tradition. The Joycean remark I traced in chapter 2, namely that Dublin if destroyed ought to be reconstructible from the pages of *Ulysses,* has ballasted the kind of research inaugurated by Richard M. Kain's use of newspaper files and *Thom's Dublin Directory* in the 1940s. "*Ulysses* criticism," in Bernard Benstock's words, "has never been quite the same since" (1991: 10). Yet if Dublin has inevitably been a priority for Joyceans, Joyce has not always been one for Dubliners. Reports of Dublin's attitude toward Joyce frequently describe a mocking, if affectionate, skepticism. Marvin Magalaner and Richard M. Kain's generalization is typical: "The Irish invariably find esoteric interpretations absurd. They prefer to regard their Jimmy as a somewhat annoying variant of the local bad boy, disrespectful, mocking, and yet withal sentimental" (1956: 209). In accounts of Joyce's Irish reception outrage often coexists with amused familiarity, an ambivalent mixture of pride in the local lad made good and surprise that he has managed to pull so many foreigners' legs. At times these reactions are not easily disentangled. Richard Ellmann has written that Dublin's disdain for *Ulysses* was mixed with a certain fascination: "A tremor went through quite a few of his countrymen, who feared the part [Joyce] might have assigned them. 'Are you in it?' or 'Am I in it?' they asked the few people known to have copies" (1982: 530). The profound imbrication of city and book—the possibility that one might have become a literary character—produces a complex reaction that continues to resonate in the contemporary celebration of Bloomsday. Even Shane Leslie, one of the fiercest early reviewers, displays a curious ambivalence, stressing the importance of the Irish and Catholic culture sadly unavailable to the book's foreign enthusiasts: "Many pages are saturated with Catholic lore and citation, which must tend to make the book more or less unintelligible to critics, who are neither of Catholic or Dublin origin." Only a Dubliner, Leslie implies, is fully competent to repudiate the novel. This would not take long, though: Leslie assures the readers of the *Dublin Review* that *Ulysses* "may safely be repudiated, before reading, by the Irish people, who certainly do not get either the rulers or writers they deserve" (1970a: 202, 201).

Our Irish Cruelty: The Sinthome in the Devil Era

The parallel between writers and rulers is ironic. The Irish Free State emerged simultaneously with *Ulysses*, but offered a different vision of Ireland. The Minister of Home Affairs Kevin O'Higgins described his generation as "probably the most conservative minded revolutionaries that ever put through a successful revolution" (Lee 1989: 105), a judgment endorsed by the historian David Fitzpatrick, who asserts that between 1916 and 1922 "social and political institutions were turned upside down, only to revert to full circle upon the establishment of the Irish Free State" (1977: 232). Terence Brown judges that the Free State "showed a prudent acquiescence before the inherited realities of the Irish social order and a conservative determination to shore up aspects of that order by repressive legislation where it seemed necessary" (1985: 14), while Dermot Keogh stresses the religious character of the new nation: "[T]he political climate of Saorstát Éireann suited and reassured members of a Catholic hierarchy which had lived through the dangers of the revolutionary period. . . . There was general political approval for the censorious attitude of the hierarchy towards sexual morality" (1994: 28). In the wake of what Keogh, following O'Higgins, calls "the conservative revolution," artistic innovation and freedom of expression were not official priorities. The country's first leader, William T. Cosgrave, said in 1924 that he had never entered the Abbey Theatre, an admission that would be repeated by Eamon de Valera during his own long period in power (Hussey 1995: 475). Gemma Hussey goes as far as to say that "It would perhaps be better to draw a veil over the early cultural experiences of twentieth-century independent Ireland" (471). Joyce himself was equally unimpressed, if we are to believe the report of Arthur Power: "Now I hear that since the Free State came in there is less freedom. The Church has made inroads everywhere, so that we are in fact becoming a bourgeois nation, with the Church supplying the aristocracy . . . and I do not see much hope for us intellectually" (Power 1974: 65). Julia Carlson sums up this view: "In the late twenties and early thirties the Irish Free State was a nation intent on purifying itself, and its people were deeply suspicious of artists and intellectuals" (1990: 8).

Yet censorship of Joyce was never as organized in Ireland as in the United Kingdom and the United States. "To his Irish countrymen he is still obscene and very likely mad," writes Ellmann at the start of *James Joyce*, adding that "they were the last of nations to lift the ban on *Ulysses*" (1982: 3). "This," retorts Bernard McGinley, "is truly an Irish fact" (1996: 34). John Ardagh's claim that "neither *Ulysses* nor any other of Joyce's works was ever formally banned in Ireland" (1994: 238) is also not quite accurate: the posthumous *Stephen Hero* was banned in November 1944, the year that Theodore Spencer published it. But *Ulysses* itself never made it on to the list of proscribed books maintained by the Censorship Board after 1929 (McGinley 1996: 45; Arnold 1991: 65–66). Carlson, a historian of Irish censorship, notes the irony in this (1990: 160), while Keogh calls it paradoxical (1994: 31). Michael Adams's history of censorship does record an early de facto ban: an ad hoc blacklist kept by Customs officials, whose existence would later be denied, operated an "exclusion order" on *Ulysses*. Yet this "was withdrawn in 1932, and the book was never banned by the Censorship Board—contrary to expectations" (1968: 31). The Customs blacklist, Adams informs us, was "based on matter which had previously been detained under the 1876 Act [the Customs Consolidation Act of 1876, a British practice retained by the Irish Free State]; there had been, for instance, an 'exclusion order' in respect of James Joyce's *Ulysses*, and this order was still in force in the Free State after the passing of the first Censorship of Publications Act [1929], and not allowed to lapse until around the year 1934" (171–72). The initial exclusion of *Ulysses*, then, was a reflection of *British* law, which was not maintained by the Free State once its own Censorship of Publications Act was in operation.

For the most part disapproval of Joyce was less official. Next to England, opines Bruce Arnold, "Ireland had more subtle ways of registering its reservations" (1991: 66). Hugh Kenner notes the nuances: "For more than ten years . . . *Ulysses* could not legally be brought into any English-speaking country in the northern hemisphere save Ireland, where they never banned it but relied on booksellers not to stock it" (1987b: 2). The Censorship Board did not take action without the initial spur of public protest (Ardagh 1994: 238), and the sheer scarcity of *Ulysses* made it unlikely for a copy, let alone the three copies required by the board, to fall into the hands of zealous citizens wanting to see it censored. Shane Leslie's disquiet in 1922 was tempered by the knowledge that *Ulysses* was an elite publication, unlikely to have a practical effect on a mass readership. In September he reassuringly remarked that "as the edition is limited and the price is rapidly ascending in the 'curious' market, it will remain out of reach of the bulk of the author's fellow-countrymen" (1970a: 201); a month later he declared himself "glad that the limited copies and their exaggerated cost will continue to prevent the vast majority of the reading public from sampling even faintly such unpleasant ware" (1970b: 210). The Censorship of Publications Act itself advised the board to take into consideration "the class of reader . . . which may reasonably be expected to read such a book or edition" (Carlson 1990: 4). The "class of reader" who had obtained a copy of *Ulysses* in this period was not likely to turn himself or herself in. J. J. Horgan, reporting on the earliest effects of the bill in September 1930, remarked that "very few people in Ireland read any modern books at all, and . . . those who do are not likely to take the trouble of acting as literary informers to the Censorship Board" (T. Brown 1985: 76). But as John Ryan's memoir indicates, the book remained out of public view: "[I]n 'with it' Rathgar of the nineteen-thirties the smart thing was to smuggle it in wrapped in the dust jacket of Mrs Beaton's Jam Making Recipes or some such fare" (1987: 51). Between 1935 and 1955, according to Aidan Higgins, "*Ulysses* was hard to come by: it was not banned but neither was it for sale in any of the bookshops—a very 'Irish' paradox, surely" (1970: 57).

Anecdotal accounts testify to the unofficial censorship of Joyce in the period following passage of the act. The writer and arts administrator Mervyn Wall, born in 1908, recounts that "In my early twenties I had bought myself *Dubliners* and *Portrait of the Artist*. One day they disappeared from my bookshelves in my bedroom. I have no doubt but that my father burnt them" (Carlson 1990: 9). Another novelist, Brian Moore (born 1921), recalls: "My father, who was a great reader, said to me once, 'James Joyce is a sewer.' He never read him, but that was the attitude" (112). John Broderick describes a slightly more official form of prohibition: "[T]he Jesuits kept them locked up in drawers where he was educated" (47–48). This detail is corroborated by John Ardagh: "[T]he Church sometimes did its own censorship. At Clongowes College, which Joyce described so sharply in *Portrait of the Artist as a Young Man*, the Jesuits in charge would sometimes confiscate pupils' copies, even as late as the 1960s, and his name could not be spoken" (1994: 238). Bernard McGinley points to evidence in an early *James Joyce Quarterly* that *Ulysses* was "effectively 'not available' in Dublin in the 1960s" (1996: 45), and the writer Seán Dunne recalls that *Ulysses* "was usually available only by special order from Dublin bookshops in the early 1960s" (Keogh 1994: 258, 437).

Despite the absence of *Ulysses* from the blacklist of the Censorship Board, then, there is plenty of evidence of hostility toward Joyce in independent Ireland after 1922. What Richard Kearney calls the "self-righteous nationalism" (1988: 259) of the new state has become almost a straw target. Even Roy Foster, no enthusiast for nationalism, has admitted that "The rigorous conservatism of the Irish Free State has become a cliché" (1989: 516). David Cairns and Shaun Richards describe the first thirty years of independence as "three decades of financial, economic, and social conservatism, in combination with cultural attitudes which, viewing the farmers as embodying the essence of the national ideal, sacrificed the material and cultural well-being of other groups to their interests" (1988: 139). "Honour thy farmer and my litters," *Finnegans Wake* mocks (Joyce 1992b: 413). The centrality of what Terence Brown calls "the populist rural values of the new state" (1985: 168) is plain from de Valera's notorious and oft-quoted Saint Patrick's Day Broadcast of 1943, which pictured "The Ireland which we have dreamed of" as "a land whose countryside would be bright with cosy homesteads, whose fields and villages would be joyous with the sounds of industry, with the romping of sturdy children, the contests of athletic youths, the laughter of comely maidens; whose firesides would be forums for the wisdom of serene old age" (Lee 1989: 334). Joyce's parodies of the extravagant lists of Celtic pastoral two decades earlier might have seemed the last word on such oration, but from the veteran of 1916 this mode was still potent. The de Valera decades stretched from Fianna Fail's victory in 1932 to the premier's successful bid for the presidency in 1959. Gemma Hussey expresses a widespread sense of the relative stasis of these years: "Through the 1930s and 1940s, and right up to the early 1960s, Ireland seemed asleep: a low level of economic activity, a gradually increasing unemployment and emigration rate, a stultifying censorship of literature and the arts, and a seemingly immortal old man in a long black coat, peering short-sightedly through schoolmasterish round glasses, were the dominant features" (1995: 158). For Declan Kiberd the period around World War II was one of "underdevelopment," in which Ireland's wartime neutrality encouraged an extended introversion "well into the 1950s" (1995: 473). "Post-war Ireland," recalls Anthony Cronin, "was a repressive, puritanical place in which even old-fashioned European liberalism seemed a dangerously innovative doctrine. There were regular condemnations of non-existent Communists and almost equally invisible free thinkers by the bishops, whose Lenten Pastorals, sometimes occupying two whole pages, were reprinted in full in the newspapers. When not occupied with the latest red scare, these were still filled with condemnations of the evil forces at large in modern life, such as Hollywood films, English Sunday newspapers, lounge bars and dance halls" (1989: 157).

What place did Joyce have in such a society? One answer is that his disdainful rejection of Ireland continued to resonate as a wise decision. "Exile," Cairns and Richards assert, "seemed to offer the only space in which critical thinking on Ireland and its identity could occur" (1988: 134). Certainly it appealed to Samuel Beckett, who famously chose France at war over Ireland at peace. John McGahern (born 1935), whose novel *The Dark* was controversially banned in 1965, expresses both understanding of and frustration with this position when he recalls that "The whole thing that I really resented when I was young was that you had to go into exile if you were an Irish writer, like Joyce and Beckett" (Carlson 1990: 64). But Joyce also continued to cast a long shadow in the literary world of the city he had left behind. It is instructive to examine, in turn, two specific milieus: the Protestant survivors of the Literary Revival, and the younger generations of Catholics.

W. B. Yeats represents for many the quintessential Irish poet. But to numerous observers his Anglo-Irishness put his nationality and allegiance in question (T. Brown 1988: 80). This uncertainty comes through in his response to *Ulysses*. In March 1922, a month after the publication of the complete novel, Yeats wrote to Olivia Shakespear: "I am reading the new Joyce—I hate it when I dip here and there but when I read it in the right order I am much impressed. However I have but read some thirty pages in that order. It has our Irish cruelty and also our kind of strength and the Martello Tower pages are full of beauty. A cruel playful mind like a great soft tiger cat—I hear, as I read, the report of the rebel sergeant in '98: 'Oh he was a fine fellow, a fine fellow. It was a pleasure to shoot him'" (1970: 284).

Yeats hates the book when reading it one way (dipping in at random), but is much impressed when reading it in another (consecutively). Despite this admiration, he seems barely able to bring himself to read it consecutively. His aesthetic response to *Ulysses* is thoroughly split. But his response also ranges out into an enigmatic sequence of images. First he admits Joyce to a collective Irish identity to which he himself already belongs: "It has *our* Irish cruelty and also *our* kind of strength" (my emphasis). The implication would appear to be that Yeats, the grand old man of the Revival, is in a position to judge who else has produced authentically Irish work, and that he has granted Joyce that honor. Today, in popular celebrations of Joyce's work produced for Bloomsday, Yeats's comment on Joyce's Irishness is still sometimes reproduced out of context. The implication, again, seems to be of a shared identity and mission.

Yet Yeats's subsequent words place all this in question. The beauty he finds in *Ulysses* coexists with cruelty, and behind the text he detects "A cruel playful mind like a great soft tiger cat." The political significance of this extraordinary image is clarified by Yeats's startling claim that the novel reminds him of "the rebel sergeant in '98," who happily shot a man he thought of as a fine fellow. What Yeats has certainly read of *Ulysses* is "Telemachus." This chapter, as recent postcolonial critics have been quick to point out, uses the martial setting of the Martello Tower to stage a confrontation between apostate Catholic Irishman (Dedalus), Anglo-Irish Catholic (Mulligan), and the English visitor Haines. It is in this encounter that Yeats appears to have found the ruthless tone of the rebel—or the tiger, toying with its prey and liable to strike at any moment. In describing *Ulysses* so vividly, Yeats remains ambiguous. At one moment he claims Joyce's accomplishment as akin to his own. Yet the cruel tiger cat and the rebel that are his images for Joyce have an otherness, a sense of threat, of which Yeats himself is wary. This is subtly analogous to Yeats's relation to the Catholic political movement, which was, at the time of his letter, in the process of assuming power in the South of Ireland. To this movement, too, Yeats's relation is ambiguous. He himself has been a republican and has sought to forge national images and narratives; but with his Ascendancy affiliations he is a kind of alien in the emerging new state, and will soon enough be orating indignantly on the rights of the Protestant race in the Senate.

John Eglinton's writings on Joyce confirm this analysis. Writing for the *Dial* in 1929, Eglinton identifies his difference from Joyce, whom he describes as a "key-personality" and "the idol of a good many of the young men of the new Ireland." Eglinton's reasoning demands quotation in full:

> He has, apparently, abjured Ireland; the subjects of all his ridicule are Irish; moreover, it is improbable that when the new censorship begins to operate, the mind of the youth will have any but furtive opportunities to form itself upon Joyce's writings. Joyce is, none the less, in several respects a champion spirit in the new national situation. In him, for the first time, the mind of Catholic Ireland triumphs over the Anglicism of the English language, and expatiates freely in the element of a universal language: an important achievement, for what has driven Catholic Ireland back upon the Irish language is the ascendancy in the English language of English literature, which, as a Catholic clergyman once truly asserted, is "saturated with Protestantism." In Joyce, perhaps for the first time in an Irish writer, there is no faintest trace of Protestantism: that is, of the English spirit. . . . [W]e are obliged to admit that in Joyce literature has reached for the first time in Ireland a complete emancipation from Anglo-Saxon ideals (1970: 459).

Eglinton, writing in the first decade following the completion of *Ulysses*, outlines a view of the book that would remain largely alien to the critical traditions I have surveyed in the previous four chapters. Pound's internationalism, Eliot's abstraction, the humanism of Budgen and Ellmann, Kennerian technicalities, even *écriture féminine*—none of these crucial moments in the reading of Joyce had acknowledged the force of the Irish Protestant view, in which Joyce terminates Anglo-Ireland. Eglinton makes explicit what is latent in Yeats: a suspicion that the ostensibly cosmopolitan Joyce in reality represents the new Catholic majority, a toppling of Anglo-Ireland's aesthetic supremacy to match the crumbling of its political hegemony.

He thus lights unerringly on what has more recently become such an insistent issue in discussions of Joyce, namely his relation to Ireland, England, and nationality. Joyce is a "champion spirit in the new national situation" of Ireland because that new situation, in the late 1920s, is one of Catholic dominance. For Eglinton, Joyce remains the only writer of English whose prose truly reflects a Catholic mind. As Eglinton would add three years later, "Joyce is, as all his writings show, Roman in mind and soul" (1990: 34). The victory of *Ulysses* is achieved not by returning to the Irish language but by wresting the English tongue away from the English mind, reinhabiting the language in the name of Ireland. In an audacious reversal, Joyce recolonizes the language of the colonizer, making it over into an idiom emancipated from "Anglo-Saxon ideals." This has become a familiar argument in recent postcolonial criticism, yet in the 1920s such an argument was novel—and, most strikingly, it was made by a Protestant for whom the Anglo-Saxon ideals were congenial. Most remarkable of all, perhaps, is the analogy that Eglinton perceives between Joyce and the new Irish Free State. Joyce is commonly viewed as having maintained a disdainful distance from the new nation. Asked if he intended to return to an independent Ireland, Joyce reportedly replied, "So that I might declare myself its first enemy?" (Ellmann 1982: 399). Yet for Eglinton *Ulysses* speaks very precisely for the new state, in a distinctively Irish Catholic idiom.

By these lights, it would seem that Protestants in the Free State should handle Joyce with care. They formed a religious and social minority; in Roy Foster's words, they represented "a dwindling and infinitesimal proportion" of the population (1989: 534). The 1926 Free State census recorded that only 7.4 percent of the populace was Protestant, and this figure was set to fall further (T. Brown 1985: 107, 309). The Catholicism of the Free State was a given. Although Protestant representation in the Senate was carefully weighted, the dwindling Anglo-Irish minority found themselves outsiders from the dominant culture sponsored by the new state. In such circumstances, a Joyce as aggressively Catholic as the one Eglinton read would be a threatening cultural symbol: yet another sign of the exclusive supremacy of Irish Ireland. But not every Protestant reading of Joyce took this line. Others were developing an argument for pluralism, in which Joyce could again be used as an example. In fact Eglinton had hinted at this argument himself in pointing out that with the imminent establishment of the Censorship Board, Joyce would be hard to get hold of in the Free State. In a new twist, then, Joyce became a case of the artistic freedom that must be defended *against* Catholic Ireland. Joyce's disciple Samuel Beckett, who attacked Free State censorship in the 1930s (1983: 84–88), is a case in point. George Russell provides a more sustained example. In 1923 he revived the *Irish Statesman* as an organ of liberal Protestantism, publishing attacks on censorship and seeking a pluralistic conception of national identity. Russell's plea of 1926 is characteristic: "We do not want uniformity in our culture or our ideals, but the balancing of our diversities in a wide tolerance" (T. Brown 1985: 120). In Richard Kearney's view, the journal "persistently brought home to its readers that the Irish national community was a pluralistic one which also contained a richly deserving Anglo-Irish component. . . . [It] was determined to keep Ireland free from self-righteous nationalism by keeping it open to cultural diversity at home and abroad" (1988: 258–59). Given the parlous status of Protestantism in the South of Ireland, the plea for pluralism was clearly expedient as well as honorable.

Russell saw a wider recognition of the value of the Literary Revival as, in Terence Brown's words, "the best hope for a resolution of differences between Irishmen. If, he believed, it could be whole-heartedly recognized by all that men and women of Anglo-Irish stock had contributed through their literary and dramatic works to Irish regeneration . . . then political differences in Ireland might lose their sharp distinctiveness, softened in the beneficent glow of culture" (1985: 123). Russell turned to Joyce as a case for his pluralism. In a 1928 essay he used *Ulysses* as an instance of the rashness of censorship, arguing that the prohibition of such a book only backfired on the censor (1990: 126). In December of the same year he granted Joyce's *Anna Livia Plurabelle* a glowing notice. Where Eglinton stresses Joyce's religious alterity, Russell puts aside this difference and seeks to express sympathy with Joyce's project, calling the work "more astonishing than anything Joyce has yet written.... [W]hatever else he may be, he is a virtuoso in the use of words" (1970: 396). Terence Brown writes that "there is ... something poignant about [Russell]'s mystified efforts to comprehend the later work of Joyce ... for which clearly he felt a temperamental distaste, within his optimistic theory about the continued vitality of the Irish Literary Renaissance" (1985: 126)—particularly as certain Catholic critics were beginning to claim the *Work in Progress* as exemplary of Catholic tradition. They effectively agreed with Eglinton, not Russell, though they shared the background of neither.

After the *Irish Statesman* had folded again in 1930, writes Michael Adams, "Its viewpoint was maintained in a somewhat modified form by the *Irish Times*" (1968: 65). The latter organ, Unionist until after independence, was generally critical of the Irish government (Keogh 1994: 126, 161). The paper presented itself as standing, in a Protestant tradition, for liberality and free speech in or against the new state. It was no coincidence that, in the words of Magalaner and Kain, it "remained a champion of Joyce, blaming his exile on the narrow attitude of the Free State toward art, reviewing instalments of the *Work in Progress,* and defending even these last stages of his career on the basis of the artist's right to express his message regardless of the public" (1956: 296). In the 1920s and early 1930s the newspaper quoted both Yeats and Russell as praising Joyce's genius; in 1933 and 1934 it complained about the Free State's illiberal failure to accommodate Joyce; and in 1939 the newspaper's reviewer boldly declared Joyce's last work "endlessly exciting" (296). The paper appears to have operated in these decades on the assumption that to the marooned Anglo-Irish dissident the Free State's enemy was a friend. A late, graphic demonstration of this pattern occurred in 1958, when the stage play *Bloomsday* was withdrawn for its affront to the moral majority (the archbishop of Dublin having been asked to open the show with a votive mass) (Keogh 1994: 238–39). When the *Irish Times* complained at this latest censorship, the furious Father Alfred O'Rahilly accused it of representing the "outlook of our Protestant, and also perhaps of our agnostic-liberal, fellow-citizens" (239). In a paradox that Eglinton had noted thirty years earlier, what some of the Anglo-Irish saw as

Joyce's Catholic authenticity did not make him a favorite of the Catholic state.

This was one reason for Joyce's appeal to a younger, Catholic-born literary generation—for whom, however, he served a contradictory double role. On the one hand, as Eglinton implied, Joyce was seen to represent Catholic Ireland in a way that Yeats could not. The reclamation—or recommunication—of the apostate is a persistent note in Catholic responses. Thomas MacGreevy's *Exagmination* essay boldly reclaims Joyce for a Catholic tradition of European scope: "To an intelligent Irishman and to Mr. Joyce least of all, Catholicism is never a matter of standing on one leg. It is not a pose, it is fundamental" (1961: 121). Mac-Greevy makes room for Joyce by loosening the image of Catholicism, stressing the creed's darkness and internal dissonance: the Free State's apparatchiks, he avers, fail to understand that "Catholicism in literature has never been merely lady-like" (123). Later Catholic commentators have been equally unwilling to disengage the writer from the faith. For John Ryan "Joyce was quintessentially an Irishman to the extent that Wilde, Shaw or Yeats could never be. This quality was the great source of his genius" (1970: 14). For Patrick Kavanagh, writes John Wilson Foster, "one could not be Irish and not a Catholic" (1991: 256). Hence Kavanagh's claim that "the outstanding quality in Joyce is his Catholicism or anti-Protestantism. . . . [W]hatever the defects of Catholicism, he saw that Protestantism was a compendium of all those defects" (1970: 49). Niall Montgomery is of the same mind: not only is Joyce "an Irish Catholic . . . the product of a Catholic school," but his work "comes at the full glory of Protestant civilization" (1970: 62). What is striking is the polemical character of these statements. All these writers could be said to be suspicious of the Irish state; in some ways they represented an enlightened alternative to it. Yet they also voice some of the most nationalistic praise of Joyce ever recorded. Scorn for Anglo-Ireland outweighs disaffection with Catholic Ireland. Whatever Joyce's attitude toward the Catholic Church, they are keen to draw out his difference from, and superiority to, Protestantism. In their own way these literary voices already indicate later positions in postcolonial criticism, in which Joyce would no longer be perceived as "holding the liberal centre" (Platt 1998: 7) but rather as a political writer whose instinctive target was the Anglo-Irish. No wonder Eglinton had been disconcerted.

And yet, simultaneously, Joyce's appeal for Dublin's literati crucially relied on his *resistance* to the shibboleths of church and nation: he offered a totemic alternative to the official culture. "Many intellectuals," asserts Dermot Keogh, "felt themselves ground to bits in de Valera's new Ireland" (1994: 75). The testimonies of Wall, Moore, and Broderick show that Joyce was viewed as unacceptable by much of the preceding generation, and remained a somewhat scandalous name until at least the 1960s. According to Anthony Cronin, familiarity with Joyce's work in the 1930s was a badge of alterity for intellectuals poised indecisively between the dominant culture and its repudiation: "You were in an ambiguous, not to say dishonest position . . . a conformist among other conformists. . . . But yet you knew about modern art and literature. You had read most of the great moderns and, above all, you had read James Joyce. That was what marked you out as different, the joke you shared against the rabblement of which you were otherwise a part" (1989: 49). Thomas MacGreevy—an "ardent Catholic" (Knowlson 1996: 90), "nationally minded" (Kiberd 1995: 462), and eventually director of the National Gallery—nonetheless "could not bear some of the increasingly stifling features" of the Free State (Knowlson 1996: 91). Cronin describes a similar unease among students of University College Dublin in the 1930s, where Vivien Mercier recalls an especially vibrant "Joyce cult" among the "overwhelmingly Catholic" undergraduates (1948: 296). Cronin presents UCD as the site of a skeptical dissent unusual during the de Valera period: "Only the intellectuals felt uncomfortable, for it was they who were most irked by the Catholic triumphalism, the pious philistinism, the Puritan morality and the peasant or *petit bourgeois* outlook of the new state. . . . It is impossible to exaggerate the importance of Joyce in their view of things" (1989: 48–49). Joyce's work thus took on a political or protopolitical significance in the Ireland where it remained taboo. In Benedict Kiely's words, "all the sideswipes that the young Joyce had made at repression and obscurantism seemed well justified in the 1940s when the repressions of a silly literary censorship were at their worst. . . . [He] was attacking not the city which he loved and celebrated but a narrow group of narrow minds that one could easily identify as being still with us" (1970: 237).

The paradoxes are dense here. Protestants (Russell, Yeats) alienated by Joyce's "Catholicism" nevertheless pressed his case against the Catholic state that he shunned. The Free State itself was aggressively Catholic but incorporated a ruralist Celtic mythos partially bequeathed to it by the largely Protestant Literary Revival (J. W. Foster 1991: 253). Catholic writers (MacGreevy, Kavanagh, Kiely) claimed Joyce as one of their own against that Protestant remnant—but echoed Russell and Yeats in siding with Joyce against the Catholic state. In this context, one can understand Brendan Kennelly's blurred invocation of "Protholics and Cathestants" (Kiberd 1995: 424). As the Christmas dinner in the *Portrait* demonstrates, there is no necessarily intrinsic connection between nationalism and a Catholic Church that had excommunicated republicans. In 1925 the future Taoiseach Seán Lemass declared that at every chance of independence for the Irish people, "the full political power of the [Catholic] Church was flung against them, and forced them back" (Lee 1989: 160). But in the mid twentieth century, Ireland's claim on Joyce was that he had given voice to the new reality of a Catholic nation. Terence Brown has demonstrated how frequently Irish responses to Joyce are enabled by the countervailing example of Yeats, who is impatiently regarded not only as an Ascendancy voice but as irredeemably backward-looking. In 1962 Sean O'Faolain introduced Joyce to the debate, putting the choice starkly: "There is no longer any question of dishing up local colour (The Noble Peasant is as dead as the Noble Savage. Poems about fairies and leprechauns, about misted lakes, old symbols of national longing, are over and done with). We need to explore Irish life with an objectivity never hitherto applied to it—and in this Joyce rather than Yeats is our inspiration" (T. Brown 1988: 81). By the early 1960s, Brown suggests, Yeats was considered "a magnificent anachronism . . . [whose] imaginative idealism could not greatly affect writers in a more prosaic age" (82). As Thomas Kinsella put it in 1966, "[Joyce's] stomach, unlike Yeats's, is not turned by what he sees shaping the new Ireland: the shamrock lumpen proletariat, the eloquent and mean-spirited tribe of Dan. Daniel O'Connell or de Valera or Paudeen do not deter him from his work; they are his subjects. He is the first major Irish voice to speak for Irish reality since the death of the Irish language" (83). For a series of Catholic writers, then, Joyce is a realistic native voice, an exemplary figure for Catholic Ireland—even as he also notably exemplifies religious and political refusal. The paradox is one that contemporary postcolonialist criticism, which includes both a liberal hostility to church and censor and a partisan affiliation to the Catholic majority against the Ascendancy caste, continues to inhabit.

The most vivid and protracted response to Joyce was that of another UCD graduate, Brian O'Nolan, who—as the novelist Flann O'Brien and the columnist Myles na gCopaleen—simultaneously assumed Joyce's mantle as laureate of the Catholic petit bourgeoisie, reprised his skepticism about the state, and struggled with his literary legacy. O'Nolan reportedly spent his life fretting in Joyce's shadow, a man under the influence in more senses than one, whom a fellow *Irish Times* columnist once called "James Joyce's literary foster child" (Cronin 1989: 176). In Anthony Cronin's view, O'Nolan's natural subject matter had already been annexed by the master: "When O'Nolan embarked on the writing of his first novel the great modernist was still alive in Paris . . . maintaining his planetary distance from Ireland and its problems, but perpetually visible in its skies all the same. . . . Joyce posed a problem for [O'Nolan]; indeed there is a sense in which he admitted this in one way or another over and over again" (ix). In a bitterly comic anecdote Donagh MacDonagh recalls how O'Nolan acquired his copy of *Ulysses:* "He stole the first volume and as the second was of no use to me I gave it to him. He never forgave me" (49). Myles na gCopaleen's column mentioned Joyce almost a hundred times, often half-seriously attacking his work (Powell 1971). With his string of pseudonyms and squirtscreen of fabrications, O'Nolan was always a divided figure: at once metafictional novelist and civil servant, suburban Catholic and urbane satirist, an expert in Gaelic whose *An Béal Bocht* (*The Poor Mouth*) lambastes the cult of the Western peasantry. His attitude toward Joyce is that of a Catholic intellectual with a split view of the independent nation: frustration at Joyce's abandonment of it coexists with a desire to follow his critical, parodic path.

Not only did O'Nolan's writing persistently recall Joyce's, but he also periodically claimed personal connections. These stretched from his claim to have authored an interview with John Joyce (Ellmann 1982: 747) to his late assertion that he had "met [Joyce] in Paris several times" (Cronin 1989: 247), a fabulation more imaginative than most of Joyce's own. In 1950 O'Nolan told the director of London's Institute of Contemporary Arts that Joyce had "asked me some years ago to make some confidential inquiries on business and family matters," but refused to let the correspondence be displayed, claiming that "I don't think it would be proper to exhibit them publicly" (Costello and van de Kamp 1987: 24). There is little reason to believe that these letters exist. Yet while asserting his literary and personal proximity in this way, O'Nolan also never ceased to resent the association. It is a sign of his continuing entanglement with his predecessor's name that in 1951 John Ryan asked O'Nolan to edit a special Joyce issue of his literary review *Envoy*. This venture was itself an exemplary attempt to think beyond the cultural parameters of independent Ireland. As Gerry Smyth points out, *Envoy* presented national questions as "incidental" and claimed that its writers took nationality for granted; the Joyce issue itself was a departure that would not have been countenanced by Sean O'Faolain's more earnest journal *The Bell* (Smyth 1998: 118). That O'Nolan agreed to be guest editor demonstrates his own acknowledgment of his inseparability from Joyce. That his own editorial likened Joyce to a man locked in a railway carriage, "resentfully drinking somebody else's whiskey" (O'Brien 1991: 173) and not realizing it was stuck in a tunnel is a sign of his unending resentment. Opining that "all true blasphemers must be believers" (169), O'Nolan chooses to stress Joyce's continued entanglement with Catholicism: "It seems to me that Joyce emerges, through curtains of salacity and blasphemy, as a truly fear-shaken Irish Catholic, rebelling not so much against the Church but against its near-schism Irish eccentricities, its pretence that there is only one Commandment, the vulgarity of its edifices, the shallowness and stupidity of many of its ministers. His revolt, noble in itself, carried him away" (174). Joyce is at once claimed as fellow Catholic, respected for his healthy skepticism, and chided for his egotistic overreaction to Ireland.

The portrait owes much to O'Nolan's own private agon with Joyce: he is loath to praise him unreservedly, and keen to establish that the master never really escaped the problematic inhabited by his successor. A like motive informs O'Nolan's last novel, *The Dalkey Archive* (1964), whose protagonist, Mick Shaughnessy—like his creator a Catholic civil servant with a touch of the artist about him—hears a rumour that Joyce is alive, and finds him working behind the bar in a seaside resort north of Dublin. The outlandish idea reflects a fascination with Joyce, the same genuine hankering to meet him that is detectable in O'Nolan's fabricated connections with the writer. Mick expresses "an admiration for all his [fictional] work, for his dexterity and resource in handling language, for his precision, for his subtlety in conveying the image of Dublin and her people, for his accuracy in setting down speech authentically, and for his enormous humour" (O'Brien 1993: 96). The praise for Joyce's dialogue, at least, echoes O'Nolan's real views (Ryan 1987: 128–29). Yet the novel's depiction of Joyce is also a debunking move, an attempt to pull his European flight back down to Dublin soil. On hearing of Joyce's location, Mick reflects that "It was surprising . . . that Joyce should go to ground so near Dublin city, in fact in the County Dublin. . . . Yet what was so funny? Perhaps Skerries was a sagacious choice. . . . The natives were quite accustomed to having strangers and visitors in their midst, and even retired people who remain on in town out of season. Most householders who had the accommodation took guests. Yes, perhaps here again one had silence, exile and cunning" (1993: 97). Joyce's modernist slogan is made bathetic by his new fate: the reclamatory re-Irishing of Joyce negates rather than celebrates him.

To similar effect, O'Nolan's *Envoy* editorial gives credence to the theory that "Joyce was at heart an Irish dawn-bursting romantic, an admirer of de Valera, and one who dearly wished to be recalled to Dublin as an ageing man to be crowned with a D Litt. from the National and priest-haunted University" (O'Brien 1991: 174). O'Nolan's portrait thus inverts the popular image of Joyce, most strikingly with respect to religion. The man Mick finds in Skerries is regarded by his neighbors as "a holy Mary Ann, just because I go to daily Mass." "If there's one thing scarce in Catholic Ireland," Joyce complains, "it is Christian charity" (1993: 128). The writer believed to be an irreligious outcast turns out to be a devout believer who never wrote *Ulysses*, whose main literary output has been "pamphlets for the Catholic Truth Society of Ireland" (165), and whose fervent hope is to join a Jesuit order, ultimately perhaps to become rector of Clongowes Wood College. The portrayal is the revenge of a man who never did leave Ireland, and whose epigraph to *The Dalkey Archive* reassures his "Guardian Angel" that he's "only fooling."

The debunking of Joyce is close to home, a cure for O'Nolan's Joycean hangover. But the personal battle also magnifies a more general complexity in the Irish response. Mockery of Joyce attests to a reluctant fascination with him. Repeatedly he is "brought home" or pulled back to earth, with the implicit or explicit claim that only Dubliners really understand him. And this gesture, a mixture of pride and iconoclasm, responds to America's appropriation of the writer. As O'Nolan's biographers have written: "[T]he Joyce of academic scholarship, which concentrated on matters of structure or myth, was not congenial to him, or to many other Dubliners of the day" (Costello and van de Kamp 1987: 119). *The Dalkey Archive* is peppered with references to trans-Atlantic interest in Joyce. Following the announcement that the writer is still alive, one character asks: "Could he be in the United States? . . . He would certainly be well-treated there, probably be given a chair at one of the universities." One of Mick Shaughnessy's reasons for seeking him out is to counter the misinformation spread by "the stupid books written *about* Joyce and his work, mostly by Americans" (O'Brien 1993: 92, 96).

This note sounds repeatedly among Joyce's Dublin successors, whose response to visiting American scholars swings between mockery and outright contempt. John Ryan's vision of "the groves of academe" fretting for Joyce's arrival (1987: 57) is a mild example. Others more directly demonstrate what John Jordan criticizes as the "snide depreciation of those of their fellows who have been successful by international standards" (1970: 136). Denis Johnston records—and seconds—Oliver Gogarty's impatience with "almost all literate North America" showing "genuine regard for every syllable of our bad boy from Belvedere," lampooning the outlandishness of American interpretations (Johnston 1970: 163–65). Bernard Share complains that visiting academics are blind to the changed reality of the city around them, and that some would even prefer the old city to be torn down: "Brute facts can sometimes be a damned nuisance" (1970: 190). Niall Montgomery, writing in 1951, duels with Harry Levin, mocks "the subtle overseas doctors in whom, under martial aid, are vested the exegetic rights in the Swiss master's work," and insists that a knowledge of the Maynooth catechism is "more helpful than the learning of Campbell and Robinson" (1970: 61–62). In his bitter poem "Who Killed James Joyce?" Kavanagh scorns the prestigious "Harvard thesis" and "Yale-man" (1970: 51–52). These were the institutions of Levin and of Ellmann and Kenner, respectively, and Ellmann for one believed that the ire was directed his way (Dick et al. 1989: xvi). Admiration and impatience coexist: commentators can hardly decide whether Joyce should be abandoned to the Americans or reclaimed for Dublin. In exaggerated form, O'Nolan's contradictions highlight the paradoxical attitudes to Joyce of many Catholic-born intellectuals: eagerly claiming Joyce as a Jesuit while also admiring his heterodoxy; drawing on his hostility to the state while stressing his irreducible ethnicity; taking pride in his local origin yet scorning foreign scholars. But O'Nolan's obsession with Joyce curiously prefigures another development: the official, belated admittance of Joyce as an icon of Irish culture, to the point where national affiliation seems to float free of religion—or the latter is displaced by the literary itself.

On 16 June 1954 a small party gathered at the Martello Tower in Sandycove to mark Bloomsday for the first time with a "Hades"-like carriage ride across the city. Anthony Cronin recalls being furtively approached by Ryan and O'Nolan with plans for the outing—"the jant," as O'Nolan called it, "which was to take place when you know, the day of your man's book" (1986: 124). The members of the elaborately conceived party were to represent Joycean figures, including the dentist Tom Joyce as "the family." Cronin recalls two events of particular interest: a song from the dentist that proved him to have his family's customary singing voice and the shock Gold Cup win for Elpenor. At 50 to 1, the horse was an even ranker outsider than Throwaway, and strangely enough took its name from the mythical character for which Paddy Dignam does duty in the novel. "What makes the result more remarkable," Cronin muses, "was that Joyce always believed his book to have strange prophetic powers of which he himself only became aware after the event" (127). Cronin is right to focus on the odd sense of coincidence and commemoration at work, for the tradition inaugurated by this first Bloomsday party plays with space and time, fictionalizing real social locations into their historical forerunners and marking the reenchantment of a certain prescribed period through a process of repetition and reenactment. (John Ryan, in his own memoir of the occasion, calls it "that enchanting day" [1987: 140].) To this extent the men of 1954 anticipated the rise of the Joycean heritage so prominent in contemporary Dublin. They could hardly have guessed what they'd started.

Vacationists in the Home Island: Bloomsday Dawns Again

It has become uncontroversial to describe Ireland in the 1950s as a drab, insular country, its major literary event the spectacle of the raincoated O'Nolan, Kavanagh and Behan apparently drinking their talents away. "[A] sense develops," writes Terence Brown, "that they were the 'tragic generation' of modern Irish letters" (1985: 237). Peter Lennon, who made his own Joycean flight to Paris during this period, recalls it harshly: "This was the late fifties, a period when the young middle class were trooping after the traditional labourers into exile. . . . The crude and incompetent patriots had created a lethargic climate; the Church a population of emotionally apprehensive, deluded people" (1994: 13). Ken Whitaker, who became secretary of the department of finance in 1956, would later describe the period in even bleaker terms: "The community was entering a dark night of the soul in which doubts were prevalent as to whether the achievement of political independence had not been futile" (Hussey 1995: 242). The morning of Whitaker's own dark night brought a White Paper entitled *Economic Development* (1958) and an initial five-year Programme for Economic Expansion, which shifted economic policy toward increased interaction with the rest of Europe. Seán Lemass, de Valera's successor, is customarily credited with modernizing the nation. "As Taoiseach in 1959–66," asserts John Ardagh, "he set in train a whole series of events, and did more than anyone else in this century to bring Ireland into the modern world" (1994: 31). Declan Kiberd recalls the period as follows: "The 1960s would be years of relative prosperity, when multinationals finally invested in Ireland; when children at last knew the benefits of free secondary education; when holidays in European resorts became possible for many; and when the long introversion of Irish intellectual life came to an end" (1995: 479). Gerry Smyth, in turn, stresses a "change in temporal and spatial perspective . . . from insularity to a re-entry into the world of international affairs . . . and from past-oriented social and cultural policy to a recognition of the need to invest in the nation's future" (1998: 97–98).

The Lemass story, like that of the Free State's insular repressiveness, has become so widely disseminated that it has begun to attract its own "revisionist" qualifications (Gibbons 1996: 82). Luke Gibbons refuses the univocal celebration of Irish modernization, but he provides an admirably succinct summary of the changes afoot:

> In 1961 Ireland applied for membership of the EEC and finally gained admittance in 1973. In 1962, it took its place in the global village of mass communications with the opening of Telefis Eireann. In the same year, the hardened arteries of Irish Catholicism were revitalized by the Second Vatican Council (1962–65) which brought an infusion of new ideas and values into the rigorist moral regime of the post-Famine era. This change was echoed in the educational arena by the publication of the 1965 report *Investment in Education*, which set out to remove the school from the sacristy, and place it in line with the need for greater technological change in Irish society. These developments took place against a wider economic backdrop which saw a shift from agriculture to industry as the mainstay of the Irish economy: in the period 1961 to 1980, employment in the agricultural sector fell from one-third to one-fifth of the workforce, while those working in industry increased from 16 to 30 per cent (1996: 82–83).

Gemma Hussey's view is not unusual: "Irish society has changed more in the two decades leading up to the 1990s than in the whole of the previous one hundred years.... An inward-looking, rural, deeply conservative, nearly 100 per cent Roman Catholic and impoverished country has become urbanized, industrialized, and Europeanized" (1995: 1). European integration has not only provided large sums of money granted to Ireland as aid, but also encouraged the circumvention of the nation's postcolonial relationship with the United Kingdom. "With the ending of economic dependence," the former premier Garret Fitzgerald has claimed, "we acquired a new self-confidence and became an equal partner with Britain, in the new multilateral context of the EC" (Ardagh 1994: 88). Accordingly, the Irish Republic has come to take its place among other European economies, with growth through the 1990s in the information-technology sector—accompanied by high unemployment and stark inequalities in the capital (White 1997: 3). The picture remains socially mixed and politically ambiguous. If the church and the conservative establishment have been in retreat from liberal proponents of free speech, feminism, and gay, abortion, and divorce rights, the most powerful motor of change has been the drive toward capitalist development, which, so Marxists have long argued, is itself the greatest foe of inefficient or outdated ideological systems. Ireland since the 1960s has been subjected to another spin in what Marshall Berman has called the maelstrom of modernity, with the mix of progress and destruction that this implies. What remains to be explored is James Joyce's place in this altered state.

Modernism has frequently been described as a hostile reaction to modernity: an indictment of mass civilization and valorization of some archaic or aesthetic alternative. But in the case of Joyce and Ireland it is possible to reverse this relationship and see the work as a proleptic manual for modernization. If Stephen Dedalus's flight to the Continent marks his frustration with the ruralist and archaic Revival, Gabriel and Gretta Conroy's European vacations and goloshes make them a rare anticipation of Kiberd's holidaying Irish. And if the ethnic makeup and entrepreneurial spirit of Leopold Bloom, like Joyce's own unsuccessful business ventures in Dublin, look forward to Lemass's postprotectionist economy, so *Finnegans Wake*'s fuzzy mingling of public-service broadcasting and public house talk might be seen to anticipate the virtual cacophony of national self-analysis after the arrival of RTE (O'Toole 1997: 145–55). Indeed, the growing interest in what Donald Theall terms the "techno-poetics" (1997) of Joyce's last work, its merging of Ireland with the polyglot atopia of the information age, reveals an affinity with the postmodern Dublin described by Jim White: "Ireland is now the place in Europe to locate for multi-national information technology firms: if your Apple crashes in Milan, Munich or Maidenhead, for instance, and you ring the help-line for assistance, the person answering your call and gently persuading you not to chuck the whole thing out of the window will be sitting in Dublin" (1997: 2).

It is possible to read Joyce as the prophet of change in Ireland, a figure whose time in his homeland has finally come. As early as 1948 John J. Slocum had unsuccessfully petitioned the Irish president to have Joyce's body reinterred in Irish soil. While acknowledging the delicacy of Joyce's standing in Ireland, Slocum cannily suggested that "in so honouring him his country would be honouring herself" (Rose and O'Hanlon 1992: 21). In the absence of the proposed disinterment, numerous commentators have still detected Joyce's more metaphorical presence. For Fintan O'Toole "The geography of Ireland at the end of the twentieth century is a version of the queer geography of Joyce's *Finnegans Wake*" (1997: 16). Certainly Joyce's acceptance has been gradual. Bernard

Share discerned a leap in Joyce's profile between the Bloomsdays of 1954 and 1969: "[M]uch more organized by now, with plenty of elegantly printed *Ulysses* maps, a Joyce Museum, junketings various, and a solemnly convened James Joyce Symposium" (1970: 189). Indeed, by June 1969 the City Arms Hotel bore a plaque declaring: "This Is The Bar Mentioned By JAMES JOYCE IN 'ULYSSES'" (Raleigh 1971: 134).

The year 1967 also saw the first International James Joyce Symposium, which would return to Dublin in 1969, 1973 and 1977, before the centenary celebration of 1982. The reminiscences of veteran Joyceans indicate that the influx of enthusiastic American scholars contrasted with—and perhaps accentuated—local skepticism. Dublin in 1967, recalls Morris Beja, "was a Jerusalem in which relatively few people aside from the pilgrims from afar seemed to care very much about its messiah" (Staley 2001: 102). Phillip Herring reflected on the symposium of 1969: "[T]he reception given some 234 Joyceans . . . twenty-eight years after the writer's death was somewhat less than enthusiastic. . . . Ireland cannot really embrace him (or us) because she does not yet feel comfortable with him (or us). . . . [T]here lingers the nagging suspicion that he smirks at Ireland from beyond the grave. . . . [L]atent hostility made us feel that we were clowns paying homage to a jester" (1969: 3–4). Thomas Staley, one of the 1967 symposium's organizers, recalls that "the uncertain attitude of some Dubliners to the Symposium was also reflected in the reports of the conference within the Irish press, a bemused but impatient mockery over the fascinated care with which scholars and critics seemed to pore over the minutest facets of the life and career of a man of whom many Irish were still not sure they fully approved" (2001: 102).

We have seen this attitude before, albeit more virulent, in Kavanagh and O'Nolan. Yet the statement that "many Irish were still not sure they fully approved" represents a major shift from Shane Leslie. Outrage had turned to mockery, on the long road to toleration. The centenary celebrations of 1982, which included a radio broadcast of the whole of *Ulysses*, suggested that Ireland had become more amenable to the public celebration of Joyce. Angela Carter's report was enthusiastic: "Dubliners wished one another: 'A Happy Bloomsday.'. . . Some said it should have been a national holiday. The entire inner city was *en fête*. . . . Thus Dublin ingeniously secularised and took back unto itself the first authentic post-modernist literary festival. . . . Nothing could have been more perfect, as the city adopted Bloomsday and revisited its own vanishing past with a tourist's eager curiosity and the devotion of a trustee" (1992: 207, 212–13). Carter observed that broader changes were also afoot: "Up go the mirror-clad slabs of office-blocks; Ireland has at last followed Joyce into Europe. . . . Everything has changed. If 16 June was Bloomsday, 26 June was Gay Pride Day" (212).

Senator David Norris, Dublin's most prominent Joycean, had a hand in both days. By the late 1990s he would describe Joyce as "one of the great liberising [*sic*] spirits of modern Ireland [who] seems now at least to have won what he always wanted—the freedom of the hearts of his fellow citizens" (1997: 7). Norris's gift for publicity would not shame the Irish popular musicians who also made a point of referring to Joyce in the late twentieth century. On the title track of a 1993 LP, the Belfast-born Van Morrison cites Joyce among a series of figures, like George Best and the singer himself, "too long in exile." The gesture not only daringly claims an affinity between Morrison and Joyce but serves as a slogan for the increasing emphasis on Joyce's Irishness. In 1987 the London-Irish band the Pogues released an LP, *If I Should Fall from Grace with God*, on whose sleeve their own images merged with a repeated photograph of Joyce. Once again the implication is of an alignment between author and musicians, a parodic insertion of the band into the literary tradition represented by Joyce. While paying tribute to Joyce and his iconic potential, the image also suggests a certain relativization of the author, from the solitude of the original photograph into a line of identically dressed Irishmen. It thus appears to draw him back into an Irish orbit, only with the ironic qualification that the band, like Joyce, have made their home and fortune in a foreign capital—a familiar Irish condition evoked on the LP in the song "Thousands Are Sailing." U2's singer Bono, making repeated references to Joyce, has also attempted to stress the latter's abiding relevance. He claims to have "understood Joyce" after watching television coverage of the Gulf War (Waters 1994: 7), and has invoked the writer as the ideal user of new technologies: "We use the word rock'n'roll, but nobody knows what it means. . . . [W]e've moved to working with a new canvas: colour, contrast, dissolves, rhythm, beat, melody and words. And saying, 'Wow! What would Salvador Dali have done, what would Joyce have done?!'" (15). If Joyce here figures as a great lost pop producer, a prototype Brian Wilson or Brian Eno, Bono has also explicitly referred to the writer's nationality as the basis of his work: "We Irish have developed a new form of the English language, more ornate, more like our native language. Even Joyce—his revenge on the English language by distorting it, mangling it, and twisting it . . . as if to spit it out, or maybe to make it our own" (232). This not only repeats the gesture of the other musicians cited in daring—in the Yeatsian "We Irish"—to align the singer with Joyce; it also offers a version of what has become a standard postcolonial emphasis. None of these figures, of course, need engage closely with Joyce's texts. Their interest here is in their general significance, in what they suggest Joyce had become several decades after *Ulysses*. The key is that he is at once unmistakably Irish and reassuringly modern: an emblem of progress yet also local. The same combination was implied in references to Joyce by President Mary Robinson, the highest-profile representative of progressive change in late-twentieth-century Ireland (Hussey 1995: 22). At the 1992 symposium in Dublin, Robinson momentarily bridged the gap between politics and academia, claiming Joyce as quintessentially Irish yet also carefully insisting that his Ireland "is not a place of regional interest [but] that fierce territory where nothing is taken for granted." His legacy, she asserted, was one of "rebellion and uncompromising self-inquiry, which prevents us from ever feeling complacent about being Irish" (Lawrence 2001: 168). Joyce again becomes the figure for an open and international Irishness. This perception has helped Joyce to attain the visibility he has in Dublin today.

"When the call to Joycean duty came I, an early convert, was at hand," recalls John Ryan (1987: 52). When the James Joyce Tower Society was founded in 1962, he was asked to be one of its two honorary secretaries. The Martello Tower, rented from the Republic's Department of Defence, became "the memorial, the museum, the place of pilgrimage," and was officially opened, eight years after the "jant," on Bloomsday 1962. Sylvia Beach came from Paris to raise the flag of Munster, on which "the Citizen waxed so warmly" (54–55). Ryan reported that the opening was attended by "the assorted cognoscenti of several continents . . . scholarly and learned heads of many nations" (55–56); and he records colorful encounters with Bavarian and Japanese Joyceans in his subsequent capacity as secretary. If the Tower reestablished a Joycean presence in Ireland, it simultaneously invited foreign experts to visit the nation: the gesture points both inward and outward. Bloomsday 1962 was the beginning of Joyce's official role as part of Irish heritage. In Patrick Wright's classic study, heritage implies a particular processing of history: "National Heritage involves the extraction of history—of the idea of historical significance and potential—from a denigrated everyday life and its restaging or display in certain sanctioned sites, events, images and conceptions. In this process history is redefined as 'the historical,' and it becomes the object of a similarly transformed and generalised public attention" (1985: 69). This usefully describes the sacralization of space and time, and the iconic use of Joyce, that I am about to consider.

The Martello Tower has remained the center of the official remembrance of Joyce, an institutionalized business focused on certain key sites. The museum contains letters, manuscripts, photographs, and rare and early editions of Joyce's work, in addition to selling such Joyce memorabilia as T-shirts, posters, postcards, and even academic works. Halfway up the visitor is offered a reconstruction of the living quarters depicted in the novel, but the top of the tower is the omphalos to which visitors are most attracted. It remains one of Dublin's major tourist attractions, but since 1994 its solitary preeminence has been supplemented by the James Joyce Centre, a restored Georgian house in North Great George's Street. Like the Martello Tower, the James Joyce Centre is an archive of Joycean materials; it also features portraits of several generations of Joyce's family, to which the writer's great-nephew Paul Joyce has added a mural illustrating every chapter of *Ulysses* in sequence. The representation of Joyce in Dublin is thus not only a matter of preserving the archive but of producing new representations and tributes: the tide of Joyceana rises. Beyond these two attractions, several other sites in the city commemorate Joyce. Marjorie Fitzgibbon's bust of the writer was unveiled in 1982 in St. Stephen's Green. O'Connell Street gained the Anna Livia Millennium Fountain in 1988. In 2001 Corporation Street, off Talbot Street, was renamed James Joyce Street as "part of an integrated development plan for the entire area" (Meade 2001: 27). Notwithstanding that development, the third major site of tribute is Fitzgibbon's statue of Joyce, erected on North Earl Street in 1990. The most common image of Joyce on postcards and in tourist brochures, the statue has done much to make Joyce usable as a piece of Dublin iconography. A photograph of the statue presents an image of the writer that is also literally an image of Dublin, effecting an elision of the two. The statue, though recent, represents a figure from a partially vanished Dublin: here and elsewhere a negotiation between old and new takes shape around Joyce.

As Joyce's nephew Ken Monaghan has noted (2001: 7), it was only in the 1990s that the public celebration of Joyce became an established fixture in Dublin life. The Martello Tower and James Joyce Centre represent a constant presence, but the nodal point of the year—for these institutions, local performers, and Joycean enthusiasts from within Dublin and without—is Bloomsday itself. By the late 1990s popular demand and commercial imperative had expanded this celebration to encompass the entire week. Typical events throughout these days include walking tours, concerts, lectures, exhibitions, and, above all, performances from Joyce's work. These range from professional dramatizations to impromptu readings by members of the public: if Bloomsday is a commercial opportunity, it is also an amateur affair, improvised in public spaces. On 16 June the city is crisscrossed with tours between key locations and dotted with recitals at appropriate spots, with some participants wearing the Edwardian dress recommended in the official literature. The event is unusual: a public party, spread across the space of the city, to which scattered groups have invited themselves, while the inhabitants of the present day tolerantly pass by. The implicit vision of Joyce is happy and humanistic, a long way not only from the struggles of 1922 but from Levin or Kenner in midcentury, or indeed MacCabe in the 1970s. The closest academic equivalent to Bloomsday's Joyce is Richard Ellmann's; indeed, the yearly celebration of a benevolent and lovable, if awkward and eccentric, artist may be among Ellmann's most unexpected legacies.

Bloomsday's central feature is the urge toward reenactment. Even for the anonymous visitor in ordinary clothes—but especially, no doubt, for those participants in boaters or crinolines—the drive is toward fidelity, the reproduction of fictional scenes (themselves, of course, not always distinguishable with absolute reliability from actual scenes in Joyce's life). The boundary between the actual and the imaginary, reality and fiction, is blurred, as contemporary devotees strive to become one with Joyce's semireal figures: eating the same breakfast as Leopold Bloom;

buying a glass of burgundy and a gorgonzola sandwich at an inflated price in Davy Byrne's at lunchtime; walking the same streets. As early as 1942, John Ryan, reading *Ulysses* for the first time, had felt something like this about his city: "Best of all, it was about Dublin and there was I, with the whole thing happening around me, albeit forty years later. It seemed incredibly modern then. . . . I felt about Dublin as the Flower People felt about the Haight-Ashbury scene in the mid-'sixties—this is where it's all at" (1987: 52). Where it's all at: the Joycean in Dublin feels *Ulysses* happening around him. Yet this sense of presence—especially another sixty years on, with the city further changed—is equally about absence, about the imaginative work of superimposing a fiction of the past onto today's reality. As Derek Attridge comments, fictional reference can feel more powerful than history: "Any reader of *Ulysses* who has visited the Martello Tower at Sandycove can testify to the way its historical reality appears to be enhanced, not diminished, through its recalling of Buck Mulligan and Stephen Dedalus; the knowledge that James Joyce once lived there for a short period has a much weaker effect on the touristic imagination" (2000: 81). Made collective on 16 June itself, the effect is an oddly ambiguous cross between, on the one hand, a religious ritual—with the imitation of exemplary or saintly figures, the long-distance pilgrimage to sacred sites, the exegesis and recital of a sacred book, and the unrealizable dream of communion with a supreme being forever beyond our reach—and, on the other, the culture of simulation notoriously associated with postmodernism. Jean Baudrillard opens *Simulations* by describing contemporary culture as one in which the "map" precedes the "territory" that it purports to denote, or even one in which the distinction between the two has vanished (1983: 1–4). The image is suggestive for Bloomsday, when Dublin seems to become rewritten as a pale imitation of a work of fiction. As early as 1937 Niall Sheridan remarked that Dublin was starting to feel like "an inferior plagiarism from *Ulysses*" (Magalaner and Kain 1956: 296). Alternatively, one could say that the contemporary commemoration of *Ulysses* allows Joyce's novel to recode the city, charging its everyday sites with esoteric significance, producing a surfeit of meaning that hovers just out of view, traceable only by the costumed figures going through the motions. Of course, the production of multiple, unsuspected levels of significance for the apparently quotidian also characterizes *Ulysses* itself, where everyday actions flip into their Homeric counterparts. Doubling this effect, Bloomsday has transformed Joyce's book into an epic subtext for the real.

In a sense, all this is an exaggeration. Those who actually dress up for Bloomsday are a tiny minority of Dublin's population on the day. The *Irish Times* of 17 June 1997 humorously described them thus: "When you think about it, Joyceans have a lot in common with Orangemen. They like to wear bowler hats; they hold a midsummer celebration which involves walking traditional routes laid down by their forefathers; and, tragically, they remain badly misunderstood by the island's majority community" (McNally 1997: 8). David Norris's annual appearances in Bloomsday coverage have made him a target for media wits. "While *Ulysses* remains widely unread in its native city," the *Irish Times* adds, "the annual festivities have an educational effect. Ask any Dubliner to name the famous literary character whose day is celebrated on June 16th and most of them will shoot back the answer—Senator David Norris" (McNally 1997: 1). The polemical paper *The Slate* takes a harsher view, dubbing Bloomsday "one of the most pretentious events in Ireland. . . . a gathering of idiots" and insisting that "In theory, the assembled morons follow the path taken around Dublin by Leopold Bloom. . . . However, most of them get lost early on, and end up walking around dangerous parts of town in their Edwardian gear, misquoting the book at the tops of their voices and generally risking a well-deserved hiding. . . . You are, of course, not allowed to take part if you have read the book" (Hughes 2002). Knockabout stuff: but it may well reflect many Dubliners' attitude toward Bloomsday, as the embarrassing cavortings of a minority. The accompanying cartoon shows Bloomsday celebrants being beaten by police—a reference to alleged police brutality at a recent "Reclaim the Streets" demonstration in Dame Street—while an unseeing Norris, dressed in Edwardian garb, sighs, "Isn't this just glorious?" The implication is that Bloomsday is damagingly out of touch with contemporary Dublin—perhaps as Joyce himself considered the Revival to be a century earlier.

Joyceans for whom the writer remains a figure of integrity and modernity may consider the association unfair. But the most persuasive charge is that Dublin's Joyce has become precisely *heritage* in Patrick Wright's sense: emphatically historical, but ultimately dehistoricized.

The cost of his civic acceptability might be the loss of his social challenge. Anthony Cronin insisted on this when he was interviewed during Bloomsday 2002, in his capacity as one of the original pilgrims of 1954—"the days," writes Aengus Fanning, "before Bloomsday became the PR industry it is now and in an age when James Joyce was a name whispered and not trumpeted in a thousand press releases." Cronin voices concern: "Some of it seems a bit hollow and hypocritical, because you know so many of those taking part have not read the book and never will read it. It has become a sort of extra national holiday. . . . Ireland has got a bit like the Catholic Church. The things that were a sin are not a sin any longer. In those days a lot of people had to ritually condemn James Joyce. . . . If you're sitting in a tea shop eating a Joycean bun, you feel you're sharing in the thing without the challenge of the reality. *Ulysses* has been turned into a jolly, beery, harmless romp. But it isn't. . . . There are some very dark places in it and on the whole its view of Ireland is not very flattering" (Fanning 2002). Cronin's frank nostalgia may be obscuring progressive change in Ireland since the 1950s, without which the national press would never have given him this platform to praise Joyce. Dubliners, understandably jaded by the annual celebrations, seem less likely than outsiders to recognize the peculiarity—and the potential for enlightenment as well as enjoyment—of a public festival built around one of the last century's most notoriously difficult writers. But Cronin does plausibly point to the risk of Bloomsday obscuring *Ulysses* itself. The public commemoration of Joyce, Cronin proposes, is as much an avoidance of as an encounter with his writing, and the challenge it might still pose to Ireland. Not for the first time, Joyce has become an occasion for the proliferation of other things.

Bloomsday is the work of dedicated enthusiasts, but Joyce's commercial value to Dublin should not be underestimated. In 1997 a shop assistant from Sweny's reported that "thousands" of bars of lemon soap had been sold, while a single bookseller professed himself confident of shifting "hundreds" of copies of the novel itself (McNally 1997: 8). Perhaps the most telling sign of Joyce's pervasiveness is not in the faithful efforts of devotees and curators but in the commercial scramble for his imprimatur—particularly among pubs and restaurants. The Joycean nod can be won either on the basis of his having frequented the place during his early years in Ireland or on the strength of a mention in his work—which tends to amount to the same thing. Davy Byrne's extracts and reprints several lines from the novel on the back of its menu card, topped with a queasy picture of the author. The Ormond Hotel promises not only "60 Bedrooms with en-suite facilities," "Direct Dial Telephone," and—most appropriately—"Temple of Sound, Dublin's Premier Dance Club," but also a lounge bar "where the image of Leopold Bloom lingers-on [sic] in the memory of that fateful day!" The hotel, decorated with Joycean plaques and signs, takes a loose acquaintance with Joyce and *Ulysses* for granted as part of the Dublin tourist's general knowledge.

Davy Byrne's and the Ormond are well known to any reader of *Ulysses*, but the book has also become valuable for a host of less memorable establishments. A wealth of Joycean endorsements appear in the official Bloomsday brochures: a special feature in the 2002 magazine introduces The Bleeding Horse, Farrington's (renamed after the less than heroic protagonist of "Counterparts"), O'Neill's (included because Corless's restaurant used to be opposite), and the North Star Hotel (unvisited in "Eumaeus"), among others (Behan 2002: 45–47). Fitzgerald's of Sandycove, decorated with stained-glass illustrations of episodes from *Ulysses*, advertises itself as "Joyce's Choice," explaining that "This house was Joyce's local and proprietor Joseph Farrell often witnessed the eccentric behaviour of the brilliant Joyce. Indeed it appears that Mr. Farrell was not at all amused by Joyce's antics and on a few occasions severely reprimanded the literary genius, a factor which may have caused this house to be omitted from literary illumination in the pages of *Ulysses*" (Logan 1997: 4). Given Joyce's penchant for prosecuting feuds in his fiction, this is a rather unconvincingly ingenious explanation for the omission. But we are also told that the proprietor Tom Fitzgerald "bears a striking resemblance to James Joyce," which can be interpreted as a desperate desire for the legitimating presence of the author himself among the ceaseless references to him. The barman who looks like Joyce, like the Whitby fish-and-chip shop owner who bears an uncanny resemblance to Elvis Presley, promises a compensation for those nomadic fans in mourning for their lost leader. With his ghost hovering around Dublin, Joyce, like Elvis, acquires something of the status of

Parnell in *Ulysses:* "Dead he wasn't. Simply absconded somewhere" (Joyce 1986: 530).

Madigan's in O'Connell Street, by contrast, pictures Joyce as a patron, superimposing the nearby statue of him over a photograph of the pub and assuring us that "the young James Joyce . . . would have been very familiar with the premises" (Logan 1997: 13). The Snug, formerly Larry O'Rourke's, makes its case with a quotation from the book— "From the cellar grating floated up the flabby gush of porter" (Joyce 1986: 47)—and boasts a brand-new "James Joyce Lounge" upstairs. The Portobello on South Richmond Street also claims to have featured in Joyce's fiction. But the vague assertion that the house "found its way into the literary fame of *Ulysses*" (Logan 1997: 27) demonstrates that almost any establishment could make a similar claim and get away with it: even most professional readers of *Ulysses* could not swear to remember every pub mentioned in the novel. If a quotation from the text itself is not required as proof of authenticity, then it appears that *Ulysses* is a blank check for any Dublin establishment looking for a way of asserting its identity— with the qualification that the claim to have been in *Ulysses* is evidently becoming less and less of a differentiating factor. The inflation of the Joycean currency, one might suspect, is devaluing it. The Irish novelist Joseph O'Connor warns that "You will always know a really lousy Dublin pub . . . because it will be called after someone in *Ulysses,* and have a faded poster of Georgian Doors sellotaped to the wall behind the bar" (1995: 153).

Perhaps the most extraordinary appropriation of Joyce, however, is *Ulysses*—the world's largest car ferry, which joined the Irish Ferries fleet in 2001. "James Joyce's Ulysses," writes Irish Ferries' marketing director, "was a book that transformed ideas of what a novel could be. In the same way we hope that our ship Ulysses will open your eyes to a new and better way to travel." Readers of Joyce who wander into Nora Barnacle's Food Emporium, the Volta Picture Theatre, Cyclops Family Entertainment, Boylan's Brasserie, or Leopold Bloom's pub may well suspect that they have walked through a cracked looking glass: Derrida's remark that we all inhabit Joyce's dream (1992: 74) has never seemed more percipient. "Joyce was far ahead of his time," the publicity release tells us: "And for that reason, naming the world's most advanced car ferry operating from the city in which his most acclaimed work is set, seems entirely appropriate" (Irish Ferries 2001). There are less authentically Joycean things than a boat from Dublin to Holyhead.

National heritage looks both inward and outward. On the one hand, the rediscovery of forms of national history involves a process of introspection in which indigenous features are positively reevaluated. This activity may well have the aim of engaging people with the past of the place they inhabit, or even encouraging patriotism or local pride (Wright 1985: 42–56; Corner and Harvey 1991: 45–58). Yet all this representational activity is also directed at the external world of foreign corporations and tourism. In an epoch of globalization, one of whose effects is widely thought to be a flattening of cultural difference—a vision in which every British high street offers the same shops, and every town in the world features a branch of McDonald's—the assertion of a local identity is a boon. Heritage, while apparently about the parochial construction of local identities, is therefore just as much about vying for the attention of a global audience. In this sense global difference and identity may be dialectical counterparts rather than stark opposites. "As global corporations scan the world for preferential locations," comments Kevin Robins, "so are particular places forced into a competitive race to attract inward investors. Cities and localities must actively promote and advertise their attractions.... In this process, local, regional or national cultures and heritage will be exploited to enhance the distinctive qualities of a city or locality. Tradition and heritage are factors that enhance the 'quality of life' of particular places and make them attractive locations for investment" (1991: 38). As Luke Gibbons has shown, one Irish version of this was visible in the 1980s in the advertising strategies of the Industrial Development Authority, which advertised the nation as one that had mercifully "missed the industrial revolution," remaining suitably unspoiled for the coming of the electronic age (Gibbons 1996: 82–93). If the imagery of this campaign is predominantly rural, Dublin offers another kind of "attractive location." What I have called the ability of Joyce's fiction to "re-encode" or "re-enchant" the city, granting legitimacy to establishments and making certain spots sacred, represents an outstanding resource for this kind of geographical differentiation or selling of place.

The stakes here are not purely economic. It may also be that the use of Joyce as a heritage icon is an attempt to find an appropriate symbol of Ireland at a time when so much traditional iconography is coming into question. In the academic sphere, the nationalist legacy has been challenged by the skeptical revisionist historiography of which Roy Foster is the leading exponent (1986). "If the claims of cultural maturity and a new European identity advanced by the 1970s can be substantiated," Foster argues, "it may be by the hope of a more relaxed and inclusive definition of Irishness, and a less constricted view of Irish history" (1989: 596). Foster's general skepticism about nationalism is perhaps in evidence in his claims that "There is little support . . . for those who see Joyce as any kind of consciously political nationalist" (1995: 3), and that "recent scholarly attempts to recruit him as a fully paid-up [nationalist] member do not convince" (1998b: 3). Terry Eagleton suspects that revisionism's antinationalist tendencies have specific historical roots, insisting that the movement "has much to do with the war in the North, the emergence of a new middle class in the republic, the transformation of a hitherto stagnant post-colonial enclave into a flourishing if grotesquely inequitable capitalist set-up, the escalating 'Europeanisation' of the country, certain historic changes in its relations with Britain and the like" (1998: 321). The link asserted here between revisionist scholarship and realpolitik became slightly more explicit in the wake of the May 1998 Irish referenda, which demonstrated the decline of nationalist sentiment in the South when 94 percent voted to drop the articles of de Valera's 1937 constitution laying claim to Ulster. Foster himself greeted the result by quoting *Ulysses:* "In the great saloon-bar conversation in James Joyce's novel *Ulysses* where 'the Citizen' interrogates Leopold Bloom about nationalism and Irishness, Joyce's humanist hero finally puts an end to it: 'But it's no use. Force, history, hatred, all that. That's not life for men and women, insult and hatred.'. . . Even those of us who are temperamentally sceptics have seen a window open, through the mechanisms of the agreement, whereby political and civic conditions in Northern Ireland might be enabled to reflect 'what really is life'" (1998a: 2).

In a postnationalist, increasingly urbanized age, Pearse and de Valera are not the figures to compel assent at home or interest abroad. By the 1960s, asserts Joseph O'Connor, "people were living lives which were very far from the ideal which Yeats and de Valera had so incongruously shared. The maidens were not dancing at the crossroads. They were watching the Rolling Stones on the latest colour TV set" (1995: 149). As the heritage analyst B. J. Graham argues, there are pragmatic as well as altruistic reasons for a muting of nationalist rhetoric on Ireland: "Tourism's heritage is far more at home with the general tenets of the revisionist model of nationalism. . . . Plurality of identity is a prerequisite both to a successful European identity and to a resolution of regional conflict. . . . [T]he heritage of a new Ireland in a new Europe has to be ideologically constructed to define Ireland's heterogeneity, not homogeneity" (1994: 153, 155).

James Joyce is one of the figures around whom this new heritage has been constructed. He operates as an icon that can bridge the gulf between heritage past and postmodern present, at once a figure of genteel Edwardian Dublin and a symbol of the modernity with which Ireland's economy has come to rival the United Kingdom's. In an era when the South's claim on the North has slackened, there is convenience in reclaiming a writer whose work can be endlessly mined for local color but who was conveniently out of the country during those immediate postcolonial years for which few have fond words. Through 1916 and the War of Independence, the absent Joyce has the ultimate alibi of having been at work on *Ulysses,* a piece of heritage perhaps more palatable in contemporary Dublin than the proclamation of the Republic itself. One condition of Joyce's iconic return to Dublin, then, is his distance from the Irish politics of the last century. Yet at the same moment, critics in Ireland and elsewhere have attempted to produce the opposite effect.

That Subject People Stuff: Postcolonial Joyce

Ezra Pound's assertion of the nonexistence of Ireland could never be taken literally by Joyce's critics. The most abstract books on Joyce find it hard not to mention Dublin, even if "*Ulysses,* Order and Myth" managed it. What the critical tradition lacked was not the acceptance of Ireland as a setting, but a belief in the seriousness of Joyce's engagement with Irish history and politics. Emer Nolan has proposed that "Joyce's most influential readers can disclose nothing but polar opposition between Joycean modernism and Irish nationalism" (1995: xi). Joyce could never quite extricate himself from Dublin, but his ceaseless literary meditation on its past did not imply a genuine interest in its political present and future.

The inversion of this view is a remarkably recent development. As late as 1991 Alan Roughley's survey *James Joyce and Critical Theory* made a scatter of Marxist comments do duty as the historicist response to Joyce. A decade later this would have seemed radically insufficient: the 1990s produced a series of books devoted to rethinking Joyce's historical contexts. Attridge and Howes' essay collection, *Semicolonial Joyce* (2000), seemed to make official the arrival—even the institutionalization—of postcolonialism in Joyce studies. Notable figures from the American Joyce industry have been involved in developing the new paradigm: Robert Spoo, Vincent Cheng, Enda Duffy, Joseph Valente. Yet the origins of this critical transformation were in Ireland itself.

Brian O'Nolan was not the only writer to see Joyce's ghost. "You are raking at dead fires," the unnamed but unmistakable figure tells Seamus Heaney at the end of "Station Island" (1984), "rehearsing the old whinges at your age. / That subject people stuff is a cod's game" (1990: 192–93). Joyce admonishes Heaney to leave behind the public anguish of political responsibility and to commit himself instead to his art. This is a familiar enough view of the writer as one who saw through and discarded nationalist rhetoric, and his starkly avant-garde search for "elver-gleams in the dark of the whole sea" (193) offers little local colour for the benefit of the tourist trade. Through his very appearance on the island of the poem, Heaney's modernist is nonetheless making a kind of return, and taking an idiosyncratic place in what Declan Kiberd calls the poem's "audacious self-identification with a 'Catholic' tradition of writing" (1995: 597). For Heaney this identification takes place in the context of the sectarian violence that has racked the North since 1969. In August that year, while Heaney in Madrid "sweated my way through / The life of Joyce" (1990: 87), ten thousand British troops were sent in to protect the besieged Catholic minority; but their continued presence came to be seen as an intervention to guard Ulster's British status. From 1970 on, the new and more militaristic "Provisional" IRA claimed the mantle of the guardian of Ulster's Catholics. As J. J. Lee comments, "The IRA was left in a monopoly position as potential protector of the Catholic community in a doomsday situation, with the army, not unreasonably, now assumed to be on the unionist side" (1989: 434). In Derry in 1972 British paratroopers shot protesters in the notorious "Bloody Sunday" incident; and in subsequent years the politics of Northern Ireland have been dominated by the violent cat-and-mouse game between republican and loyalist paramilitary groups. A number of initiatives intended to bring peace and equality to the province have been inconclusive, though the 1990s brought the substantial developments of an IRA ceasefire and the Good Friday agreement of 1998.

One epiphenomenon of the Troubles was a swathe of critical writing, more orchestrated and coherent than in the era of maverick scribes like Denis Donoghue and Conor Cruise O'Brien. Richard Kearney of University College Dublin led the way with the journal *The Crane Bag* (1977–86), whose first issue expressed the hope "that the creativity of art and the commitment of politics might converge to challenge the assumption that the aesthetic and political are two mutually exclusive areas," for "even if history is irretrievably past, its meaning is still in the process of becoming" (1988: 264–65). An even greater urgency was evident in Derry's Field Day Theatre Company, formed in 1980 by a collective that included the playwright Brian Friel and the poet-critics Seamus Heaney, Seamus Deane, and Tom Paulin (Field Day Theatre Company 1985: vii; Ardagh 1994: 254–55). Field Day soon widened its activities to produce a series of pamphlets on Irish writing and history. Among the aims of these movements, both South and North, was the rereading of Ireland's literature in a postcolonial context that was now felt to be unavoidable. The Troubles had brought the politics of Irish literature back to the fore. A rethinking of the images of Ireland offered by the literary tradition might provide at least a figurative space beyond the conflict. A rigorous examination of that tradition was seen as imperative.

Joyce, along with Yeats, featured prominently in this work. Terence Brown (1988: 84–88) has shown how the *Crane Bag* and Field Day analyses reprised the existing opposition between these two archetypal figures, envisaged as archaic revivalist and unabashed modernist. Of all the new Irish critics, Richard Kearney has most clearly endorsed this opposition, allying Joyce's modernism with national modernization: "Modernism rejects both the aims and idioms of revivalism. It affirms a radical break with tradition and endorses a practice of cultural self-reflection where inherited concepts of identity are subjected to question. . . . The modernist mind prefers discontinuity to continuity, diversity to unity, conflict to harmony, novelty to heritage. . . . The modernist tendency in Irish culture is characterised by a determination to *demythologize* the orthodox heritage of tradition" (1988: 12–13).

There are no prizes for guessing where Kearney's sympathies lie. His volume *Transitions* traces this great divide through various forms of twentieth-century Irish culture, never more clearly than in the opposition between Yeats and Joyce: "Instead of seeking to transcend the fragmentation of modern consciousness by invoking a timeless mythic past, Joyce embraced the 'filthy modern tide' and resolved to create in its wake altogether different possibilities of experience. Whereas Yeats moved back towards a pre-modern culture, Joyce moved forward to a postmodern one" (1988: 31). Kearney thus comes close to the sense, described earlier, that Joyce and Irish (post)modernization go hand in hand. If the Europeanized Joyce is a symbol of the economic benefits of Europe, his "deconstruction of the 'phallogocentric fallacy'" (47) anticipates the importation of intellectual aid that Kearney, drawing frequently on Colin MacCabe's poststructuralist reading of Joyce, announces: "I see no good reason why the critical methods of contemporary European thought—hermeneutics, existentialism, structuralism, psychoanalysis, dialectics or deconstruction—cannot be usefully employed in the interpretation of Irish culture" (17–18). Kearney's position in *Transitions* is not far from the paean to modernity suspiciously described by Luke Gibbons: "It is considered progressive to extend an uncritical welcome to multinational investment as a positive step in helping people to think in global terms, and socialists have been among the most vocal supporters of calls to become post-national 'Young Europeans'" (1996: 95). John Wilson Foster is equally dubious of Kearney's stance: "Literature and art constitute a kind of EEC in cultural terms, a multinational corporation of the pen and the brush" (1991: 237).

Seamus Deane, his generation's foremost Irish critic, registered a similar skepticism in an influential pamphlet on the Joyce/Yeats question entitled "Heroic Styles" (1984). Joyce, writes Deane, "is, if you like, our most astonishing 'modernist' author and Yeats is his 'anachronistic' counterpart" (1985: 56–57). Unlike Kearney, however, Deane is unable to give Joyce his blessing on that basis: "The pluralism of his styles and languages, the absorbing nature of his controlling myths and systems, finally gives a certain harmony to varied experience. But, it could be argued, it is the harmony of indifference, one in which everything is a version of something else, where sameness rules over diversity. . . . Joyce anticipated the capacity of modern society to integrate almost all antagonistic elements by transforming them into fashions, fads—styles, in short" (56). Deane is dubious about Joyce's seeming complicity with the coming times, unwilling to go as far as Kearney in exchanging the remains of an Irish identity for European cosmopolitanism. Like Kearney, Deane scrutinizes myths of Irish identity, but in "Heroic Styles" he remains wary of embracing Joycean modernity if it means—as Heaney's Joyce seems to recommend in "Station Island"—a dilution of political commitment.

Yet Deane was not about to give up on Joyce. Andrew Gibson, trying to historicize Joyce in the late 1980s, had "little to work with apart from scattered writings by Seamus Deane" (2002: vii). Through the 1980s Deane, more than any other critic, made the public case for an Irish Joyce—not only in Field Day publications but in contributing the essays "Joyce and Nationalism" to MacCabe's collection of *New Perspectives* (1982), and "Joyce the Irishman" to Attridge's *Cambridge Companion* (1990). While theory was taking off in Britain—and taking Joyce studies with it—Deane's austere, sometimes gnomic prose made the case for contextualization. On this basis Deane became general editor of Joyce's work for Penguin's "Twentieth-Century Classics" series. This commission was noteworthy: a major British publisher had explicitly placed Joyce in the hands of an Irishman—more precisely, a neonationalist theorist of postcolonialism from Catholic Derry. Deane edited the *Portrait* and *Finnegans Wake* himself, while the remaining texts were handled by other major Irish critics: *Dubliners* by Terence Brown, *Poems and Exiles* by J. C. C. Mays, and *Ulysses* by Declan Kiberd. To date this has been among the largest gestures in the "re-Irishing" of Joyce.

The simplest point in Deane's commentaries has been the importance of Ireland to understanding Joyce, "formed by the Ireland he repudiated" (1990: 31). His late experiments are "anticipated in the conflict between Irish, Hiberno-English and standard English which is a feature of the Irish writing Joyce knew" (32). The *Portrait* is "among the most important of Irish novels because it is the first to examine the distorted relationship between the Irish community and oppression" (1992a: vii).

Finnegans Wake's "critique of writing" has its roots in "the phenomenon of the Irish experience of mutilation and catastrophe" (1992b: xiv). Such statements already take us beyond the critical tradition. Yet in assessing their implications one must avoid glib simplicities. In the detail of Deane's accounts, Joyce's relation to the country becomes vexed and varied. Deane persistently circles back to troublesome issues, Joycean pathologies: the necessity and difficulty of translation (xl–xlvi); the impossible desire to be self-created (1990: 47–48). To return Joyce to an Irish context is not (as it is for the tourist industry, developing simultaneously with Deane's work) to celebrate a national treasure, but to recover the roots of his difficulty.

Ireland and Joyce, moreover, can never simply be restored to one another. Deane is a generalist in Irish studies, the author of a *Short History* of the whole national literature (1986). Accordingly, unlike a card-carrying Joycean, he does not see Joyce as the center of the Irish literary tradition (though he does read him in the context of Mangan, Wilde, and the Revival) but rather as an extraordinary offshoot of it, whose distance from (and consequent reimagination of) Ireland is among his most salient features. In other words, the "native" recovery of Joyce allows exile to regain its full weight. For Joyce, Deane writes, "Ireland was a negative idea" (1990: 39). Dublin "had to be both nowhere and everywhere, absence and presence"; the Irish self "must be invented"; Joyce "salutes and bids farewell to the Ireland he had left and to the Ireland he created in its absence from it and its absence from him" (42, 45, 53). The *Portrait* is accordingly read as proleptic: Stephen Dedalus "is going to make Ireland part of History by making it open to the future" (1992a: xli). Deane's Joyce is thus not at home in Ireland, though he is not thinkable apart from it. Deane stresses Joyce's separation from the Revival, conceived of as archaic alongside his modernity: "It is just this fancy-dress version of tradition that Joyce flees from, most particularly because it is so loyal to an idea of Ireland and the Irish as an essentialist place and people, given over to a destiny that is inscribed in the past and will be reinscribed in the future" (xxxix). Yet even here he is ambivalent, writing elsewhere that "Joyce was, and knew himself to be, part of the Irish Revival" (1990: 53). He offers us an Irish Joyce beyond Ireland, and beyond any simple escape from it; a figure to admire, but too complex for Deane fully to shed his own ambivalence.

Declan Kiberd is more unequivocally prepared to celebrate Joyce. In a *Crane Bag* essay of 1984 he bids to square the circle, combining modernity and a nationalism that had seemed irredeemably organicist: "There was, however, a second form of Irish revival, an alternative to the one led by Yeats and de Valera. It was pioneered by men like [James] Connolly and James Joyce, men who began with the courageous admission that there is no such thing as an Irish identity, ready-made and fixed, to be carried as a passport into eternity" (T. Brown 1988: 84). The familiar opposition between Joyce and Yeats returns, posed not as an ethnic difference (hence the association of Yeats and de Valera) but as a political one. Kiberd's Joyce speaks not for the given Catholic nation but for its European emancipation. As Brown shrewdly notes (84), "Europe" now signifies "socialism" where for MacGreevy and Corkery it had connoted "Catholicism." Even here, though, the emancipatory road is a "form of Irish revival": modernity is not simply to be opposed to nation. This is the twist in Kiberd's blockbuster *Inventing Ireland* (1995), which aims to reclaim not only Joyce, but most of the previous century's other major Irish writers, for a broad church of national renaissance. Writers and artists, Kiberd avers, have shown Ireland the way, legislating for imaginative freedom before the politicians passed their actual censorship laws. Literature is Ireland's utopia, the place where its consciousness has been most valiantly forged. Even if the reality of independence has betrayed much of that promise, Kiberd is prepared to argue for its achievements—and this involves a reversal of the Arnoldian canard that Ireland is dreamy and archaic. The aim of the Easter Rising, he quotes a veteran as saying, was to "put an end to the rule of the fairies in Ireland" (1995: 1). Toward the end of a book packed with inversions and hybridity, Kiberd argues that Ireland is "arguably more advanced than Britain" in its accommodation of nationalism and its "fully modern form of the state": "The extraordinary modernity of Irish thinking and writing deserves to be stressed, when too many commentators have emphasized only backwardness" (645). Joyce, above all, exemplifies this twist: "He did not become modern to the extent that he ceased to be Irish; rather he began from the premise that to be Irish was to be modern anyway" (266–67). Modernism and nationalism can thus be reconciled after all, and Kiberd is able to claim Joyce, alongside a suddenly rehabilitated Yeats, as part of a proud national literature. "[B]oth the 1916 Rising and *Ulysses*", Kiberd ventures, "can be interpreted in rather similar ways: as attempts to achieve, in the areas of politics and literature, the blessings of modernity *and* the liquidation of its costs. In other words, the Irish wished to be modern and counter-modern in one and the same gesture" (330).

Kiberd is Joyce's greatest utopian reader, abler than any at finding the emancipatory gift that his writing leaves to Ireland. In this respect he was a good student of Richard Ellmann. His reading of *Ulysses* is full of resounding affirmations of community, the human body, and even—extraordinarily, after the impact of theory in Joyce studies—of oral tradition triumphing over a reifying writing (355). He offers Joyce a more direct, energetic agency than does Deane, and envisages him involved in a guerilla struggle in which literary form takes on the British Empire. In Kiberd's view Joyce developed a new kind of genre, a postnovel whose name we do not yet know (342–43): in this, as in other respects, he sees the Irish writer as proleptic of the postcolonial literatures of Asia and South America. Kiberd, like Deane, sees Joyce as quintessentially modern, awake to a disenchanted world rather than the dreams of the Revival (336–37). Yet his reading is less notable for making this distinction than for the syncretism with which Joyce is drawn into the capacious movement for national liberation. For all Kiberd's doubts about the nostalgia of Revivalism, Yeats and Synge emerge as exemplary figures alongside Joyce. *Inventing Ireland* is an ecumenical epic: this is part of its utopianism. But other postcolonial studies of Joyce have emphasized not unity but division.

Emer Nolan's *James Joyce and Nationalism* (1995) challenges the critical tradition on the relation between its title's terms. From the modernists Pound and Eliot, through the American veterans Ellmann and Kenner, to recent poststructuralists, Nolan finds a refusal to think seriously about Joyce's relation to Irish politics. Against this consensus she proposes that Joyce was in fact committed not merely to gradualist nationalism but to revolutionary republicanism. The argument's centerpiece is a revisionist account of "Cyclops" that seeks to show how the prejudices of earlier readers have obscured Joyce's real sympathies. Nolan is perhaps the first critic to entertain in public the idea that Joyce supports the citizen in his debate with Leopold Bloom. The nationalists, she argues, speak a vivid Hiberno-English that "provides a parallel to literary modernism" (1995: 110). The proximity between their comical invective and the parodies of *Ulysses* itself problematizes the view that "Cyclops" is satirizing a nationalist discourse that anyway echoes Joyce's own earlier statements on Irish history. The attempt to invert these critical valences is a peculiarly difficult task. Perhaps it is because "Cyclops" is such a limit case that Nolan stakes so much on it; in practice even her provocative treatment of the issue remains tentative. (Indeed, she has subsequently been more critical of the citizen, declaring him and Bloom "two sides of the same coin" [2000: 91]). Alongside her support for nationalism, her case involves an even more striking departure from critical consensus: a new skepticism toward Bloom, who is taken as the bland figure of a cosmopolitan modernity that Joyce seeks to question. Bloom is accused of generalization, homogenization, dehistoricization—in all of which he contrasts with Stephen Dedalus, who is, in turn, elevated as an exemplary figure. Nolan proposes that Dedalus's interior monologue produces historical snapshots that arrest time and generate a fugitive political wisdom (1995: 72–73); indeed, the citizen's language is shown to perform a similar operation (102).

Nolan's polemical rereading thus sets itself against existing Joyce criticism, producing an artist whose political engagement has been distorted by liberal appropriations. Her work carries a strong implication of reclamation, whereby Joyce is returned to a national context in which he can be properly understood. She denies that "a certain reading of Joyce might facilitate a revelation of his true Irishness, or that his works might be handed back to Irish people cleansed of their difficulty and their political complexity," but insists that "the Irish have by now endured as much sentimentalizing blarney at the hands of Joyceans as they have ever perpetrated on unsuspecting literary tourists and scholars" (1995: xiv). Vincent Cheng has also picked at stereotypes of the Irish, arguing for Joyce's critique of the "binary trap" created by colonialism. Yet the emphasis of Cheng's *Joyce, Race, and Empire* (1995) differs significantly from that of Nolan. For Cheng Irish nationalism is essentially the child of empire, doomed to replicate the homogenizing and racist paradigm it seeks to displace. Joyce offers a liberating alternative, "denying the convenient, constructed essentialisms of binary distinctions based on absolute and inherent difference" (1995: 290). Cheng's and Nolan's contemporaneous works were the major postcolonial readings to date. But if they contributed to a new consensus—namely, that Joyce's politics must be taken seriously—their emphases diverged. Nolan sought to reclaim from critical dismissal the Irish nationalism that Cheng viewed as an essentialist mirror of empire; Cheng's postcolonialism worked toward a reassertion of the tolerant Joyce who could see beyond local difference. The question they raised was whether the new Joyce would turn out to be liberal or partisan. Would the reassertion of an Irish context reemphasize Joyce's cosmopolitanism in contrast to his homeland, or demonstrate his immersion in native culture?

The most uncompromising answer came not from Dublin but from London. Len Platt's *Joyce and the Anglo-Irish* (1998) takes up a theme that Nolan had only adumbrated: Joyce's relation to the cultural nationalism of the Revival. Platt sees *Ulysses* as radically distinct from this formation in its replacement of pious mythology with abrasive modernity. In itself, Platt admits (1998: 232), this is a very familiar view. The novelty here is that Joyce breaks with the Revival not in enlightened disdain for its nationalism, but in native disgust at its opportunistic falsity. He writes against Revivalism not to promote cosmopolitanism but rather to attack his ethnic and class enemy. Joyce is more Irish than the Revival: *Ulysses* is an epic of anti-Protestantism. Stephen Dedalus again emerges as the heroic figure he had not been since Kenner's intervention in the 1940s (Platt 1998: 97), for he articulates colonial dispossession and a specifically Catholic riposte to it. His performance in the library "interrogates notions of Catholic inferiority and implicitly insists on restoring Church scholasticism to a meaningful place in Ireland's intellectual tradition" (80), as had Joyce's own Triestine lectures (22–30). Platt's reading revives a view of Joyce that we have already witnessed in the responses of Yeats and Eglinton, Kavanagh and Montgomery, but whose political implications were never assimilated by the critical tradition. "In 'Circe,'" Platt declares with some relish, "Joyce really wipes the floor with Protestant revivalism" (177–78). Readers of a sensitive disposition are advised to look away. This is among the most unabashedly partisan treatments Joyce has ever received; and Platt is insistent upon the intensity of Joyce's involvement in the polemic. Unlike recent American scholars of Joyce's conception of history, he views Joyce not as a detached theorist but as a cultural combatant with no interest in transcending his own preconceptions of the Anglo-Irish: "Joyce had a very considerable investment in historical reconstruction, a motivation that was powerful, committed, even raw"; he was "engaged in a furious war over cultural politics" (16–17). Among Platt's most original contributions is this visceral, frankly one-sided view of Joyce's politics, beside which other accounts of his "commitment" look anemic. It may be that Platt's approach responds more accurately to the politics of late-colonial Ireland than other, more decorous critical idioms. It may also be that in a period of Irish reclamations of Joyce, this approach is enabled by Platt's very distance from contemporary Ireland, where his book's sectarian resonances would be nearer the knuckle.

Platt's approach is echoed and developed by Andrew Gibson, who has fostered a political reading of Joyce distinguished by its attention to social history. *Joyce's Revenge* (2002) is Gibson's statement, the product of fifteen years of research: in the plenitude of its detail and the subtlety of its argument it represents the culmination thus far of the "Irish turn" in the reading of Joyce. Gibson's work differs from Platt's in two main ways. One is its focus on England, rather than Anglo-Ireland, as Joyce's prime target. For Gibson *Ulysses* responds not only to centuries of colonialism but also to a very historically specific burst of English cultural nationalism that had evolved during Joyce's own lifetime. (The focus on this formation is an implicit riposte to the Anglocentric view, in which only Ireland could need a nationalist movement.) The extravagant styles of *Ulysses*—the bad writing of "Eumaeus" is an exemplary case—emerge as deliberate contaminations and perversions of English modes whose original forms had insisted on purity, sanity, and correctness. Joyce thus performs not so much a de-Anglicization of Ireland as a recolonization of the imperial culture. Gibson's second difference from Platt is his emphasis on Joyce's own effort to transcend the limits of anticolonialism. Gibson's Joyce understands that resistance to empire is necessary yet also disabling; his strenuous critique of colonial culture is accompanied by a certain utopian aspiration beyond it. Gibson sees *Ulysses* as beginning with Irish *ressentiment*, yet working to be free of it. If it is a sustained piece of resistance to England, it also "moves towards conciliation and reconciliation" (2002: 19). In Brecht's terms, this Joyce understands that "Anger, even against injustice / Makes the voice hoarse" (1976: 320); and the laughter of *Ulysses* is an attempt to escape this bind.

Gibson's Joyce thus contains echoes of others. Like Platt's, he is engaged in a ferocious cultural battle; simultaneously, like Kiberd's, he seeks a utopian path "beyond nationalism to liberation." The complexity of this project is not lost on Gibson, who repeatedly stresses the arduous delicacy of Joyce's labor—most clearly in his identification of three "Joycean virtues": "historical specificity; work; and the clear-eyed recognition of difficulty or entanglement" (2002: 18). Like other critics before him, Gibson here makes a gesture of fidelity, visibly seeking to emulate the virtues he ascribes to Joyce. Above all, he responds to the novel's "historical specificity" with an insistence on particularity (4, 8, 42–43, 139, 151) and a barrage of historical sources hitherto untouched by the critical tradition. While his general argument combines existing postcolonial positions into a significant new synthesis, it may be this densely particularizing method that is Gibson's chief legacy to the study of Joyce. Following his work, a number of familiar themes may be available for reconsideration in more rigorously historical terms.

Within the existing field of Irish-centered readings of Joyce, there is a clear consensus about Joyce's active hostility toward colonialism. But beyond this most general principle major questions remain open. There is still room for disagreement, for instance, over Joyce's relationship to three key formations: nationalism, Anglo-Ireland, and Catholicism. Thus, the complicity of Irish nationalism with its colonial antagonist has become a truism, but Nolan has questioned Joyce's distance from it, and his well-known investment in Parnell (Gibson 2002: 4–6) confirms the need for further scrutiny. Gibson and, emphatically, Platt identify the Anglo-Irish as usurpers despised by Joyce, but this reading is in tension with Kiberd's syncretic utopianism or Cheng's denunciation of ethnic division. Cheng's more recent attack on Irish Ireland's illiberal refusal of authenticity to "a Yeats or a Bloom" (2001: 18) clearly conflicts with the English critics' qualified sympathy for D. P. Moran. The character of the Revival—its claim to authenticity, its relation to nationalism, and Joyce's own view of it—has not been settled: unsurprising, given the movement's extent and influence. Meanwhile, the body that escapes largely unscathed from the English historicists' rigorous polemics is the Catholic Church itself. Platt and Gibson view Joyce not only as the representative of a rising Catholic middle class but, more specifically, as defending and deploying Catholic theology against Protestant civilization. In this respect secular criticism has returned to the assertion of Joyce's religious allegiance that was long ago made by Noon, Sullivan, and Kenner. Catholicism is now associated with radicalism, as indeed it customarily is in contemporary British perceptions of Northern Ireland. A case has been made for reexamining Joyce's own religious convictions (McGinley 1996: 34; Morrison 1999). In postcolonial criticism, though, the Catholic Church's status as one of Ireland's two imperial masters has been notably soft-pedaled. Platt and Gibson mention it only intermittently, and Gibson characteristically ascribes Catholic repressiveness to the British influence (2002: 202–3). Even in his finely detailed analysis of Father Conmee (82–86), the Church's only meaningful crime is its complicity with England. Rejection of the British Empire is a given in Joyce studies. How far its dialectic of enlightenment and cruelty is matched by the record of the other empire appears to be off the agenda. One emphasis has thus gone missing: Joyce's role as one of the great secularizing figures of modern Ireland and beyond.

These debates continue the critical history I have examined in this chapter. Like that history, they are not easily separable from the modern history of Ireland itself. One lesson of recent criticism has been that Joyce's writing must be understood in relation to Irish history; it may now be that this also applies to the reading of Joyce. It is also evident, however, that Joyce cannot be returned to a unitary and predictable "Ireland." Since his own youth, Joyce has provoked contention as much as consensus in his homeland. The fact that it ceased to be his only homeland only intensified this. ("Exile," in fact, is another venerable trope that deserves rigorous reintegration into current criticism.) In Ireland—as elsewhere, from Pound to Derrida—Joyce has been not only a subject in his own right but the occasion for other questions and enterprises. This is true even of the easily mocked heritage industry, which Emer Nolan (1995: xiv) has carefully distinguished from its English counterparts. Dublin's commemoration of Joyce combines financial opportunism and political convenience; but it is also a testament to transformations in Ireland that Joyce himself helped to inspire. The National Library of Ireland's recent acquisition of important manuscript material also reflects social change, and will contribute to Ireland's growing prominence in the interpretation of Joyce. The "Irish turn" in Joyce criticism has helped us to understand the centrality of colonialism, and the struggle against it, in texts that had long been seen in international or abstract terms. The densely particularized reading of that history in Joyce's work continues to be a priority, and may have only just begun. We will know if a Joycean utopia ever arrives: these questions will no longer seem more urgent than listening to his rendition of the Blooms' cat or the sound of the sea. What is certain is that Ireland has not finished with Joyce, even if he has by now become a nightmare from which many Dubliners would like to awake.

Works Cited

Index

Works Cited

Aaron, Daniel (1979) *Writers on the Left: Episodes in American Literary Communism.* New York: Octagon; orig. pub. New York: Harcourt Brace Jovanovich, 1961.
Adams, Michael (1968) *Censorship: The Irish Experience.* Dublin: Scepter.
Allen, Walter (1958) *The English Novel.* Harmondsworth, Eng.: Pelican; orig. pub. London: Phoenix House, 1954.
"Aramis" (1970) "The Scandal of *Ulysses.*" *Sporting Times,* no. 34 (1 April 1922): 4. In *James Joyce: The Critical Heritage,* ed. Deming, 192–94.
Ardagh, John (1994) *Ireland and the Irish.* London: Hamish Hamilton.
Arnold, Bruce (1991) *The Scandal of "Ulysses": The Sensational Life of a Twentieth-Century Masterpiece.* New York: St. Martin's.
Ashworth, G. J., and Larkham, P. J., eds. (1994) *Building a New Heritage: Tourism, Culture and Identity in the New Europe.* London: Routledge.
Attridge, Derek (1988) *Peculiar Language: Literature as Difference from the Renaissance to James Joyce.* London: Methuen.
——, ed. (1990) *The Cambridge Companion to James Joyce.* Cambridge: Cambridge University Press.
—— (2000) *Joyce Effects.* Cambridge: Cambridge University Press.
Attridge, Derek, and Daniel Ferrer, eds. (1984) *Post-Structuralist Joyce: Essays from the French.* Cambridge: Cambridge University Press.
Attridge, Derek, and Marjorie Howes, eds. (2000) *Semicolonial Joyce.* Cambridge: Cambridge University Press.
Baldick, Chris (1987) *The Social Mission of English Criticism, 1848–1932,* rev. ed. Oxford: Clarendon; 1st ed. 1983.
—— (1996) *Criticism and Literary Theory, 1890 to the Present.* London: Longman.
Barthes, Roland (1967) *Writing Degree Zero,* trans. Annette Lavers. London: Jonathan Cape; orig. pub. Paris: Seuil, 1953.
—— (1973) *Mythologies,* trans. Annette Lavers. St. Albans, Eng.: Paladin; orig. pub. Paris: Seuil, 1957.
Baudrillard, Jean (1983) *Simulations.* New York: Semiotext(e).

Beckett, Samuel (1983) *Disjecta: Miscellaneous Writings and a Dramatic Fragment*, ed. Ruby Cohn. London: John Calder.

———, et al. (1961) *Our Exagmination Round His Factification for Incamination of Work in Progress*. London: Faber; orig. pub. Paris: Shakespeare and Company, 1929.

Begnal, Michael H. (1991) "A Skeleton Key to Campbell and Robinson." In *Re-Viewing Classics of Joyce Criticism*, ed. Dunleavy, 36–45.

——— (1992) "*Finnegans Wake* and the Nature of Narrative." In *Critical Essays on James Joyce's "Finnegans Wake,"* ed. McCarthy, 119–28.

Behan, Maria (2002) "Drinking in Joyce." In *James Joyce Bloomsday Magazine 2002*, ed. Meade, 45–47.

Beja, Morris, ed. (1973) *"Dubliners" and "A Portrait of the Artist as a Young Man": A Casebook*. London: Macmillan.

Beja, Morris, Phillip Herring, Maurice Harmon, and David Norris, eds. (1986) *James Joyce: The Centennial Symposium*. Urbana: University of Illinois Press.

Belsey, Catherine (1980) *Critical Practice*. London: Methuen.

Benjamin, Walter (1973) *Illuminations*, ed. Hannah Arendt and trans. Harry Zohn. London: Fontana.

Bennett, Arnold (1970) "James Joyce's *Ulysses*." *Outlook* (29 April 1922): 337–39. In *James Joyce: The Critical Heritage*, ed. Deming, 219–22.

Benstock, Bernard (1991) "The Fabulous Voyaging of Richard M. Kain." In *Re-Viewing Classics of Joyce Criticism*, ed. Dunleavy, 8–22.

———, ed. (1982) *The Seventh of Joyce*. Bloomington: Indiana University Press.

———, ed. (1988) *James Joyce: The Augmented Ninth*. Syracuse, N.Y.: Syracuse University Press.

Bergonzi, Bernard (1986) *The Myth of Modernism and Twentieth-Century Literature*. New York: St. Martin's.

Bérubé, Michael (1992) *Marginal Forces/Cultural Centers: Tolson, Pynchon, and the Politics of the Canon*. Ithaca, N.Y.: Cornell University Press.

Bloom, Harold, ed. (1986) *James Joyce: Modern Critical Views*. New York: Chelsea House.

Bolt, Sydney (1992) *A Preface to James Joyce*, 2nd ed. Harlow: Longman; 1st ed. 1981.

Booth, Wayne C. (1961) *The Rhetoric of Fiction*. Chicago: University of Chicago Press.

Bordwell, David (1989) *Making Meaning: Inference and Rhetoric in the Interpretation of Cinema*. Cambridge, Mass.: Harvard University Press.

Bourdieu, Pierre (1993) *The Field of Cultural Production: Essays on Art and Literature*, ed. Randal Johnson. Cambridge: Polity.

Bowie, Malcolm (1979) "Jacques Lacan." In *Structuralism and Since*, ed. Sturrock, 116–53.
Brannigan, John, Geoff Ward, and Julian Wolfreys, eds. (1998) *Re: Joyce: Text, Culture, Politics*. Basingstoke, Eng.: Palgrave Macmillan.
Brecht, Bertolt (1964) *Brecht on Theatre: The Development of an Aesthetic*, ed. John Willett. London: Methuen.
——— (1976) *Poems, 1913–1956*. London: Eyre Methuen.
Brion, Marcel (1961) "The Idea of Time in the Work of James Joyce." In Beckett et al., *Our Exagmination*, 23–33.
Bristol, Michael (1996) *Big-Time Shakespeare*. London: Routledge.
Brown, Dennis (1990) *Intertextual Dynamics within the Literary Group—Joyce, Lewis, Pound and Eliot: The Men of 1914*. Basingstoke, Eng.: Macmillan.
Brown, Richard (1985) *James Joyce and Sexuality*. Cambridge: Cambridge University Press.
——— (1992) *James Joyce: A Post-Culturalist Perspective*. Basingstoke, Eng.: Macmillan.
——— (1996) "Marilyn Monroe Reading *Ulysses:* Goddess or Post-Cultural Cyborg?" In *Joyce and Popular Culture*, ed. Kershner, 170–79.
Brown, Terence (1985) *Ireland: A Social and Cultural History, 1922–1985*. London: Fontana.
——— (1988) *Ireland's Literature: Selected Essays*. Mullingar, Ire.: Lilliput.
Budgen, Frank (1961) "James Joyce's *Work in Progress* and Old Norse Poetry." In Beckett et al., *Our Exagmination*, 35–46.
——— (1989) *James Joyce and the Making of "Ulysses."* Oxford: Oxford University Press; orig. pub. London: Grayson and Grayson, 1934.
Burgess, Anthony (1973) *Joysprick: An Introduction to the Language of James Joyce*. London: André Deutsch.
———, ed. (1965) *A Shorter "Finnegans Wake."* London: Faber.
Bush, Ronald (1996) "James Joyce: The Way He Lives Now." *James Joyce Quarterly* 33, no. 4 (summer): 523–29.
Cairns, David, and Shaun Richards (1988) *Writing Ireland: Colonialism, Nationalism and Culture*. Manchester: Manchester University Press.
Campbell, Joseph, and Henry Morton Robinson (1944) *A Skeleton Key to "Finnegans Wake."* London: Faber.
Carlson, Julia, ed. (1990) *Banned in Ireland: Censorship and the Irish Writer*. Athens: University of Georgia Press.
Carroll, David, ed. (1990) *The States of "Theory": History, Art and Critical Discourse*. New York: Columbia University Press.
Carter, Angela (1992) *Expletives Deleted*. London: Vintage.

Cheng, Vincent J. (1995) *Joyce, Race and Empire*. Cambridge: Cambridge University Press.
——— (2001) "'Terrible Queer Creatures': Joyce, Cosmopolitanism, and the Inauthentic Irishman." In *James Joyce and the Fabrication of an Irish Identity*, ed. Michael Patrick Gillespie, 11–38. Amsterdam: Rodopi.
Collins, Joseph (1970) "James Joyce's Amazing Chronicle." *New York Times Book Review*, 28 May 1922, 6, 17. In *James Joyce: The Critical Heritage*, ed. Deming, 222–26.
Connor, Steven (1996) *James Joyce*. Exeter, Eng.: Northcote House.
——— (1997) *Postmodernist Culture: An Introduction to Theories of the Contemporary*, 2nd ed. Oxford: Blackwell; 1st ed. 1989.
Corner, John, and Sylvia Harvey, eds. (1991) *Enterprise and Heritage: Crosscurrents of National Culture*. London: Routledge.
Costello, Peter (1994) *James Joyce: The Years of Growth, 1882–1915*. London/Basingstoke: Papermac/Macmillan; orig. pub. London: Kyle Cathie, 1992.
Costello, Peter, and Peter van de Kamp (1987) *Flann O'Brien: An Illustrated Biography*. London: Bloomsbury.
Coward, Rosalind, and John Ellis (1977) *Language and Materialism: Developments in Semiology and the Theory of the Subject*. London: Routledge and Kegan Paul.
Cronin, Anthony (1959) "The Master Builder." *Times Literary Supplement*, 20 November, 669–70.
——— (1986) *Dead as Doornails: Bohemian Dublin in the Fifties and Sixties*. Oxford: Oxford University Press; orig. pub. London/Dublin: Calder and Boyers/Dolmen Press, 1976.
——— (1989) *No Laughing Matter: The Life and Times of Flann O'Brien*. London: Grafton.
Culler, Jonathan (1988) *Framing the Sign*. Oxford: Blackwell.
Currie, Mark (1998) "Revisiting Poststructuralist Joyce." In *Re: Joyce*, ed. Brannigan et al., 258–64.
Deane, Seamus (1985) "Heroic Styles: The Tradition of an Idea." In *Ireland's Field Day*, ed. Field Day Theatre Company, 45–58.
——— (1986) *A Short History of Irish Literature*. London: Hutchinson.
——— (1990) "Joyce the Irishman." In *The Cambridge Companion to James Joyce*, ed. Attridge, 31–53.
——— (1992a) Introduction to *A Portrait of the Artist as a Young Man*, by James Joyce, ed. Deane, vii–xliii.
——— (1992b) Introduction to *Finnegans Wake*, by James Joyce, ed. Deane, vii–xlix.

DeKoven, Marianne (1991) *Rich and Strange: Gender, History, Modernism*. Princeton: Princeton University Press.
Delaney, Frank (1983) *James Joyce's Odyssey: A Guide to the Dublin of "Ulysses."* London: Paladin; orig. pub. London: Hodder and Stoughton, 1981.
Deming, Robert, ed. (1970) *James Joyce: The Critical Heritage*. 2 vols. London: Routledge and Kegan Paul.
Derrida, Jacques (1978) *Edmund Husserl's "The Origin of Geometry": An Introduction*, trans. John P. Leavey, Jr., and ed. David B. Allison. Stony Brook, N.Y.: Nicolas Hays.
——— (1984) "Two Words for Joyce." In *Post-Structuralist Joyce*, ed. Attridge and Ferrer, 145–59.
——— (1992) *Acts of Literature*, ed. Derek Attridge. London: Routledge.
Dettmar, Kevin J. H., ed. (1992) *Rereading the New: A Backward Glance at Modernism*. Ann Arbor: University of Michigan Press.
——— (1996a) *The Illicit Joyce of Postmodernism*. Madison: University of Wisconsin Press.
——— (1996b) "*Ulysses* and the Preemptive Power of Plot." In *Pedagogy, Praxis, "Ulysses"*, ed. Newman, 21–46.
Dick, Susan, Declan Kiberd, Dougald Macmillan, and Joseph Ronsley, eds. (1989). *Omnium Gatherum: Essays for Richard Ellmann*. Gerrards Cross, Eng.: Colin Smythe.
Docker, John (1994) *Postmodernism and Popular Culture: A Cultural History*. Cambridge: Cambridge University Press.
Doyle, Brian (1989) *England and Englishness*. London: Routledge.
Dunleavy, Janet Egleson (1991) *Re-Viewing Classics of Joyce Criticism*. Urbana: University of Illinois Press.
Eagleton, Terry (1976a) *Criticism and Ideology: A Study in Marxist Literary Theory*. London: NLB, 1976.
——— (1976b) *Marxism and Literary Criticism*. London: Methuen.
——— (1980). "Molly's Piano." *New Statesman* 100 (19 September): 21.
——— (1983) *Literary Theory: An Introduction*. Oxford: Blackwell.
——— (1990) *The Ideology of the Aesthetic*. Oxford: Blackwell.
——— (1997) *Marx*. London: Phoenix.
——— (1998) *Crazy John and the Bishop, and Other Essays on Irish Culture*. Cork: Cork University Press.
Easthope, Antony (1988) *British Post-Structuralism Since 1968*. London: Routledge.
Edel, Leon (1977) *The Life of Henry James*. 2 vols. Harmondsworth, Eng.: Peregrine.

Eglinton, John (1970) "Dublin Letter." *Dial* 86 (May 1929): 417–20. In *James Joyce: The Critical Heritage*, ed. Deming, 459.

——— (1990) "The Beginnings of Joyce." In *James Joyce: Interviews and Recollections*, ed. E. H. Mikhail, 32–37. Basingstoke, Eng.: Macmillan.

Eliot, T. S. (1948) "A Message to the Fish." *Horizon* 3 (March 1941): 173–75. In *James Joyce*, ed. Givens, 468–71.

——— (1975) *Selected Prose*, ed. Frank Kermode. London: Faber.

——— (1988) *The Letters of T. S. Eliot*. Vol. 1: *1898–1922*, ed. Valerie Eliot. London: Faber.

Ellmann, Richard (1972) *Ulysses on the Liffey*. London: Faber, 1972.

——— (1973) *Golden Codgers: Biographical Speculations*. Oxford: Oxford University Press.

——— (1975) "Pieces of *Ulysses*" (review of *James Joyce's "Ulysses": Critical Essays*, ed. Hart and Hayman). *Times Literary Supplement*, 3 October, 1118.

——— (1977) *The Consciousness of Joyce*. London: Faber.

——— (1982) *James Joyce*, rev. ed. Oxford: Oxford University Press; 1st ed. 1959.

——— (1986) Preface to *Ulysses*, by James Joyce, ix–xiv.

——— (1989) *a long the riverrun: Selected Essays*. Harmondsworth, Eng.: Penguin; orig. pub. London: Hamish Hamilton, 1988.

Empson, William (1959) "The Joyce Saga: Before Bloomsday and After." *New Statesman*, 31 October, 585–86.

——— (1984) *Using Biography*. London: Chatto and Windus.

Enright, D. J. (1943) "Cormac's Ruined House: A Survey of the Modern Irish Novel." *Scrutiny* 11, no. 3 (spring): 180–88.

Evans, Ifor (1963) *A Short History of English Literature*, 2nd ed. Harmondsworth, Eng.: Pelican.

Evans, Malcolm (1989) *Signifying Nothing: Truth's True Contents in Shakespeare's Texts*, 2nd. ed. Hemel Hempstead, Eng.: Harvester Wheatsheaf.

Fairhall, James (1993) *James Joyce and the Question of History*. Cambridge: Cambridge University Press.

Fanning, Aengus (2002) "Remembrance of Bloomsdays Past." *Sunday Independent*, 16 June, 11.

Ffrench, Patrick (1995) *The Time of Theory: A History of "Tel Quel," 1960–1983*. Oxford: Clarendon.

Field Day Theatre Company, ed. (1985) *Ireland's Field Day*. London: Hutchinson.

Finney, Michael (1978) "Eugene Jolas, *transition,* and the Revolution of the Word." In *In the Wake of the "Wake,"* ed. Hayman and Anderson, 39–53.

Fitch, Noel Riley (1985) *Sylvia Beach and the Lost Generation.* Harmondsworth, Eng.: Penguin, 1985; orig. pub. New York: Norton, 1983.

Fitzpatrick, David (1977) *Politics and Irish Life, 1913–21: Provincial Experience of War and Revolution.* Dublin: Gill and Macmillan.

Flaubert, Gustave (1997) *Selected Letters,* ed. Geoffrey Wall. Harmondsworth, Eng.: Penguin.

Foster, John Wilson (1991) *Colonial Consequences: Essays in Irish Literature and Culture.* Dublin: Lilliput.

Foster, Roy (1986) "We Are All Revisionists Now." *Irish Review* 1: 1–5.

——— (1989). *Modern Ireland, 1600–1972.* Harmondsworth, Eng.: Penguin; orig. pub. London: Allen Lane, 1988.

——— (1995) Review of Peter Costello, *James Joyce: The Years of Growth, Odyssey* 7 (spring): 2–3.

——— (1998a) "Ulster Chooses Life." *Independent on Sunday,* 24 May, sec. 2, pp. 1–2.

——— (1998b) "Homage to a Spoilt God." *Independent on Sunday,* 26 July, sec. 2, p. 3.

Foucault, Michel (1991) *The Foucault Reader,* ed. Paul Rabinow. Harmondsworth, Eng.: Penguin; orig. pub. New York: Pantheon, 1984.

French, Marilyn (1982). *The Book as World: James Joyce's "Ulysses."* London: Abacus; orig. pub. Cambridge, Mass.: Harvard University Press, 1976.

Friedman, Melvin J. (1991). "Ellmann on Joyce." In *Re-Viewing Classics of Joyce Criticism,* ed. Dunleavy, 130–41.

Friedman, Susan Stanford, ed. (1993). *Joyce: The Return of the Repressed.* Ithaca, N.Y.: Cornell University Press.

Fussell, Paul (1975). *The Great War and Modern Memory.* Oxford: Oxford University Press.

Gaudier-Brzeska, Henri (1914) "Vortex. Gaudier-Brzeska." *Blast* 1 (June): 155–58.

Gébler Davies, Stan (1975) *James Joyce: A Portrait of the Artist.* London: Davis-Poynter.

Gibbons, Luke (1996) *Transformations in Irish Culture.* Cork: Cork University Press.

Gibson, Andrew, ed. (1995) *Reading Joyce's "Circe."* Amsterdam: Rodopi.

———, ed. (1996) "*Ithaca.*" Amsterdam: Rodopi.

———, (1997) Review of Vincent J. Cheng, *Joyce, Race and Empire, New Odyssey* 4, no. 1 (winter/spring): 2–3.

——— (2002) *Joyce's Revenge: History, Politics and Aesthetics in "Ulysses."* Oxford: Oxford University Press.

Gilbert, Sandra M., and Susan Gubar (1985) "Sexual Linguistics: Gender, Language, Sexuality." *New Literary History* 16: 515–43.

Gilbert, Stuart (1959) "In the Wake of His Life Flowed His Art." *Saturday Review*, 24 October, 43–44.

——— (1961) "Prolegomena to Work In Progress." In Beckett et al., *Our Exagmination*, 47–75.

——— (1963) *James Joyce's "Ulysses,"* rev. ed. Harmondsworth, Eng.: Peregrine; 1st ed. London: Faber, 1930.

——— (1993) *Reflections on James Joyce: Stuart's Gilbert's Paris Journal*, ed. Thomas F. Staley and Randolph Lewis. Austin: University of Texas Press.

Gillespie, Michael Patrick (1989) *Reading the Book of Himself: Narrative Strategies in the Works of James Joyce*. Columbus: Ohio State University Press.

——— (1991) "Kenner on Joyce." In *Re-Viewing Classics of Joyce Crticism*, ed. Dunleavy, 142–54.

Givens, Seon, ed. (1948) *James Joyce: Two Decades of Criticism*. New York: Vanguard.

Glasheen, Adaline (1977) *Third Census of "Finnegans Wake."* Berkeley: University of California Press.

Gogarty, Oliver St. John (1970) "They Think They Know Joyce." *Saturday Review of Literature* 33 (18 March 1950): 8–9, 36–37. In *James Joyce: The Critical Heritage*, ed. Deming, 764–65.

Goldberg, S. L. (1961) *The Classical Temper: A Study of James Joyce's "Ulysses."* London: Chatto and Windus.

Gorman, Herbert (1941) *James Joyce: A Definitive Biography*. London: John Lane/The Bodley Head.

Graff, Gerald (1987) *Professing Literature: An Institutional History*. Chicago: University of Chicago Press.

Graham, B. J. (1994) "Heritage Conservation and Revisionist Nationalism in Ireland." In *Building a New Heritage*, ed. Ashworth and Larkham, 135–58.

Grant, Damian (1970) *Realism*. London: Methuen.

Gross, John (1976) *Joyce*, corrected impression. London: Fontana-Collins; orig. pub. 1970.

Gupta, Suman (1993) "The Construction of Criticism: Critical Responses to James Joyce's *Ulysses*, 1922–1941." Ph.D. diss, Oxford University.

Hart, Clive, and David Hayman, eds. (1974) *James Joyce's "Ulysses": Critical Essays*. Berkeley: University of California Press.

Harvey, David (1989) *The Condition of Postmodernity*. Oxford: Blackwell.

——— (1996) *Justice, Nature and the Geography of Difference*. Oxford: Blackwell.

Harwood, John (1995) *Eliot to Derrida: The Poverty of Interpretation.* Basingstoke, Eng.: Macmillan.
Hawkes, Terence (1977) *Structuralism and Semiotics.* London: Methuen.
Hayman, David (1982) *"Ulysses": The Mechanics of Meaning,* rev. ed. Madison: University of Wisconsin Press; orig. pub. Englewood Cliffs, N.J.: Prentice-Hall, 1970.
Hayman, David, and Elliott Anderson, eds. (1978) *In The Wake of the "Wake."* Madison: University of Wisconsin Press.
Heaney, Seamus (1990) *New Selected Poems, 1966–1987.* London: Faber.
Heath, Stephen (1972) *The Nouveau Roman: A Study in the Practice of Writing.* London: Elek.
——— (1975) Note to Phillipe Sollers, "Joyce and Co.," *Tel Quel* 64 (winter): 3–13.
——— (1984) "Ambiviolences: Notes for Reading Joyce." In *Post-Structuralist Joyce,* ed. Attridge and Ferrer, 31–68.
Henke, Suzette A. (1990) *James Joyce and the Politics of Desire.* London: Routledge.
——— (1991) "Exagmining Beckett and Company." In *Re-Viewing Classics of Joyce Criticism,* ed. Dunleavy, 60–81.
Herr, Cheryl (1986) *Joyce's Anatomy of Culture.* Urbana: University of Illinois Press.
——— (1994) "'Penelope' as Period Piece." In *Molly Blooms,* ed. Pearce, 63–79.
——— (1996) "Ireland from the Outside." In *Joyce and the Subject of History,* ed. Wollaeger, Luftig, and Spoo, 195–210.
Herring, Phillip F. (1969) "Some Thoughts on the Second International James Joyce Symposium." *James Joyce Quarterly* 7, no. 1 (fall): 3–9.
——— (1989) "Richard Ellmann's *James Joyce.*" In *The Biographer's Art: New Essays,* ed. Jeffrey Meyers, 106–27. Basingstoke, Eng.: Macmillan.
Higgins, Aidan (1970) "Tired Lines, or Tales My Mother Told Me." In *A Bash in the Tunnel,* ed. Ryan, 55–60.
Hillis Miller, J. (1982) "From Narrative Theory to Joyce; From Joyce to Narrative Theory." In *The Seventh of Joyce,* ed. Benstock, 3–4.
Holderness, Graham, ed. (1988) *The Shakespeare Myth.* Manchester: Manchester University Press.
Holderness, Graham, and Bryan Loughrey (1991) "Shakespearean Features." In *The Appropriation of Shakespeare,* ed. Marsden, 183–201.
Huddleston, Sisley (1970) "*Ulysses.*" *Observer,* no. 6823 (5 March 1922), 4. In *James Joyce: The Critical Heritage,* ed. Deming, 213–16.
Hughes, Barry (2002) "Spaz Guide To: Bloomsday." *Slate,* June.
Hulme, T. E. (1960) *Speculations: Essays on Humanism and the Philosophy of Art,* ed. Herbert Read. London: Routledge and Kegan Paul.

Hussey, Gemma (1995) *Ireland Today: Anatomy of a Changing State.* Harmondsworth, Eng.: Penguin; orig. pub. Dublin: Town House and Country House, 1993.

Huyssen, Andreas (1986) *After the Great Divide: Modernism, Mass Culture and Postmodernism.* Bloomington: Indiana University Press.

Inglis, Fred (1995) *Raymond Williams.* London: Routledge.

Irish Ferries (2001). *Ulysses—a Voyage of Discovery* (publicity brochure).

Jackson, Holbrook (1970) "Ulysses à la Joyce." *To-Day* 9 (June 1922): 47–49. In *James Joyce: The Critical Heritage,* ed. Deming, 198–200.

Jameson, Fredric (1979) *Fables of Aggression: Wyndham Lewis, the Modernist as Fascist.* Berkeley: University of California Press.

——— (1982) "*Ulysses* in History." In *James Joyce and Modern Literature,* ed. McCormack and Stead, 126–41.

Johnson, Jeri (1993) Introduction to *Ulysses,* by James Joyce. Oxford: Oxford University Press, ix–xxxvii.

Johnson, Lesley (1979) *The Cultural Critics: From Matthew Arnold to Raymond Williams.* London: Routledge and Kegan Paul.

Johnston, Denis (1970) "A Short View of the Progress of Joyceanicity." In *A Bash in the Tunnel,* ed. Ryan, 163–67.

Jolas, Eugene (1948) "My Friend James Joyce." In *James Joyce,* ed. Givens, 3–18.

——— (1961) "The Revolution of Language and James Joyce." In Beckett et al., *Our Exagmination,* 77–92.

Jones, Peter, ed. (1972) *Imagist Poetry.* Harmondsworth, Eng.: Penguin.

Jordan, John (1970) "Joyce without Fears: A Personal Journey." In *A Bash in the Tunnel,* ed. Ryan, 135–46.

Joyce, James (1975) *Selected Letters,* ed. Richard Ellmann. London: Faber.

——— (1986) *Ulysses,* corrected text, ed. Hans Walter Gabler. Harmondsworth, Eng.: Penguin.

——— (1992a) *A Portrait of the Artist as a Young Man,* ed. Seamus Deane. Harmondsworth, Eng.: Penguin; orig. pub. New York: Huebsch, 1916, and London: Egoist Press, 1917.

——— (1992b) *Finnegans Wake,* ed. Seamus Deane. Harmondsworth, Eng.: Penguin; orig. pub. London: Faber, 1939.

Kain, Richard M. (1947) *Fabulous Voyager: A Study of James Joyce's "Ulysses."* New York: Viking.

Kant, Immanuel (1987) *Critique of Judgment,* trans. Werner S. Pluhar. Indianapolis: Hackett.

Kaufmann, Michael Edward (1992) "T. S. Eliot's New Critical Footnotes to Modernism." In *Rereading the New,* ed. Dettmar, 73–85.

Kavanagh, Patrick (1970) "Who Killed James Joyce?" In *A Bash in the Tunnel*, ed. Ryan, 49–52.
Kearney, Richard (1988) *Transitions: Narratives in Modern Irish Culture*. Manchester: Manchester University Press.
Kelly, Joseph (1998) *Our Joyce: From Outcast to Icon*. Austin: University of Texas Press.
Kenner, Hugh (1962) *The Stoic Comedians: Flaubert, Joyce and Beckett*. Berkeley: University of California Press.
——— (1974) "Circe." In *Reading Joyce's "Ulysses": Critical Essays*, ed. Hart and Hayman, 341–62.
——— (1975) *The Pound Era: The Age of Ezra Pound, T. S. Eliot, James Joyce and Wyndham Lewis*. London: Faber; orig. pub. Berkeley: University of California Press, 1971.
——— (1976) "The Pedagogue as Critic." In *The New Criticism and After*, ed. Thomas Daniel Young, 36–46. Charlottesville: University of Virginia Press.
——— (1978) *Joyce's Voices*. Berkeley: University of California Press.
——— (1982a) "Notes Towards an Anatomy of 'Modernism.'" In *A Starchamber Quiry: A James Joyce Centennial Volume, 1882–1982*, ed. E. L. Epstein, 1–42. London: Methuen.
——— (1982b) "The Impertinence of Being Definitive." *Times Literary Supplement*, 17 December, 1383–84.
——— (1983) *A Colder Eye: The Modern Irish Writers*. London: Allen Lane.
——— (1984) "The Making of the Modernist Canon." In *Canons*, ed. Robert von Hallberg, 363–75. Chicago: University of Chicago Press.
——— (1987a) *Dublin's Joyce*. New York: Columbia University Press; 1st ed. Bloomington: Indiana University Press, 1956.
——— (1987b) *"Ulysses,"* rev. ed. Baltimore, Md.: Johns Hopkins University Press; 1st ed. Hemel Hempstead, Eng.: George Allen and Unwin, 1980.
——— (1987c) *The Mechanic Muse*. Oxford: Oxford University Press.
——— (1991) Introduction to *Axel's Castle*, by Edmund Wilson. New York: Collier Books, ix–xxii.
——— (1993) "Joyce and Modernism." In *Approaches to Teaching Joyce's "Ulysses,"* ed. McCormick and Steinberg, 21–30.
Keogh, Dermot (1994) *Twentieth-Century Ireland: Nation and State*. Dublin: Gill and Macmillan.
Kermode, Frank (1959) "Puzzles and Epiphanies." *Spectator*, 13 November, 675–76.
——— (1997) *Not Entitled: A Memoir*. London: Flamingo; orig. pub. New York: Farrar, Straus & Giroux, 1995.

Kershner, R. B., ed. (1996) *Joyce and Popular Culture*. Gainesville: University of Florida Press.

Kettle, Arnold (1973) "The Consistency of James Joyce." In *The Pelican Guide to English Literature*. Vol. 7: *The Modern Age*, 3rd. ed., ed. Boris Ford, 319–32. Harmondsworth, Eng.: Pelican, 1973.

Kiberd, Declan (1995) *Inventing Ireland: The Literature of the Modern Nation*. London: Jonathan Cape.

——— (1998) "John Bull's Other Irishman." Paper presented at the conference "Aesthetics/Gender/Nation: Perspectives on the Work of Terry Eagleton." Oxford University, 21 March.

Kiely, Benedict (1970) "The Artist on the Giant's Grave." In *A Bash in the Tunnel*, ed. Ryan, 235–41.

Knowlson, James (1996) *Damned to Fame: The Life of Samuel Beckett*. London: Bloomsbury.

Kristeva, Julia (1984) *Revolution in Poetic Language*, trans. Margaret Waller. New York: Columbia University Press; orig. pub. Paris: Seuil, 1974.

Larbaud, Valéry (1970) "James Joyce." *Nouvelle Revue Française* 18 (April 1922): 385–405. In *James Joyce: The Critical Heritage*, ed. Deming, 252–62.

Lawrence, Karen R. (1990) "Joyce and Feminism." In *The Cambridge Companion to James Joyce*, ed. Attridge, 237–58.

——— (2001) "Building the Foundation: Women in the IJJF." *Joyce Studies Annual* 12 (summer): 163–71.

Leavis, F. R. (1933) "Joyce and 'The Revolution of the Word.'" *Scrutiny* 2, no. 2 (September): 193–201.

——— (1962a) *The Great Tradition*. Harmondsworth, Eng.: Peregrine; orig. pub. London: Chatto and Windus, 1948.

——— (1962b) *The Common Pursuit*. Harmondsworth, Eng.: Peregrine; orig. pub. London: Chatto and Windus, 1952.

——— (1964) *D. H. Lawrence: Novelist*. Harmondsworth, Eng.: Peregrine; orig. pub. London: Chatto and Windus, 1955.

Lee, J. J. (1989) *Ireland: Politics and Society, 1912–1985*. Cambridge: Cambridge University Press.

Lennon, Peter (1994) *Foreign Correspondent: Paris in the Sixties*. London/Basingstoke: Picador/Macmillan.

Leonard, Garry. (1994) "Molly Bloom's 'Lifestyle': The Performative as Normative." In *Molly Blooms*, ed. Pearce, 196–234.

Lernout, Geert (1990) *The French Joyce*. Ann Arbor: University of Michigan Press.

Leslie, Shane (1970a) "*Ulysses*." *Dublin Review* 171 (September 1922): 112–19. In *James Joyce: The Critical Heritage*, ed. Deming, 200–203.

——— (1970b) "*Ulysses.*" *Quarterly Review* 238 (October 1922): 219–34. In *James Joyce: The Critical Heritage*, ed. Deming, 206–11.
Levenson, Michael (1984) *A Genealogy of Modernism: A Study of English Literary Doctrine, 1908–1922.* Cambridge: Cambridge University Press.
Levin, Harry (1960) *James Joyce: A Critical Introduction*, rev. ed. Faber: London; 1st ed. Norfolk, Conn.: New Directions, 1941.
——— (1963) *Contexts of Criticism.* New York: Atheneum.
——— (1966) *Refractions: Essays in Comparative Literature.* Oxford: Oxford University Press.
Levin, Jonathan (1992) "'Entering the Modern Composition': Gertrude Stein and the Patterns of Modernism." In *Rereading the New*, ed. Dettmar, 137–63.
Levin, Richard, and Charles Shattuck (1948) "First Flight to Ithaca: A New Reading of Joyce's *Dubliners.*" In *James Joyce*, ed. Givens, 47–94.
Levine, Jennifer (1978) "Rejoycings in *Tel Quel.*" *James Joyce Quarterly* 16, nos. 1–2 (fall/winter): 17–26.
——— (1990) "*Ulysses.*" In *The Cambridge Companion to James Joyce*, ed. Attridge, 131–59.
Levitt, Morton P. (1991) "Harry Levin's *James Joyce* and the Modernist Age: A Personal Reading." In *Re-Viewing Classics of Joyce Criticism*, ed. Dunleavy, 90–105.
Lewis, Wyndham (1982) *Blasting and Bombardiering.* London: John Calder; orig. pub. London: Eyre and Spottiswoode, 1937; revised edition London: Calder and Boyars, 1967.
——— (1993) *Time and Western Man*, ed. Paul Edwards. Santa Rosa: Black Sparrow Press; orig. pub. London: Chatto and Windus, 1927.
Lidderdale, Jane, and Mary Nicholson (1970) *Dear Miss Weaver: Harriet Shaw Weaver, 1876–1961.* London: Faber.
Litz, A. Walton (1961) *The Art of James Joyce: Method and Design in "Ulysses" and "Finnegans Wake."* London: Oxford University Press.
——— (1974) "Pound and Eliot on *Ulysses:* The Critical Tradition." In *Fifty Years "Ulysses,"* ed. Staley, 5–18.
——— (1986) "*Ulysses* and Its Audience." In *James Joyce: The Centennial Symposium*, ed. Beja et al., 220–30.
Llona, Victor (1961) "I Dont Know What To Call It But Its Mighty Unlike Prose." In Beckett et al., *Our Exagmination*, 93–102.
Lodge, David (1977) *The Modes of Modern Writing.* London: Edward Arnold.
——— (1981a) *Working with Structuralism.* London: Routledge and Kegan Paul.

——— (1981b) "*Middlemarch* and the Idea of the Classic Realist Text." In *The Nineteenth-Century Novel: Critical Essays and Documents*, ed. Arnold Kettle, 218–38. London: Heinemann.

Logan, Chris, ed. (1997) *Bloomsday: A Celebration of James Joyce, 1904–1997*. Dublin: Ireland USA Contacts.

Lyotard, Jean-François (1990) "After the Sublime: The State of Aesthetics." In *The States of "Theory,"* ed. Carroll, 297–304.

MacCabe, Colin (1972) "Uneasiness in Culture." *Cambridge Review* 93, no. 2208 (2 June): 174–77.

——— (1974) "Readings in French." *Cambridge Review* 95, no. 2219 (March): 86–89.

——— (1975) Review of Jonathan Culler's *Structuralist Poetics*. *Cambridge Review* 96, no. 2227 (30 May): 185–86.

——— (1979) *James Joyce and the Revolution of the Word*. Basingstoke, Eng.: Macmillan.

——— (1980) *Godard: Images, Sounds, Politics*. Basingstoke, Eng.: Macmillan.

———, ed. (1982) *James Joyce: New Perspectives*. Brighton, Eng.: Harvester Wheatsheaf.

——— (1985) *Tracking the Signifier. Theoretical Essays: Film, Linguistics, Literature*. Minneapolis: University of Minnesota Press, 1985.

MacGreevy, Thomas (1961) "The Catholic Element in *Work in Progress*." In Beckett et al., *Our Exagmination*, 117–27.

MacKillop, Ian (1995) *F. R. Leavis: A Life in Criticism*. London: Allen Lane.

Maddox, Brenda (1988) *Nora*. London: Hamish Hamilton.

Magalaner, Marvin, and Richard M. Kain (1956) *Joyce: The Man, the Work, the Reputation*. New York: New York University Press.

Mahaffey, Vicki (1995) *Reauthorizing Joyce*. Gainesville: University of Florida Press.

Mais, S. P. B. (1970) "An Irish Revel: And Some Flappers." *Daily Express*, 25 March 1922, n.p. In *James Joyce: The Critical Heritage*, ed. Deming, 191.

"Man About Town" (1970) "A New *Ulysses*." *Evening News*, 8 April 1922, 4. In *James Joyce: The Critical Heritage*, ed. Deming, 194–95.

Marcus, Laura (1995) *Auto/biographical Discourses: Theory, Criticism, Practice*. Manchester: Manchester University Press.

Marsden, Jean I., ed. (1991) *The Appropriation of Shakespeare: Post-Renaissance Reconstructions of the Works and the Myth*. Hemel Hempstead, Eng.: Harvester Wheatsheaf.

Martindale, C. C. (1970) "*Ulysses*." *Dublin Review* 171 (1922): 273–76. In *James Joyce: The Critical Heritage*, ed. Deming, 204–6.

Mason, Ellsworth (1989) "Ellmann's Road to Xanadu." In *Omnium Gatherum*, ed. Dick et al., 4–12.

Materer, Timothy (1979) *Vortex: Pound, Eliot and Lewis*. Ithaca, N.Y.: Cornell University Press.

McAlmon, Robert (1961) "Mr. Joyce Directs an Irish Word Ballet." In Beckett et al., *Our Exagmination*, 103–16.

McCarthy, Patrick A. (1991) "Stuart Gilbert's Guide to the Perplexed." In *Re-Viewing Classics of Joyce Criticism*, ed. Dunleavy, 23–35.

———, ed. (1992) *Critical Essays on James Joyce's "Finnegans Wake."* New York: G. K. Hall.

McCormack, W. J., and Alistair Stead, eds. (1982) *James Joyce and Modern Literature*. London: Routledge and Kegan Paul.

McCormick, Kathleen, and Erwin R. Steinberg, eds. (1993) *Approaches to Teaching Joyce's "Ulysses."* New York: Modern Language Association.

McGinley, Bernard (1996) *Joyce's Lives: Uses and Abuses of the Biografiend*. London: North London University Press.

McLuhan, Marshall (1954) "Joyce, Mallarmé and the Press." *Sewanee Review* 62: 38–55.

McMillan, Dougald (1975) *transition, 1927–38: The History of a Literary Era*. London: Calder and Boyars.

McNally, Frank (1997) "Pun my word, it's Orange hats and lemon soap for Jim's joys," *Irish Times*, 17 June, 1, 8.

Meade, Declan, ed. (2001) *James Joyce Bloomsday Magazine 2001*. Dublin: James Joyce Centre.

———, ed. (2002) *James Joyce Bloomsday Magazine 2002*. Dublin: James Joyce Centre.

Mercier, Vivian (1948) "Dublin Under the Joyces." In *James Joyce*, ed. Givens, 285–301.

Meyers, Jeffrey (1995) *Edmund Wilson: A Biography*. Boston: Houghton Mifflin.

Monaghan, Ken (2001) "That Time Again . . . ." In *James Joyce Bloomsday Magazine 2001*, ed. Meade, 7.

Montgomery, Niall (1970) "Joyeux Quicum Ulysses . . . Swissairis Dubellay Gadelice." In *A Bash in the Tunnel*, ed. Ryan, 61–72.

Morrison, Steven (1999) "Heresy, Heretics and Heresiarchs in the Works of James Joyce." Ph.D. diss., University of London.

Mulhern, Francis (1979) *The Moment of "Scrutiny."* London: NLB.

Murry, John Middleton (1970) "Ulysses." *Nation and Athanaeum* 31 (22 April 1922): 124–25. In *James Joyce: The Critical Heritage*, ed. Deming, 195–98.

Nadel, Ira (1991) "The Incomplete Joyce." *Joyce Studies Annual* 2 (summer): 86–100.

Newman, Charles (1985) *The Post-Modern Aura: The Act of Literature in an Age of Inflation*. Evanston, Ill.: Northwestern University Press.

Newman, Robert, ed. (1996) *Pedagogy, Praxis, "Ulysses": Using Joyce's Text to Transform the Classroom*. Ann Arbor: University of Michigan Press.

Nicholls, Peter (1995) *Modernisms: A Literary Guide*. Basingstoke, Eng.: Macmillan.

Nicholson, Robert (1988) *The "Ulysses" Guide: Tours Through Joyce's Dublin*. London: Methuen.

Nolan, Emer (1995) *James Joyce and Nationalism*. London: Routledge.

——— (2000) "State of the Art: Joyce and Postcolonialism." In *Semicolonial Joyce*, ed. Attridge and Howes, 78–95.

Norris, David (1997) "Joyce's Dublin." In *Bloomsday*, ed. Logan, 5–7.

Norris, Margot (1974) *The Decentered Universe of "Finnegans Wake."* Baltimore, Md.: Johns Hopkins University Press.

——— (1992) "The Postmodernization of *Finnegans Wake* Reconsidered." In *Rereading the New*, ed. Dettmar, 343–62.

North, Michael (1999) *Reading 1922: A Return to the Scene of the Modern*. Oxford: Oxford University Press.

Noyes, Alfred (1970) "Rottenness in Literature." *Sunday Chronicle*, 29 October 1922, 2. In *James Joyce: The Critical Heritage*, ed. Deming, 274–75.

O'Brien, Flann (1991) *Stories and Plays*. London: Paladin.

——— (1993) *The Dalkey Archive*. London: Flamingo; orig. pub. London: MacGibbon and Kee, 1964.

O'Connor, Joseph (1995) *The Secret World of the Irish Male*. London: Minerva.

O'Faolain, Sean (1970) "Correspondence: *Anna Livia Plurabelle*." *Irish Statesman* 11 (5 January 1929): 354–55. In *James Joyce: The Critical Heritage*, ed. Deming, 396–98.

O'Toole, Fintan (1997) *The Lie of the Land: Irish Identities*. London: Verso.

Packard, Vance (1960) *The Hidden Persuaders*. Harmondsworth, Eng.: Penguin.

Parrinder, Patrick (1982) "The Strange Necessity: James Joyce's Rejection in England, 1914–1930." In *James Joyce*, ed. MacCabe, 151–67.

——— (1984) *James Joyce*. Cambridge: Cambridge University Press.

——— (1991) *Authors and Authority: English and American Criticism, 1750–1990*. Basingstoke, Eng.: Macmillan.

Peake, C. H. (1977) *James Joyce: The Citizen and the Artist*. London: Edward Arnold.

Pearce, Richard, ed. (1994) *Molly Blooms: A Polylogue on "Penelope" and Cultural Studies*. Madison: University of Wisconsin Press.

Pinkney, Tony (1989a) Editor's introduction ("Modernism and Cultural Theory") to *The Politics of Modernism*, by Williams, 1–29.
——— (1989b) "Editorial: The Politics of Modernism." *News From Nowhere*, no. 7 (winter): 3–8.
Plath, Sylvia (1966). *The Bell Jar.* London: Faber; orig. pub. London: William Heinemann, 1963.
Platt, Len (1998). *Joyce and the Anglo-Irish: A Study of Joyce and the Literary Revival.* Amsterdam: Rodopi.
Pound, Ezra (1914) "The New Sculpture." *Egoist*, 16 February, 67–68.
——— (1915) "Affirmations II: Vorticism." *The New Age*, 14 January, 277–78.
——— (1954) *Literary Essays of Ezra Pound*, ed. T. S. Eliot. London: Faber.
——— (1967) *Pound/Joyce: The Letters of Ezra Pound to James Joyce, with Pound's Critical Essays and Articles about Joyce*, ed. Forrest Read. New York: New Directions.
——— (1982) *Selected Letters, 1907–1941*, ed. D. D. Paige. London: Faber.
Powell, David (1971) "An annotated Bibliography of Myles na Gopaleen's (Flann O'Brien's) 'Cruiskeen Lawn' Commentaries on James Joyce." *James Joyce Quarterly* 9, no. 1 (fall): 50–62.
Power, Arthur (1974) *Conversations with James Joyce*, ed. Clive Hart. London: Millington.
Prendergast, Christopher (1972) "Myth, Ideology and Semioclastics." *Cambridge Review* 93, no. 2208 (2 June): 170–74.
Rainey, Lawrence (1998) *Institutions of Modernism.* New Haven, Conn.: Yale University Press.
Raleigh, John Henry (1971) "'Afoot in Dublin In Search of the Habitations of some Shades.'" *James Joyce Quarterly* 8, no. 2 (winter): 129–41.
Rehm, George (1970) "*Ulysses.*" *Chicago Tribune* (European edition), 13 February 1922, 2. In *James Joyce: The Critical Heritage*, ed. Deming, 212–13.
Restuccia, Frances L. (1989) *Joyce and the Law of the Father.* New Haven, Conn.: Yale University Press.
Robbins, Bruce (1993) *Secular Vocations: Intellectuals, Professionalism, Culture.* London: Verso.
Robertson, William K. (1989) "A Portrait of James Joyce's Biographer." In *Omnium Gatherum*, ed. Dick et al., 42–48.
Robins, Kevin (1991) "Tradition and Translation: National Culture in Its Global Context." In *Enterprise and Heritage*, ed. Corner and Harvey, 21–44.
Rodker, John (1961) "Joyce and His Dynamic." In Beckett et al., *Our Exagmination*, 139–46.

Roe, David (1989) *Gustave Flaubert*. Basingstoke, Eng.: Macmillan.
Rose, Danis, and John O'Hanlon, eds. (1992) "Ireland and James Joyce: Documents from the National Archive." *Joyce Studies Annual* 3 (summer): 3–31.
Roughley, Alan (1991) *James Joyce and Critical Theory*. Hemel Hempstead, Eng.: Harvester Wheatsheaf.
Russell, George (AE) (1970) "Anna Livia Plurabelle." *Irish Statesman* 11 (29 December 1929): 339. In *James Joyce: The Critical Heritage*, ed. Deming, 395–96.
——— (1990) "The Censorship Bill." *Irish Statesman* 10 (1928): 486–87. In *Banned in Ireland*, ed. Carlson, 125–29.
Ryan, John, ed. (1970) *A Bash in the Tunnel: James Joyce by the Irish*. Brighton, Eng.: Clifton.
——— (1987) *Remembering How We Stood: Bohemian Dublin at the Mid-Century*. Mullingar, Ire.: Lilliput; orig. pub. Dublin: Gill and Macmillan, 1975.
Schaum, Melita (1988) *Wallace Stevens and the Critical Schools*. Tuscaloosa: University of Alabama Press.
Scholes, Robert (1974) *Structuralism in Literature: An Introduction*. New Haven, Conn.: Yale University Press.
——— (1992) *In Search of James Joyce*. Urbana: University of Illinois Press.
Schwartz, Lawrence H. (1988) *Creating Faulkner's Reputation: The Politics of Modern Literary Criticism*. Knoxville: University of Tennessee Press.
Scott, Bonnie Kime (1984) *Joyce and Feminism*. Bloomington: Indiana University Press.
——— (1987) *James Joyce*. Brighton, Eng.: Harvester.
———, ed. (1988) *New Alliances in Joyce Studies*. Newark: University of Delaware Press.
——— (1991) "A Consensus on Glasheen's *Census*." In *Re-Viewing Classics of Joyce Criticism*, ed. Dunleavy, 46–59.
Segall, Jeffrey (1993) *Joyce in America: Cultural Politics and the Trials of "Ulysses."* Berkeley: University of California Press.
Selden, Raman (1993) *A Reader's Guide to Contemporary Literary Theory*, 3rd ed.. Hemel Hempstead, Eng.: Harvester Wheatsheaf; 1st ed. 1985.
Seldes, Gilbert (1970) "Ulysses." *Nation* 115, no. 2982 (30 August 1922): 211–12. In *James Joyce: The Critical Heritage*, ed. Deming, 235–39.
Senn, Fritz (1984) *Joyce's Dislocutions: Essays on Reading as Translation*, ed. John Paul Riquelme. Baltimore, Md.: Johns Hopkins University Press.
——— (1991) "Rereading *The Books at the Wake*." In *Re-Viewing Classics of Joyce Criticism*, ed. Dunleavy, 82–89.

——— (1995) *Inductive Scrutinies: Focus on Joyce*, ed. Christine O'Neill. Dublin: Lilliput.
Serio, John (1988) Foreword to *Wallace Stevens and the Critical Schools*, by Schaum, ix–xii.
Share, Bernard (1970) "Downes's Cakeshop and Williams's Jam." In *A Bash in the Tunnel*, ed. Ryan, 189–92.
Sheehan, Paul (2002) *Modernism, Narrative and Humanism*. Cambridge: Cambridge University Press.
Sinfield, Alan (1989) *Literature, Politics and Culture in Postwar Britain*. Oxford: Blackwell.
Slocombe, George (1970) "*Ulysses*." *Daily Herald* 921 (17 March 1922): 4. In *James Joyce: The Critical Heritage*, ed. Deming, 217–18.
Smith, Stan (1994) *The Origins of Modernism: Eliot, Pound, Yeats and the Rhetorics of Renewal*. Hemel Hempstead, Eng.: Harvester Wheatsheaf.
Smyth, Gerry (1998) *Decolonisation and Criticism*. London: Pluto.
Sollers, Philippe (1978). "Joyce & Co.," trans. Stephen Heath. In *In The Wake of the "Wake,"* ed. Hayman and Anderson, 107–21.
Staley, Thomas F., ed. (1974) *Fifty Years "Ulysses."* Bloomington: Indiana University Press.
——— (2001) "Adventures in the Joyce Trade." *Joyce Studies Annual* 12 (summer): 100–110.
Sturrock, John, ed. (1979) *Structuralism and Since*. Oxford: Oxford University Press.
Sutherland, John (1985) "The Politics of English Studies in the British University, 1960–1984." In *Historical Studies and Literary Criticism*, ed. Jerome J. McGann, 126–40. Madison: University of Wisconsin Press.
Taylor, Gary (1990) *Reinventing Shakespeare: A Cultural History from the Restoration to the Present*. London: Vintage.
Theall, Donald F. (1997) *Joyce's Techno-Poetics*. Toronto: University of Toronto Press.
Tindall, William York (1969) *A Reader's Guide to "Finnegans Wake."* London: Thames and Hudson.
Travis, Alan (1998) "How They Tried to Kill Off Ulysses." *Guardian*, 15 May, sec. 1, p. 3.
Tredell, Nicolas (1994) *Conversations with Critics*. Manchester, Eng.: Carcanet.
Trotter, David (1992) "A Horse Is Being Beaten: Modernism and Popular Fiction." In *Rereading the New*, ed. Dettmar, 191–219.
——— (1993) *The English Novel in History, 1895–1920*. London: Routledge.

van Boheemen, Christine (1988) "Deconstruction after Joyce." In *New Alliances in Joyce Studies*, ed. Scott, 29–36.

van Boheemen-Saaf, Christine (1998) "Purloined Joyce." In *Re: Joyce*, ed. Brannigan et al., 246–57.

Vanderham, Paul (1998) *James Joyce and Censorship: The Trials of "Ulysses."* Basingstoke, Eng.: Macmillan.

Waters, John (1994) *Race of Angels: Ireland and the Genesis of U2*. Belfast: Blackstaff.

Watt, Ian (1987) *The Rise of the Novel: Studies in Defoe, Richardson and Fielding*. London: Hogarth; orig. pub. London: Chatto and Windus, 1957.

Waugh, Patricia, ed. (1997) *Revolutions of the Word: Intellectual Contexts for the Study of Modern Literature*. London: Arnold/Hodder Headline.

Wells, H. G. (1970) "James Joyce." *Nation* 20 (24 February 1917): 710, 712; and *New Republic* 10 (10 March 1917): 158–60. In *James Joyce: The Critical Heritage*, ed. Deming, 86–88.

White, Jim (1997) "Viva Dublina!" *Guardian*, 17 March , sec. 2, pp. 1–3.

Widdowson, Peter, ed. (1989) *Hardy in History: A Study in Literary Sociology*. London: Routledge.

Wilde, Oscar (1992) *Complete Works*. London: Magpie.

Williams, Raymond (1975) *The Long Revolution*. Harmondsworth, Eng.: Penguin; orig. pub. London: Chatto and Windus, 1961.

——— (1979) *Politics and Letters: Interviews with "New Left Review."* London: Verso.

——— (1981) *Culture*. Glasgow: Fontana.

——— (1984) *Writing in Society*. London: Verso.

——— (1987) *The English Novel from Dickens to Lawrence*. London: Hogarth; orig. pub. London: Chatto and Windus, 1970.

——— (1989a) *The Politics of Modernism*. London: Verso.

——— (1989b) *Resources of Hope*, ed. Robin Gable. London: Verso.

——— (1989c) *What I Came to Say*, ed. Neil Belton, Francis Mulhern, and Jenny Taylor. London: Hutchinson Radius.

Williams, William Carlos (1961) "A Point for American Criticism." In Beckett et al., *Our Exagmination*, 171–85.

Wilson, Edmund (1961) *Axel's Castle*. Glasgow: Fontana; orig. pub. New York: Charles Scribner's Sons, 1931.

Wollaeger, Mark A., Victor Luftig, and Robert Spoo, eds. (1996) *Joyce and the Subject of History*. Ann Arbor: University of Michigan Press.

Wollen, Peter (1982) *Readings and Writings: Semiotic Counter-Strategies*. London: Verso.

Woolf, Virginia (1978) *A Writer's Diary*, ed. Leonard Woolf. London: Grafton.
Wright, Patrick (1985) *On Living in an Old Country*. London: Verso.
Yeats, William Butler (1964) *Selected Prose*, ed. A. Norman Jeffares. London: Macmillan.
────── (1970) Letter to Olivia Shakespear (8 March 1922). In *James Joyce: The Critical Heritage*, ed. Deming, 284.
Young, Robert, ed. (1981) *Untying the Text: A Post-Structuralist Reader*. London: Routledge and Kegan Paul.

Index

Aaron, Daniel, 73
Abbey Theatre, 186
Abin, César, 55
Adams, Michael, 186–87, 194
Adams, Robert M., 138
Aldington, Richard, 11, 43
Allen, Walter: *The English Novel*, 85
Althusser, Louis, 152, 162
Anderson, Laurie, 180
Anderson, Margaret, 18–21, 26, 34
Anderson, Sherwood, 54
"Aramis" (reviewer, *Sporting Times*) 25–28, 164
Ardagh, John, 186, 188, 203
Aristotle, 112
Arnold, Bruce, 22–24, 97–98, 187
Arnold, Matthew, 224
Artaud, Antonin, 159–60
Atherton, James, 138
Attridge, Derek, 8, 21, 104, 165–73, 177, 211; *Cambridge Companion to James Joyce*, 175, 222; "The Ideology of Character," 170–71; *Joyce Effects*, 166; "Judging Joyce," 172–73; *Peculiar Language*, 171–72; *Post-Structuralist Joyce* (with Daniel Ferrer), 155, 165–66; *Semicolonial Joyce* (with Marjorie Howes), 219
Austen, Jane, 89

Bakhtin, Mikhail, 179
Baldick, Chris, 5, 16–17, 153, 159–60
Barnes, Djuna, 83, 174
Barthes, Roland, 127–28, 151, 152, 160, 163–64, 167; *Mythologies*, 114, 155;

S/Z, 152; *The Pleasure of the Text*, 160; *Writing Degree Zero*, 13, 127–28
Bateson, Gregory, 142
Baudrillard, Jean, 180; *Simulations*, 211
Bauerle, Ruth, 138
Beach, Sylvia, 23–24, 100, 173, 208
Beckett, Samuel, 55, 57–58, 67, 81, 98, 130, 135, 147, 152, 189, 193; *Watt*, 124
Begnal, Michael H., 145–46
Behan, Brendan, 203
Beja, Morris, 3, 138, 206
Bell, Adrian, 79; "Change in the Farm," 79
Bell, 199
Belsey, Catherine, 162
Benjamin, Walter, 125–26, 180
Bennett, Arnold, 17–18, 26–29, 32, 35, 43, 164
Benstock, Bernard, 100, 138, 184
Benstock, Shari, 138
Bérard, Victor, 65
Bergson, Henri, 46, 49, 58
Berman, Marshall, 205
Bérubé, Michael, 93, 95
Best, George, 207
Bhabha, Homi K., 180
biography, 100–111; as humanist genre, 102, 109
Blake, William, 62, 99
Blast, 34, 37, 41–42, 131
Bloom, Harold, 98
Bloomsday, 202, 206–7, 208–16
Bloomsday (play), 194
Bolshevism, literary, 33, 165
Bolt, Sydney, 54

Bono, 207–8
Booth, Wayne C., 117
Bordwell, David, 160
Bourdieu, Pierre, 23
Bowen, Zack, 138
Bowie, Malcolm, 162
Boyle, Robert, 119, 142
Brecht, Bertolt, 159–60, 228
Brion, Marcel, 55, 58–59
Broderick, John, 188, 196
Brooks, Cleanth, 96
Brown, Dennis, 34–36
Brown, Richard, 3, 21, 32, 175
Brown, Terence, 185, 188, 193–94, 197, 203, 220, 222, 224
Budgen, Frank, 18, 53–54, 55, 85, 99, 103, 111, 134, 138, 152, 192; *James Joyce and the Making of "Ulysses,"* 54, 68–76
Burgess, Anthony: *Joysprick*, 92; *A Shorter "Finnegans Wake,"* 61, 92, 146
Bush, Ronald, 98, 105–6

Cairns, David, 188–89
Cambridge, University of, 77–86, 151–52, 156–58, 165, 167, 170
Cambridge Review, 152–57
Campbell, Joseph, and Henry Morton Robinson, 201; *A Skeleton Key to "Finnegans Wake,"* 96, 145–46
Carlson, Julia, 186
Carlyle, Thomas, 88
Carter, Angela, 206–7
censorship, 6, 18–22, 61, 64–65, 80–81, 154, 185–89, 191, 193–94, 196
Cheng, Vincent J., 182, 219, 229; *Joyce, Race, and Empire*, 226–27
Chicago Tribune, 54
Cixous, Hélène, 149, 166, 179
cold war, 91, 95
Collins, Joseph, 26–29
communitarianism, 121
Connolly, James, 224
Connor, Steven, 3, 7, 104, 181

Conrad, Joseph, 131
Corkery, Daniel, 224
Cosgrave, William T., 186
Costello, Peter, 103–4; *James Joyce: The Years of Growth*, 103
Cousins, Gretta, 174
Coward, Rosalind, and John Ellis: *Language and Materialism*, 159
Crane Bag, 220, 224
Criterion, 43
Cronin, Anthony, 92, 104–5, 189, 196, 198, 202, 213
Culler, Jonathan, 42, 119, 155–56; *Structuralist Poetics*, 154, 156
cultural studies, 180–81

Daily Express, 25, 27, 33
Daily Mail, 40–41
Dali, Salvador, 207
Dante Alighieri, 92
Davies, Stan Gébler, 97, 103–4; *James Joyce: A Portrait of the Artist*, 103
Deane, Seamus, 220, 221–23, 225; "Heroic Styles," 221; "Joyce and Nationalism," 222; "Joyce the Irishman," 222; *A Short History of Irish Literature*, 223
deconstruction, 169–72, 177–78, 221
de Valera, Eamon, 186, 188–89, 196–97, 200, 203, 217, 224
Defoe, Daniel, 99
DeKoven, Marianne, 38, 49
Delaney, Frank, 75
DeLillo, Don, 180
Deming, Robert H., 87, 105
Derrida, Jacques, 129, 143–45, 149–52, 166–69, 171, 176, 179, 181–82, 215, 230; *Acts of Literature*, 166; "Structure, Sign and Play in the Discourse of the Human Sciences," 144; "Two Words for Joyce," 166, 168; "*Ulysses* Gramophone," 166, 169

Dettmar, Kevin J. H., 166, 171
Dial, 40, 191
Dickens, Charles, 6, 33, 58, 76, 86
Docker, John, 82, 161
Donoghue, Denis, 220
Doonesbury, 180
Dostoyevsky, Fyodor, 35, 88–89, 135
Doyle, Arthur Conan: *The Stark-Munro Letters*, 99
Doyle, Brian, 5
Dublin Review, 185
Duff, Charles, 61
Duffy, Enda, 219
Dunne, Seán, 188

Eagleton, Terry, 5, 7, 28, 65, 77, 82, 96, 133, 151, 162, 217
Easthope, Antony, 161–62
Edel, Leon, 102; *The Life of Henry James*, 104
Edwards, Paul, 49
Eglinton, John, 6–7, 191–96, 227
Egoist, 12, 18, 78
Einstein, Albert, 46
Eliot, George, 132, 135; *Middlemarch*, 161
Eliot, T. S., 15, 24, 33–35, 38–40, 42–51, 54, 58, 60, 61, 63–64, 77, 82–84, 89, 91, 92, 96, 99, 112, 116, 120, 125, 130, 137, 142, 147–49, 158, 164, 168, 175, 178, 192, 225; *After Strange Gods*, 83–84; *Prufrock and Other Observations*, 35; "Tradition and the Individual Talent," 117; "*Ulysses*, Order and Myth," 42–46, 51, 54, 83, 218; *The Waste Land*, 43–45, 82, 90, 116
Ellmann, Maud, 166
Ellmann, Richard, 7, 20, 48, 86–87, 92–94, 97–136 *passim*, 137–39, 152–54, 162, 168, 176, 180, 184–85, 201–2, 225; *The Consciousness of Joyce*, 98, 108, 114, 119; *James Joyce*, 100–115 *passim*, 134, 137–38, 174, 186; humanism, 108–15, 120–21, 129, 134, 152–53, 192,
210; *a long the riverrun*, 100; politics, 114, 136; *Ulysses on the Liffey*, 99, 112–14, 142, 152; *Yeats: The Man and His Masks*, 100
Emerson, Ralph Waldo, 88
Empson, William, 105, 110, 120
Eno, Brian, 207
Envoy, 199–200
Ernst, Morris, 64–65
Evans, Ifor: *A Short History of English Literature*, 85
Evans, Malcolm, 5
Evening News (London), 28
Evening Telegraph (Dublin), 96

Fairhall, James, 75
Fanning, Aengus, 213
Farrell, Joseph, 214
Faulkner, William, 4
feminism, 49–50, 173–80
Ferrer, Daniel, 165
Ffrench, Patrick, 150
Field Day Theatre Company, 220, 222
Finney, Michael, 59, 61
Fitzgerald, Garret, 204
Fitzgerald, Tom, 214
Fitzgibbon, Marjorie, 209
Fitzpatrick, David, 185
Flaubert, Gustave, 11–13, 16, 35, 39–40, 42, 43, 79, 84, 89, 119, 124–25, 126, 127, 135; *Bouvard and Pécuchet*, 40; *Madame Bovary*, 40, 42; *A Sentimental Education*, 40; *Three Tales*, 40
Ford, Boris, 85
Ford, Ford Madox, 12, 131
Forrester, Joseph, 20
Foster, John Wilson, 195, 221
Foster, Roy, 188, 192, 217
Foucault, Michel, 74–75, 151, 153, 179
Frank, Joseph, 148
French, Marilyn, 134; *The Book as World*, 111

Freud, Sigmund, 20, 143, 162, 179
Friedman, Melvin J., 102
Friel, Brian, 220
Fussell, Paul, 36
Futurism, 39

Gabler, Hans Walter, 118
Galsworthy, John, 16
Gaudier-Brzeska, Henri, 12, 37
Gibbons, Luke, 203–4, 216, 221
Gibson, Andrew, 46, 182, 222; *Joyce's Revenge*, 228–30
Gide, André, 89
Gilbert, Sandra, 175
Gilbert, Stuart, 53–54, 56, 58, 69–70, 72, 75–76, 99, 103, 105, 112, 178; *James Joyce's "Ulysses,"* 54, 60–68, 83
Gillespie, Michael Patrick, 7
Givens, Seon: *Two Decades of Criticism*, 117
Glasheen, Adaline, 138; *A Census of "Finnegans Wake,"* 138
Godard, Jean-Luc, 160–61
Gogarty, Oliver St. John, 92, 112, 201
Goldberg, S. L., 166; *The Classical Temper*, 157
Goldman, Arnold, 99
Gorman, Herbert, 112; *James Joyce*, 102
Graff, Gerald, 95
Graham, B. J., 218
Grant, Damian, 13
Griffith, Arthur, 16
Groden, Michael, 138
Gross, John, 111, 156
Gubar, Susan, 175
Gupta, Suman, 42

Hardy, Thomas, 4, 86
Hart, Clive, 69, 100, 108, 115, 138, 166; *Structure and Motif in "Finnegans Wake,"* 146
Harvey, David, 52–53
Harwood, John, 10

Hauptmann, Gerhard, 174
Hawkes, Terence, 161; *Structuralism and Semiotics*, 160
Hayman, David, 108, 115, 138; *"Ulysses": The Mechanics of Meaning*, 126
H.D., 11
Heaney, Seamus, 219, 221; "Station Island," 219, 222
Heap, Jane, 18–20
Heath, Stephen, 7, 151–62, 166–67, 170, 177; "Ambiviolences," 151–56; *The Nouveau Roman*, 159
Heidegger, Martin, 143
Henke, Suzette A., 62, 173; *James Joyce and the Politics of Desire*, 178–79
Herr, Cheryl Temple, 114, 173, 180; *Joyce's Anatomy of Culture*, 180
Herring, Phillip, 101, 138, 206
Higgins, Aidan, 187
Hodgart, Matthew, 138
Holderness, Graham, 4, 183
Homer, 70, 95, 99, 118; *The Odyssey*, 43–44, 63, 65–67, 68–69, 89, 141, 181
Horgan, J. J., 187
Howes, Marjorie, 8, 219
Huddleston, Sisley, 25–26, 30
Hugo, Victor, 88
Hulme, T. E., 11, 39, 45, 49
humanism, 71–76, 108–15, 120–21, 129, 134, 139, 142
Husserl, Edmund, 159; *The Origin of Geometry*, 150
Hussey, Gemma, 186, 189, 204
Hutcheon, Linda, 128
Huyssen, Andreas, 37–38, 42

Ibsen, Henrik, 88–89, 109, 121, 174
Imagism, 10–15. See also Pound, Ezra
Inglis, Fred, 165
International James Joyce Foundation, 172
IRA (Irish Republican Army), 219–20
Ireland, 6–8, 14–18, 48–51, 56–57, 89–90,

131, 181–82, 183–231; Catholic responses to Joyce, 195–202; distrust of American criticism, 201–2; heritage and Joyce, 208–18, 230; initial response to Joyce, 185–90; Northern Ireland, 217–20, 230; Protestant responses to Joyce, 190–95; postcolonial criticism, 192, 198, 218–31; in post-Lemass era, 203–8; Protestant responses to Joyce, 190–95
Irigaray, Luce: *Speculum of the Other Woman*, 38
Irish Homestead, 118
Irish Statesman, 56–57, 193–94
Irish Times, 194, 198, 212

Jackson, Holbrook, 25, 27, 29, 164
Jakobson, Roman, 141
James, Henry, 43, 102; *The Ambassadors*, 126
James Joyce Centre (Dublin), 209–10
James Joyce Museum (Dublin), 208–10
James Joyce Quarterly, 101, 188
James Joyce's "Ulysses": Critical Essays (Hart and Hayman), 60, 108, 115
Jameson, Fredric, 24, 48, 170
Johnson, Jeri, 75–76
Johnson, Lesley, 77, 99
Johnston, Denis, 201
Jolas, Eugene, 53, 54–60, 61–62, 73, 81, 89, 182
Jolas, Maria, 54
Jordan, John, 201
Joyce, Eva, 105
Joyce, James: *Anna Livia Plurabelle*, 193–94; *Critical Writings*, 98; *Dubliners*, 9–16, 34, 35, 39–40, 66–67, 117–18, 128–29, 131, 144, 171, 177, 188, 222; *Exiles*, 121, 222; *Finnegans Wake / Work in Progress*, 53–231 passim; "I Hear an Army Marching on the Land," 11; as national or international, 6–8, 14–18, 45–46, 48–49, 52–57, 80, 89–90, 110–11, 135–36, 181–82, 191–92, 200–202, 218–31; and novel genre, 41–43, 45, 69–71, 147–49, 225; obscenity, 17–22, 25–28, 50; *A Portrait of the Artist as a Young Man*, 10–18, 21, 25, 32, 35, 39, 43, 64, 67, 100, 106–7, 109, 117, 125, 131, 170, 176, 188, 197, 222–23; static and kinetic modes of reading, 20–22, 26–28, 32, 44–45, 64, 81, 91, 149, 164, 178; *Stephen Hero*, 176, 186; *Ulysses*, passim
Joyce, John Stanislaus, 198
Joyce, Lucia, 174
Joyce, Nora Barnacle, 103, 105
Joyce, Paul, 209
Joyce, Stanislaus, 107; *My Brother's Keeper*, 98
Joyce, Tom, 202

Kain, Richard M., 94, 117, 184; *Fabulous Voyager*, 96
Kant, Immanuel: sublime, 30–32, 44; *Critique of Judgment*, 30–32
Kaufmann, Michael Edward, 43–44
Kavanagh, Patrick, 195, 197, 203, 206, 227; "Who Killed James Joyce?," 201–2
Kearney, Richard, 149, 188, 193, 220–22; *Transitions*, 221
Kelly, Joseph, 5, 45, 101
Kennelly, Brendan, 197
Kenner, Hugh, 5–6, 7, 24, 72, 75, 76, 89, 92–93, 95, 97–136 passim, 138, 161–62, 172, 182, 187, 192, 201, 210, 225, 227; Catholicism, 119–21, 230; counter-humanism, 119–30, 134; debt to modernism, 130–33; *Dublin's Joyce*, 66, 97–98, 116–17, 119–25, 127–28, 131–32, 174; on "International Modernism," 135–36; "The Impertinence of Being

Kenner, Hugh (*continued*)
  Definitive," 105–6; "Joyce and Modernism," 132; *Joyce's Voices*, 118–19, 127–29, 131–33, 135; "The Making of the Modernist Canon," 134; *The Mechanic Muse*, 125–26, 132; politics, 121–23; *The Pound Era*, 98, 115, 117–19, 130, 132, 134; *The Stoic Comedians*, 98, 119, 124–25, 127, 134–35; technology, 122–26; textuality, 126–30, 180; *"Ulysses,"* 119, 131–33
Kenyon Review, 117
Keogh, Dermot, 185, 196
Kermode, Frank, 86–87, 105, 114–15
Kettle, Arnold, 85
Kiberd, Declan, 14–15, 94, 149, 189, 203, 205, 219, 222, 224–25, 229; *Inventing Ireland*, 224–25
Kiely, Benedict, 196–97
Kinsella, Thomas, 197
Kristeva, Julia, 149, 151, 159–60, 163–64, 166–67, 179; *Revolution in Poetic Language*, 163

Lacan, Jacques, 143, 149, 162, 166, 168, 179
Laforgue, Jules, 35
Larbaud, Valery, 24, 43
Lawrence, D. H., 42, 77, 81–86, 134–35, 142, 156–58, 167
Lawrence, Karen R., 173, 175–78
Leavis, F. R., 7, 53, 77–86, 89, 94, 134–35, 153, 157–58, 164, 167, 170; *Culture and Environment*, 80; *D. H. Lawrence, Novelist*, 77, 84, 134, 157; *The Great Tradition*, 83–84, 157; "Joyce and 'The Revolution of the Word'," 78–82, 135, 158; *Mass Civilization and Minority Culture*, 80; *New Bearings in English Poetry*, 82
Lee, J. J., 219–20
Lemass, Seán, 197, 203, 205
Lennon, Peter, 203

Lernout, Geert, 5, 87, 149
Leslie, Shane, 25–29, 33, 72, 120, 185, 187, 206
Levenson, Michael, 12, 36, 37, 45
Levin, Charles, and Charles Shattuck: "First Flight to Ithaca," 66–67
Levin, Harry, 3, 5–6, 53, 87–96, 97–98, 109–10, 116–17, 136, 146, 149, 170, 178, 201, 210; *James Joyce*, 3, 87–91; "James Joyce et l'Idée de la Littérature Mondiale," 89; "What Was Modernism?," 88
Levin, Jonathan, 44
Levine, Jennifer, 148–49, 153, 163
Lévi-Strauss, Claude, 142, 143, 151
Levitt, Morton P., 87
Lewis, Wyndham, 9, 10, 12, 34–39, 43, 46–51, 54, 56, 58–59, 84, 116, 130, 175, 177; *Blasting and Bombardiering*, 39; *The Enemy*, 36, 46; *Tarr*, 35, 43; *Time and Western Man*, 46–51
Linati, Carlo, 112
Little Review, 18–22, 78
Litz, A. Walton, 3, 24, 40, 92, 98–101, 112, 118, 138
Llona, Victor, 55–56
Lodge, David, 141
Long, Michael, 165
Loughrey, Bryan, 4
Lyotard, Jean-François, 30–32, 50

MacCabe, Colin, 7, 139–40, 151–65, 166–68, 170, 174, 177, 184, 210, 221; *James Joyce: New Perspectives*, 157–58, 165, 222; *James Joyce and the Revolution of the Word*, 128, 157, 161–65, 179; "Realism and the Cinema," 161; "Uneasiness in Culture," 152–56, 164
MacDonagh, Donagh, 198
MacGreevy, Thomas, 195–97, 224
Maddox, Brenda, 103
Magalaner, Marvin, 117, 184
Mahaffey, Vicki, 173, 181

Mais, S. P. B., 27, 29, 33
Mallarmé, Stéphane, 159–60
Mangan, James Clarence, 223
Manganiello, Dominic: *Joyce's Politics*, 114
Mann, Thomas, 89, 96
Marcus, Laura, 101–2
Marinetti, F. T., 39
Marx, Karl, 162
Marx Brothers, 74
Mason, Ellsworth, 92, 98, 100, 107
Mays, J. C. C., 222
McAlmon, Robert, 56
McCormack, W. J., and Alistair Stead: *James Joyce and Modern Literature*, 165
McGahern, John, 189; *The Dark*, 189
McGinley, Bernard, 88, 100–101, 103–5, 107, 186, 188
McLuhan, Marshall, 123; "Joyce, Mallarmé and the Press," 123; *The Mechanical Bride*, 125
McMillan, Dougald, 54, 55, 58
"Men of 1914," 34–51, 58–60, 76, 84, 88, 118, 130, 134, 178. *See also* Eliot, T. S.; Lewis, Wyndham; Pound, Ezra
Mercier, Vivien, 196
Miller, Henry, 83
Milton, John: *Paradise Lost*, 135
modernism: and American academy, 86–96; anticipates theory, 167–70; and Cambridge, 156–58; and Irish modernity, 205, 224–25; Joyce and emergence of, 9–51; Kenner and, 130–36; Leavis and, 81–84; and novel genre, 41–43; political, 159–61; and technology, 124–26; *transition* and, 58–60; and war, 35–37. *See also* "Men of 1914" *and individual authors*
Modern Language Association, 184
Moeller, Philip, 20, 22, 27
Molly Blooms (Pearce), 180

Monaghan, Ken, 210
Monroe, Harriet, 15
Montgomery, Niall, 195, 201, 227
Moore, Brian, 188, 196
Moore, George, 25, 29
Moore, Marianne, 35
Moran, D. P., 229
Morrison, Van, 207
Movement, The, 87
Mulhern, Francis, 77, 84
Murray, Josephine, 174
Murry, John Middleton, 29, 32–33, 164–65

Nadel, Ira, 105
na gCopaleen, Myles. *See* O'Nolan, Brian
Nation, 15
National Library of Ireland, 8, 230
National Review, 131
New Age, 10, 15
New Criticism, 23–24, 90, 95–96, 113, 119, 126, 148
Newman, Charles, 91–92
New Masses, 73
New Statesman, 105
New York Times, 26–27
Nicholls, Peter, 37–38, 41–42
Nicholson, Robert, 184
Nietzsche, Friedrich, 88
Nolan, Emer, 111, 114, 182, 218, 229–30; *James Joyce and Nationalism*, 225–27
Noon, William T., 119, 142, 230
Norris, David, 207, 212
Norris, Margot, 143–49, 154, 163, 173; *The Decentred Universe of "Finnegans Wake,"* 143–49
North, Michael, 14, 47, 50, 52, 56; *Reading 1922*, 10
Noyes, Alfred, 33–34

O'Brien, Conor Cruise, 220
Observer, 25

O'Connell, Daniel, 197
O'Connell, John, 107
O'Connell, William, 106
O'Connor, Joseph, 215, 217
O'Faolain, Sean, 56–57, 197, 199
O'Higgins, Kevin, 185
O'Neill, Christine, 129
O'Nolan, Brian (Flann O'Brien), 106, 198–202, 203, 206, 219; *An Béal Bocht (The Poor Mouth)*, 198; *The Dalkey Archive*, 183, 199–201
O'Rahilly, Alfred, 194
O'Toole, Fintan, 181, 205
Our Exagmination Round his Factification for Incamination of Work in Progress (Beckett et al), 54, 55–59, 62, 103, 145, 152

Packard, Vance: *The Hidden Persuaders*, 122–23
Parnell, Charles Stewart, 215, 229
Parrinder, Patrick, 67, 82, 84, 101, 130; *James Joyce*, 111
Paul, Elliot, 54
Paulin, Tom, 220
Peake, C. H., 68, 75, 134; *James Joyce: The Citizen and the Artist*, 111
Pearse, Patrick, 217
Picasso, Pablo, 137
Pinkney, Tony, 9, 49–50, 114
Platt, Len: *Joyce and the Anglo-Irish*, 227–30
Plekhanov, Georgy, 91
Pogues, The: *If I Should Fall from Grace with God*, 207
Porter, Charles, 80
poststructuralism, 7, 139, 144–45, 148, 149–73, 225. *See also* theory
Pound, Ezra, 7, 9–18, 24, 33–42, 45–46, 48–51, 57–59, 72, 84, 89, 96, 99, 114, 116, 122, 130–31, 136, 147–48, 164, 175, 182, 191–92, 218, 225, 230; *The Cantos*, 41, 84, 130; "The Non-Existence of Ireland," 15
Power, Arthur, 186
Powys, John Cowper, 21
Presley, Elvis, 214
Proust, Marcel, 49, 96

Quinn, John, 19–22, 24, 27, 50, 64

Rabelais, François, 56
Radek, Karl, 73
Rainey, Lawrence, 23–24, 28, 32
Ransom, John Crowe, 95–96
Reagan, Ronald, 179
Rehm, George, 27–28
Restuccia, Frances L., 76
Richards, I. A., 156
Richards, Shaun, 188–89
Ricks, Christopher, 165
Robbins, Bruce, 95
Robins, Kevin, 216
Robinson, Mary, 208
Rolling Stones, 218
Roughley, Alan: *James Joyce and Critical Theory*, 219
RTE (Radio Telefís Éireann), 204–5
Russell, George, 193–94, 197
Ryan, John, 187, 195, 199, 201–2, 208, 211

Saussure, Ferdinand de, 139, 144, 151
Schaum, Melita, 4
Scholes, Robert, 87, 94, 100, 117, 138, 140–43, 149; *Structuralism in Literature*, 140; "*Ulysses:* A Structuralist Perspective," 140–43
Scott, Bonnie Kime, 138, 173–78; *James Joyce*, 176; *Joyce and Feminism*, 173–76
Screen, 151, 160–61
Scrutiny, 77–84, 135, 158
Segall, Jeffrey, 5, 73, 96, 98, 116, 119, 122

Selden, Raman: *A Reader's Guide to Contemporary Literary Theory*, 160
Senn, Fritz, 100, 126, 129, 138, 166, 179–80
Serio, John, 4–5
Seward, A. C., 81
Shakespear, Olivia, 190
Shakespeare, William, 4–6, 58, 78–79, 168, 183–84
Share, Bernard, 201, 205–6
Shaw, George Bernard, 17, 24, 195
Sheehan, Paul, 41, 147
Sheridan, Niall, 211
Simpsons, The, 181
Sinfield, Alan, 82, 91, 95, 151
Sinn Féin, 16, 48
Slate, 212
Slocombe, George, 28
Slocum, John J., 205
Smyth, Gerry, 199, 203
socialism, 33, 62, 72–73, 85–86, 114, 121, 136, 159–60, 165, 177, 219, 221, 224
Sollers, Philippe, 150–52, 164, 166
Spencer, Theodore, 94, 186
Spengler, Oswald, 46
Spoo, Robert, 219
Sporting Times, 25, 64
Staley, Thomas F., 138, 206; *Fifty Years "Ulysses,"* 140
Stein, Gertrude, 49
Stendhal, 11
Sterne, Lawrence, 17
Stevens, Wallace, 4
Steyn, Stella, 55
structuralism, 113, 139–50, 156, 221
Sturrock, John: *Structuralism and Since*, 160
Sullivan, Kevin, 119, 230; *Joyce Among the Jesuits*, 103
Sunday Chronicle, 33
Swift, Jonathan, 17, 41, 64

Synge, John Millington, 225; *The Playboy of the Western World*, 16

Tate, Allen, 96
Tel Quel, 150–52, 154
Thackeray, William Makepeace, 89
Theall, Donald, 205
theory, 7, 49–50, 60, 129–30, 137–82, 222, 225; complex relation to Joyce, 139–41, 143–45, 149–50, 162–63, 167–73, 178; defined, 139
Thom's Dublin Directory, 89, 94, 184
Thornton, Weldon, 138
Times (London), 6
Times Literary Supplement, 104–5, 108, 115
Tindall, William York, 92, 138
Tolstoy, Leo, 89, 135; *War and Peace*, 118
transition, 7, 49, 54–60, 66, 76, 78, 80–82, 136, 145, 158, 178
Trotsky, Leon, 33
Trotter, David, 10, 41–42, 170
Turgenev, Ivan, 89

U2, 207–8
University College Dublin, 196, 198, 220

Valente, Joseph, 219
van Boheemen-Saaf, Christine, 150, 169
Vanderham, Paul, 5, 19–20, 64–65
Vorticism, 12, 36–38. *See also* Lewis, Wyndham

Wall, Mervyn, 188, 196
Warren, Robert Penn, 96
Watt, Ian, 70–71
Waugh, Patricia, 58
Weaver, Harriet Shaw, 22, 35, 100, 173–74
Wells, H. G., 15–18, 25, 32, 35, 40, 48, 50

Whitaker, Ken: *Economic Development*, 203
White, Jim, 205
Whitehead, A. N., 46
Widdowson, Peter, 4–5
Wilde, Oscar, 9, 195, 223
Wilder, Thornton, 138
Williams, Raymond, 52–53, 70–71, 77, 85–86, 121, 151; *Culture*, 34; *The English Novel from Dickens to Lawrence*, 85–86; *The Long Revolution*, 85
Williams, William Carlos, 94
Wilson, Brian, 207
Wilson, Edmund, 89, 99; *Axel's Castle*, 73–74, 137
Wimsatt, W. K., 92, 113
Wollen, Peter, 160–61
Woolf, Virginia, 44, 101, 114
Woolsey, John, 19, 65, 68
Wordsworth, William, 121
World Wide Web, 139, 181
Worthington, Mabel P., 138
Wright, Patrick, 209, 212

Yeats, George, 100
Yeats, W. B., 16, 24, 48, 49, 92, 94, 100, 112, 114, 158, 161, 183, 190–92, 194–95, 197, 208, 217, 220–21, 224–25, 227, 229; *A Vision*, 112

Zola, Émile, 13, 25, 89

Irish Studies in Literature and Culture

Joyce's Critics: Transitions in Reading and Culture
Joseph Brooker

Locked in the Family Cell: Gender, Sexuality, and Political Agency in Irish National Discourse
Kathryn A. Conrad

Riot and Great Anger: Stage Censorship in Twentieth-Century Ireland
Joan FitzPatrick Dean

The Wee Wild One: Stories of Belfast and Beyond
Ruth Schwertfeger